Lecture Notes in Computer Science   10190

Commenced Publication in 1973
Founding and Former Series Editors:
Gerhard Goos, Juris Hartmanis, and Jan van Leeuwen

More information about this series at http://www.springer.com/series/8851

Ngoc Thanh Nguyen · Ryszard Kowalczyk
Alexandre Miguel Pinto · Jorge Cardoso (Eds.)

Transactions on Computational Collective Intelligence XXVI

 Springer

Editors-in-Chief

Ngoc Thanh Nguyen
Institute of Informatics
Wroclaw University of Technology
Wroclaw
Poland

Ryszard Kowalczyk
Swinburne University of Technology
Hawthorn, SA
Australia

Guest Editors

Alexandre Miguel Pinto
University of Lisbon
Lisbon
Portugal

Jorge Cardoso
Huawei German Research Center
Munich
Germany

and

University of Coimbra
Coimbra
Portugal

ISSN 0302-9743   ISSN 1611-3349   (electronic)
Lecture Notes in Computer Science
ISSN 2190-9288   ISSN 2511-6053   (electronic)
Transactions on Computational Collective Intelligence
ISBN 978-3-319-59267-1   ISBN 978-3-319-59268-8   (eBook)
DOI 10.1007/978-3-319-59268-8

Library of Congress Control Number: 2017942988

Printed on acid-free paper

This Springer imprint is published by Springer Nature
The registered company is Springer International Publishing AG
The registered company address is: Gewerbestrasse 11, 6330 Cham, Switzerland

Transactions on Computational Collective Intelligence XXVI

Preface

It is our pleasure to present the XXVI volume of the LNCS *Transactions on Computational Collective Intelligence*. This Special Issue is the compilation of selected papers of the First International KEYSTONE Conference 2015 (IKC 2015), part of the Keystone COST Action IC1302 (www.keystone-cost.eu). COST (European Cooperation in Science and Technology – www.cost.eu) is a pan-European intergovernmental framework. Its mission is to enable breakthrough scientific and technological developments leading to new concepts and products and thereby contribute to strengthening Europe's research and innovation capacities. It allows researchers, engineers, and scholars to jointly develop their own ideas and take new initiatives across all fields of science and technology, while promoting multi- and interdisciplinary approaches. COST aims at fostering a better integration of countries that are less research-intensive to the knowledge hubs of the European research area. The COST Association, an international not-for-profit association under the Belgian law, integrates all management, governing, and administrative functions necessary for the operation of the framework. The COST Association currently has 36 member countries.

This volume collects and analyzes the main results achieved by the research areas covered by KEYSTONE (the Action: *S*emantic *Key*word-Based Search on *S*tructured data *S*ources). For Action members, the conference was also the place to discuss the results obtained during the first two years of activities. The research theme of IKC 2015 was "Keyword-Search on Massive Datasets." It is an emerging and challenging theme. In particular, since large-scale data sources usually comprise very large schemas and billions of instances, keyword search over such datasets face several challenges related to scalability and interpretation of the keyword query intended meaning. Whereas state-of-the-art keyword search techniques work well for small or medium-size databases in a particular domain, many of them fail to scale on heterogeneous databases that are composed of thousands of instances. The discovery of semantically related data sources is another critical issue, hindered by the lack of sufficient information on available datasets and endpoints. Browsing and searching for data at this scale is not an easy task for users. Semantic search can support the process aiming at leveraging semantics to improve the accuracy and recall of search mechanisms.

This volume inaugurates the year 2017, the seventh year of TCCI activities. In the past 25 issues, we have published 253 high-quality papers. This issue contains 10 papers.

In the first paper "Professional Collaborative Information Seeking: Towards Traceable Search and Creative Sensemaking," Andreas Nuernberger et al. propose an adapted model for professional collaborative information seeking. The authors also introduce a system that has been specifically developed to support collaborative technology search.

The second paper entitled "Exploiting Linguistic Analysis on URLs for Recommending Web Pages: A Comparative Study" by Sara Cadegnani et al. analyzes and compares three different approaches to leverage information embedded in the structure of websites and the logs of their web servers to improve the effectiveness of web page recommendation. Their proposals exploit the context of users' navigations, i.e., their current sessions when surfing a specific website. These approaches do not require either information about the personal preferences of the users to be stored and processed or complex structures to be created and maintained.

In the third paper, "Large-Scale Knowledge Matching with Balanced Efficiency-Effectiveness Using LSH Forest" by Michael Cochez et al., the authors investigate the use of LSH Forest (a self-tuning indexing schema based on locality-sensitive hashing) for solving the problem of placing new knowledge tokens in the right contexts of the environment. They argue and show experimentally that LSH Forest possesses the required properties and could be used for large distributed set-ups. Further, they show experimentally that for their type of data minhashing works better than random hyperplane hashing.

The fourth paper, "Keyword-Based Search of Workflow Fragments and Their Composition" by Khalid Belhajjame et al., presents a method for identifying fragments that are frequently used across workflows in existing repositories, and therefore are likely to incarnate patterns that can be reused in new workflows. They present a keyword-based search method for identifying the fragments that are relevant for the needs of a given workflow designer. They go on to present an algorithm for composing the retrieved fragments with the initial (incomplete) workflow that the user designed based on compatibility rules that they identified, and showcase how the algorithm operates using an example from eScience.

The fifth paper, entitled "Scientific Footprints in Digital Libraries" by Claudia Ifrim et al., analyzes citation lists to not only quantify but also understand impact by tracing the "footprints" that authors have left, i.e., the specific areas in which they have made an impact. They use the publication medium (specific journal or conference) to identify the thematic scope of each paper and feed from existing digital libraries that index scientific activity, namely, Google Scholar and DBLP. This allows them to design and develop a system, the Footprint Analyzer, which can be used to successfully identify the most prominent works and authors for each scientific field, regardless of whether their own research is limited to or even focused on the specific field. Various real-life examples demonstrate the proposed concepts, and results from the developed system's operation prove the applicability and validity.

In the sixth paper titled "Mining and Using Key-words and Key-phrases to Identify the Era of an Anonymous Text," Dror Mughaz et al. determine the time frame in which the author of a given document lived. The documents are rabbinic documents written in Hebrew-Aramaic languages. The documents are undated and do not contain a bibliographic section, which constitutes a substantial challenge. The authors define a set of key phrases and formulate various types of rules – "Iron-clad," Heuristic, and Greedy – to define the time frame. These rules were tested on two corpora containing response documents, and the results are promising. They are better for larger corpora than for smaller corpora.

The next paper, "Toward Optimized Multimodal Concept Indexing" by Navid Rekabsaz et al., presents an approach for semantic-based keyword search and focuses especially on its optimization to scale to real-world-sized collections in the social media domain. Furthermore, the paper presents a faceted indexing framework and architecture that relates content to semantic concepts to be indexed and searched semantically. The authors study the use of textual concepts in a social media domain and observe a significant improvement from using a concept-based solution for keyword searching.

In the eighth paper, entitled "Improving Document Retrieval in Large-Domain Specific Textual Databases Using Lexical Resources," Ranka Stanković et al. propose the use of document indexing as a possible solution to document representation. They use metadata for generating a bag of words for each document with the aid of morphological dictionaries and transducers. A combination of several tf-idf-based measures was applied for selecting and ranking of retrieval results of indexed documents for a specific query and the results were compared with the initial retrieval system that was already in place. In general, a significant improvement has been achieved according to the standard information retrieval performance measures, where the InQuery method performed the best.

In the ninth paper, "Domain-Specific Modeling: A Food and Drink Gazetteer," Andrey Tagarev et al. build a food and drink (FD) gazetteer for classification of general, FD-related concepts, efficient faceted search or automated semantic enrichment. For general domains (such as the FD domain), re-using encyclopedic knowledge bases like Wikipedia may be a good idea. The authors propose a semi-supervised approach that uses a restricted Wikipedia as a base for the modeling, achieved by selecting a domain-relevant Wikipedia category as root for the model and all its subcategories, combined with expert and data-driven pruning of irrelevant categories.

The last paper, "What's New? Analyzing Language-Specific Wikipedia Entity Contexts to Support Entity-Centric News Retrieval" authored by Yiwei Zhou et al., focuses on the problem of creating language-specific entity contexts to support entity-centric, language-specific information retrieval applications. First, they discuss alternative ways such contexts can be built, including graph-based and article-based approaches. Second, they analyze the similarities and the differences in these contexts in a case study including 220 entities and five Wikipedia language editions. Third, they propose a context-based entity-centric information retrieval model that maps documents to aspect space, and apply language-specific entity contexts to perform query expansion. Last, they perform a case study to demonstrate the impact of this model in a news retrieval application. The study illustrates that the proposed model can effectively improve the recall of entity-centric information retrieval while keeping high precision and can provide language-specific results.

We would like to thank all the authors for their valuable contributions to this issue and all the reviewers for their opinions, which contributed greatly to the high quality of the papers. Our special thanks go to the team at Springer, who have helped to publish the many TCCI issues in due time and in good order.

February 2017   Alexandre Miguel Pinto
                                                                          Jorge Cardoso

Transactions on Computational Collective Intelligence

This Springer journal focuses on research in computer-based methods of computational collective intelligence (CCI) and their applications in a wide range of fields such as the Semantic Web, social networks, and multi-agent systems. It aims to provide a forum for the presentation of scientific research and technological achievements accomplished by the international community.

The topics addressed by this journal include all solutions to real-life problems for which it is necessary to use computational collective intelligence technologies to achieve effective results. The emphasis of the papers published is on novel and original research and technological advancements. Special features on specific topics are welcome.

Contents

Professional Collaborative Information Seeking: Towards Traceable Search and Creative Sensemaking

Dominic Stange[✉], Michael Kotzyba, and Andreas Nürnberger

DKE Group, Faculty of Computer Science,
University of Magdeburg, Magdeburg, Germany
{dominic.stange,michael.kotzyba,andreas.nuernberger}@ovgu.de

Abstract. The development of systems to support collaborative information seeking is a challenging issue for many reasons. Besides the expected support of an individual user in tasks such as keyword based query formulation, relevance judgement, result set organization and summarization, the smooth exchange of search related information within a team of users seeking information has to be supported. This imposes strong requirements on visualization and interaction to enable user to easily trace and interpret the search activities of other team members and to jointly make sense of gathered information in order to satisfy an initial information need. In this paper, we briefly motivate specific requirements with a focus on collaborative professional search, review existing work and propose an adapted model for professional collaborative information seeking. In addition, we discuss the results of a use case study and point out major challenges in professional collaborative search. Finally, we briefly introduce a system that has been specifically developed to support collaborative technology search.

Keywords: Collaborative search · Information behaviour · Search user interface

1 Introduction

With the increasing amount of digitally stored data and information the requirements and expectations on information search systems, in particular web search engines, steadily grow. To achieve an appropriate user experience, search systems not only have to retrieve web documents related to the explicit given keyword based search query, but also have to consider the user's context and ideally support the whole search process, i.e., all steps from query formulation over relevance judgement to result set organization and summarization. Current search engines already provide several features to support users regarding context, e.g., by

---

This is a revised and extended version of a contribution to the 1st International KEYSTONE Conference (IKC 2015), Coimbra Portugal, 8–9 September 2015 [32].

N.T. Nguyen et al. (Eds.): TCCI XXVI, LNCS 10190, pp. 1–25, 2017.
DOI: 10.1007/978-3-319-59268-8_1

considering the location, previously used search queries or already visited result pages, to adapt query suggestions or the search result set, cf. [6]. But if the user's information need gets more complex and the search goes beyond a simple fact finding task the support provided by existing systems is still rather limited.

In this paper, we focus on search systems for domain experts, also called professionals. This group of users usually not only need to retrieve simple facts or explore an area of interest, but have to satisfy a complex information need with a real-world problem in mind. For professionals the search is rather a creative process in which domain specific information is collected and used to derive solutions for an application domain. For example, a frequent task in the business area is to perform an extensive technology research to keep up to date, know about state-of-the-art methods and hence to be competitive. In addition, since the tasks to be solved by professionals are usually complex, they often have to be processed by a team of experts in order to solve the task in reasonable time and appropriate quality. Therefore, adequate support methods for collaborative information seeking (CIS) tasks are needed. Unfortunately, we still lack tools and methods to support complex search tasks [15] and collaborative search tasks [20], especially for professional searchers.

Different models for information seeking, or more general information behaviour, have been proposed. These models underline the complexity of the search process, describe essential components and consider the search process from different perspectives. However, the majority of the models rather consider information seeking as a process that is performed by an individual and not a group of users. Therefore these models have to be adapted and extended to be applicable to support the design and evaluation of search systems that enable collaborative information seeking by a team of professionals. To make CIS feasible, a search user interface (SUI) is required that covers all steps of the search process and its phases, such as planning, exploration, sensemaking and summarization. That is, the search system should enable the team of searchers to trace the seeking process and to collaborate in understanding structure and meaning of the revealed information [15]. Hence, in this work we start with a discussion of aspects and issues of complex information seeking processes and then propose two SUI concepts that focus on supporting traceability and creative sensemaking in collaborative search. Furthermore, while research in the area of information seeking is traditionally motivated from the library and information sciences community, focusing on behavioural aspects of information acquisition processes – therefore providing a more abstract and theoretical approach –, research in the area of (exploratory) search is focusing on characterizing and modeling search processes in order to develop methods and tools to actually support a user in information seeking processes (mainly driven by research in information retrieval). In the following, we aim at providing an integrated view on research from both perspectives and therefore use information seeking terminology when focusing on behavioural aspects and search terminology when focusing on concrete user support technology.

The structure of this work is as follows: Sect. 2 provides a brief overview of information seeking, established models and illustrates their relation to collaborative search. In Sect. 3 we address the process of CIS from different perspectives, describe important aspects and provide an adapted model for professional collaborative search. In Sect. 4 we present results of a requirement analysis that was conducted in form of a case study at a large automotive company. Afterwards, we provide two suggestions for SUIs, that support traceability and creative sensemaking in Sect. 5, including a discussion on our general design decisions. The last section summarizes the paper and provides an outlook towards prospective, collaborative search systems.

2   Review on Related Work

2.1   Information Behavior and Seeking Models

Information behaviour models provide the most general approach to describe a user during information acquisition and exploration. The models are used to characterize seeking behaviour, context information, possible dialog partners and the search system itself. The literature provides a huge variety of models that address different levels and aspects of information behaviour. In Wilson [45] several models are summarized. A further overview can be found in Knight and Spink [23]. Wilson's nested model of information behaviour (cf. [45]) defines information seeking behaviour in the framework of information behaviour and considers these models as a subset. That is, information behaviour models additionally describe intervening variables, activating mechanisms and different information sources to embed information seeking behaviour. Models of information seeking behaviour cover all methods describing a user who is conducting a search to discover and yield access to information sources, i.e., all used strategies and tactics. In Wilson's first model of information behaviour [44] (cf. Fig. 1), the user recognizes an information need and starts seeking for information on different formal or informal information sources. Alternatively, the user can seek for information exchange with other people. If successful, the user may use the gained information to further refine the information seeking behaviour or to transfer information to other people. Furthermore, successfully gained information may be used to evaluate the current state of satisfaction and to (re-)formulate the information need. However, the model considers information (seeking) behaviour rather as an individual process: The user's behaviour is motivated by an individual information need, he/she seeks individually for information and merely exchanges or transfers information with other people to satisfy the individual need. Neither the need itself nor the actions performed within the seeking process, such as keyword query formulation or information acquisition, are linked or synchronized with others. Furthermore, the information use remains an individual process or is performed with others outside the information seeking process executed with the system.

Information-seeking can also be considered from the cognitive or mental perspective that allows to describe the seeking process in several phases.

For example, Kuhlthau [25, 26] proposed a phenomenological model with six *stages*: Initiation, Selection, Exploration, Formulation, Collection and Presentation. Ellis (et al.) [11–13] discussed a model with empirically supported categories, termed *features*: Starting, Chaining, Browsing, Differentiating, Monitoring, Extracting, Verifying and Ending. If the models' perspectives coincide, they even can be aggregated, c.f. [45]. As in Wilson's model, Kuhlthau and Ellis also describe information seeking rather as an individual process. After the search initiation and (first) exploration, the user starts to differentiate the retrieved information sources, maybe uses an adapted query formulation that better describes the information need and starts individually to extract or collect relevant information. However, especially in a collaborative setting this cognitive process describes an essential aspect of collective search, namely the current state of understanding and sensemaking within the team. e.g., if all team members know about the already explored information and additionally get a prepared, current view of the examined sources, it is easier to differentiate sources for the next steps, to collect valuable new information and hence to increase the team's sensemaking. Further theoretical models can be found in [5].

In contrast to the cognitive or mental perspective, information seeking can also be studied in relation to conducted information activities. That is, all interactions with the information system and its components, such as result information acquisition, comparison or planning, are addressed. To consider these activities for collaboration is essential as well, since the individual information needs and the resulting information seeking behaviour of the professionals need to be coordinated to contribute to the team's goal to solve a complex task. An established model for search activities was proposed by Marchionini [27] based on the concept of *exploratory search*. Exploratory search is usually motivated from the uncertainty of a user in his/her information need or lack of knowledge

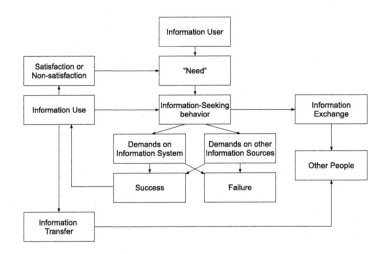

Fig. 1. Wilson's model of information behaviour from 1981 [44] in a variation according to [45].

to tackle it. It combines a standard lookup-search with the activities learning and investigation. A discussion of methods to support exploratory search can be found in [18] and a further activity pattern related investigation in [10].

2.2 Collaborative Information Seeking

Collaborative search can be defined as a special case of a social search [14], in which all participants share an information need and actively conduct a specific search together in order to achieve a common search goal [19]. This social perspective is also discussed in [3,39]. While in [17] different roles and dimensions of collaboration are discussed, such as intent (explicit and implicit), depth of mediation, concurrency and location, Shah provides in [38] a more general introduction and definition of *collaborative information seeking*. Poltrock's et al. [33] definition of collaborative information seeking as "the activities that a group or team of people undertakes to identify and resolve a shared information need" (p. 239) nicely agrees with the information activity related perspective as discussed above. Reddy and Jansen [34] study the collaborative information seeking behaviour of two healthcare teams in a business setting. They found that collaborative information behaviour differs from individual information behaviour on several dimensions and present a model in which they contrast the context (individual vs. collaborative information behaviour) with the actual behaviour (information seeking vs. searching). Capra et al. [8] study search strategies in a collaborative search task. Their results show that collaboration in a search task occurs at various stages. They present three higher-level search strategies how collaborative information seeking is carried out: Participants acted on their own, unaware of their collaborators (independent strategy); participants used their collaborators' previous work to do additional work in the same space (parallel strategy); and participants used knowledge of what their collaborators have done to take new directions (divergent strategy). In her early assessment Morris [29] advocates four aspects (coverage, confidence, exposure, and productivity) in which dedicated collaborative search systems can influence a user's search experience in an exploratory search task. A collaborative search system has been proposed by Morris et al. [31]. They study how personalization of web search can be achieved based on a membership in a group that works on the same task. They show how three techniques (groupization, smart splitting, and group hit-highlighting) can enhance the individual search experience in a collaborative context.

2.3 Professionals as Information Users

Professional searchers satisfy most of the characteristics described by Knight and Spink [23]. They are not necessarily information professionals, i. e., are "unlikely to have any formal training in developing appropriate search queries or retrieval strategies", "likely to use a wider variety of search strategies, with more inconsistent results", and "more likely to be the 'information user' of the information they are seeking." However, they often have a lot of domain expertise which influences individual search strategies and often leads to more successful findings than having little expertise [21,43]. The circumstance of being rather an information user also makes it more likely that experts use simple structured search queries (but with expert knowledge related terms) to address their information needs. This is, in contrast to patent search experts, for example, who often have a good education in working with search technologies but do not necessarily have to be domain experts in the topic they investigate. That means, even in a complex search scenario experts often resort to using rather standard search tools, like Web and Intranet search engines, and only a limited scope of query formulation strategies and techniques.

Professionals often perform a complex, exploratory search task to gather domain-related information for an underlying problem-solving task [27]. This search task is usually open-ended and has an uncertain process and outcome (c.f. Marchionini [27]). Furthermore, problem-solving often requires collaboration in exploring the information space together, collecting domain-related information, making sense of it and using it. Professionals within an organization are often part of communities and typically know each other personally. Therefore, in addition to the exploratory nature of this task, there are further characteristics which can be attributed to the business setting in which a proferssional search is performed. The domain-related problems that need to be solved by the community often exist over a longer period of time which results in a continuous information need. That is, the search topics need to be updated, which leads to repeatedly executed search tasks dealing with similar or overlapping contents.

Powerful (web) search technologies have made a lot of business-relevant information available for domain experts of a company to explore, collect, and use in their problem-solving tasks. This business-relevant information is also constantly being published in a huge amount and diversity. Hence, search technologies for professionals also need to consider aspects of big data in order to support their users appropriately. For example, the *volume* of scientific articles, patents or reports about developments in physics, medicine, automation, robotics etc. that need to be explored for an exhaustive research is immense. Additionally, the *variety* of information sources and formats might be important to estimate source characteristics such as quality or processibility. Last but not least, the *velocity* in which information is generated, e. g., about new innovative technologies, influences the information acquisition processes of organizations. For more information about the "3 Vs" of big data see, e. g., McAfee and Brynjolfsson [28].

3 Towards an Integrated Model for Collaborative Professional Search

In this section we discuss crucial aspects of CIS for professionals in more detail, provide a model that links essential components for the design of novel search systems and discuss resulting requirements and challenges. As discussed above, existing information seeking models focus on individual seeking processes. The model presented in Fig. 2 is based on Wilson's information behaviour model [44] (c.f. Fig. 1) and provides an integrated extension regarding collaborative information seeking with an emphasis on a group of domain experts. After the emergence of a complex task, the group of professionals has to discuss and define the corresponding, shared information need. Even if the need cannot be specified precisely (due to the exploratory character of the task), the group has to divide it in subneeds that can be (at least initially) processed by an individual. In the next step, each domain expert can start to satisfy his/her resulting individual information need by performing individual information seeking. Since the information seeking occurs in the context of a collaborative task the collaborative information seeking behaviour component emphasises that search-related and collaborative activities have to be taken into account when the experts reveal new information. Here, it is important that each member of the group is able to follow, organize and participate in the seeking process and understand the revealed information. The organization can be enabled by the collaborative activities illustrated on the right. The control component comprises all activities to promote and regulate the seeking process. Awareness allows the users to review the current state and progress of the search task and assess individual contributions of the group. Coordination addresses all means to synchronise the collaborative seeking activities between the users. Communication refers to exchanging information among the members of the group which can involve different organisational aspects and may be directly, i. e., offline using other technologies than the search system. The left part of the collaborative box in Fig. 2 shows the search task-related activities, planning, exploration, sensemaking and information use. By exploration the team reveals structural information that can influence the individual information need or the information seeking behaviour directly. Sensemaking and information use allow to reveal new findings and key aspects that influence the information need on a semantic level. Especially the information use makes it possible to perform a relevance evaluation. Insights about structure, semantics and relevance influence the searcher's individual information need and, thus, the resulting individual seeking behaviour. By performing additional collaborative actions, however, the co-searchers also affect the group's information seeking behaviour. That is, by sharing insights about planning, exploration, sensemaking, or information use individuals shape their joint search experience. What is

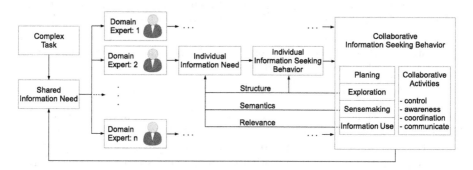

Fig. 2. Illustration of collaborative information seeking with an emphasis on a group of domain experts.

needed are lean ways to couple collaborative with search-related activities in a search task. We describe our approach of achieving this connection by addressing requirements and challenges in the following sections.

3.1   Requirements

Problem-Solving Context: The type of professional search we want to address is often part of a so-called *known genuine decision task* (c.f. Byström and Järvelin's [7] categorization). In our case, the structure of the result is often known a priori but the procedures for performing the task, i.e., the needed information and the process are unknown. This kind of task often goes along with a complex information need. There has been some debate about what constitutes a complex information need. Aula and Russell [2] present an interpretation that fits to our professional search scenario. Among other criteria they argue that complex search often requires exploration and more directed information finding activities, where the searcher often uses multiple sources of information. Additionally, a complex search often requires note-taking because of the searcher's limited ability to hold all gathered information in memory. Besides, relevant information is typically spread across lots of resources in the information space. This makes the information space sparse with facts, as opposed to a dense information space where a single resource may contain all relevant information to sufficiently answer the information need. Hence, considering the problem-solving context is crucial in supporting CIS.

Collaboration: Professional search often concerns a community of experts that face similar problems and thus have similar, overlapping information needs. A professional search tool, therefore, should allow these experts to work together in these tasks. Most experts within such a community know each other personally, which distinguishes it from other scenarios where collaborative search is analysed. The collaboration is explicit, active, remote (mostly), and asynchronous. In the context of a collaborative exploratory search, it is important to note that it may not be known beforehand, who will take part in the search task. It may happen that some experts join the team while others have already started gathering and using information. Based on Reddy and Jansen [34], reasons why users engage in collaboration are (1) the complexity of information need, (2) fragmented information resources (sources reside in multiple and dispersed systems), (3) the lack of domain expertise and (4) the lack of immediately accessible information.

Updates: Professionals are often required to update their knowledge about the domains they are responsible for which is why they have to repeatedly perform search tasks about various, sometimes overlapping search topics. Professional search requires the ability to investigate, update and extend previous search tasks. In Kotov et al. [24] such tasks are considered cross-session tasks which often evolve over time. The information need in a cross-session task is typically complex and progressively refined with each new update.

Traceability and Creative Sensemaking: When it comes to search-related activities that are performed by the whole group of collaborating searchers exploring an information space, making sense of collected information and using this information in a problem solving situation should be *traceable* for each individual, so that he/she understands how the various contributions of the searchers relate to each other. Every team member needs to be able to understand their joint search strategy in order to make better or more relevant contributions and benefit from each others' domain knowledge and search expertise. The second requirement in professional search is *sensemaking* in context of the underlying genuine decision task in which the search process is embedded in. Sensemaking can be understood as the "process of searching for a representation and encoding data in that representation to answer task-specific questions" [35]. It is an integral part of many information seeking models because it describes how a searcher (mentally) models, interprets, disambiguates, and interacts with the information that is gathered during search. The requirements on traceability and sensemaking can be defined as follows: Traceability in collaborative search describes the team's ability to understand the structure, semantics, and relevance of their collaborative information seeking behaviour. Traceability concerns especially the search-related activities exploration, sensemaking, and information use. Co-searchers should be able to understand how they explore the information space as a team, what information they collect in the resources they discover, and how they synthesise/interpret this information with respect to their search goal. Creative sensemaking can be defined as satisfying (complex) information needs in a problem solving context to "form a coherent functional whole" and reorganize "elements into a new pattern or structure through generating, planning, or producing" (cf. taxonomy of learning in [1]). The core task is to make sense of the gathered information of a search task and create solutions to the underlying domain problem. Therefore, creative sensemaking inherits some properties of information use as well. Since professional search is often embedded in a problem-solving task creatively using the collected information and generating new ideas, concepts, or solutions to solve the problems is very important. Creative sensemaking is central to search tasks with complex information needs where solutions in an application domain have to be generated based on the collected information.

Traceability and creative sensemaking are still rarely addressed in (collaborative) search settings. They are, however, particularly important in order to support experts engaged in a professional search task. Since the type of professional search we outlined above refers to an explicit collaboration between experts, one approach of supporting them is to design specially-tailored user interfaces that provide new types of visualizations and interaction methods.

3.2 Challenges

Most of the current collaborative search systems are designed to "allow participants to find, save, and share documents, and see the activities of others in the collaboration group" (Hearst [20]). However, there are reasons why collaborative search tools have not become widely accepted (yet). Hearst [20] argues that in order for users to move from a solitary to a collaborative search tool there "must be enough additional value as yet in the tools offered." In particular, Shah [37] mentions cost factors that one should keep in mind when designing collaborative search tools, e.g., the *cost of learning* a new system, *adaption/adoption costs* when using a collaborative system, and the *collaborative costs* when being part of group task. Capra et al. [9] study how searchers perform ongoing, exploratory searches on the web and share their findings with others. Their results show that searchers employ a variety of tools and techniques that go "beyond the functionalities offered by today's search engines and web browsers", e. g., note-taking, information management, and exchange. The study by Kelly and Payne [22] confirms these results. They also find that (collaborative) searchers want to "repurpose" their search results at the end of the task to arrange them into a more meaningful way. Shah [36] proposed guidelines for the design of a collaborative search tool that focus on behavioural aspects of collaboration. These include that a tool should allow for effective communication, encourage individual searchers to make contributions, coordinate the individual actions and needs, and provide means to explore and negotiate individual differences. When it comes to concrete features that a collaborative search tool should support, various authors have contributed their ideas:

- *Awareness:* "knowing what other people are doing" during collaborative information behaviour activities [30,34].
- *Communication:* share information with other members of the collaboration team bilaterally or in conference [34].
- *Division of Labour:* reduce individual effort by avoiding redundant actions and allow for effective "divide-and-conquer" techniques [20,30].
- *Feedback:* with respect to collaborative search includes a "feeling of accomplishment"; Co-searchers should be able to step back and get an understanding of what actions are required next and by whom [20].
- *Overview:* refers to a visualization of the "land-scape" that the team has covered in their collaborative search task that also allows them to depict what they still have to do [20]. "Users must have access to a visualization of not only their search process, but also of their collaborators. ... [This] will allow users to discuss each other's searches and provide feedback on how to improve them." [34]
- *Persistence:* makes the context, content, and task of a search session available for future access and for others in a collaboration; In particular, it is the precondition for remote and asynchronous collaborative search [30].
- *Personalization:* means to provide "structure to let individuals define what their personal constraints or preferences are" when they engage in collaborative search [20].

There are still many features missing in today's collaborative search tool stack [20]. Therefore, in the next section we discuss our line of thought during the design of our collaborative search system. The issues pointed out above are backed by a small user study carried out among experts of a large automotive company who perform technology scouting.

4   Requirements Analysis: A Case Study in Technology Scouting

In order to validate and extend our theoretical analysis, we conducted a small case study with domain experts employed at a large automotive company. The study questions are related to the complex task of technology scouting. In the following, the task of technology scouting is first discussed in more detail. Afterwards we present the results of the study.

4.1   Use Case in Technology Scouting

According to Georghiu [16] technology scouting in a business setting constitutes an aspect of technology intelligence in which an organization aims to "develop an understanding of current activities, emerging trends and future directions of key companies, technologies and other players of interest." In particular technology scouting is the "purposeful searching for specific technology entities of high interest." In our understanding the outcome of technology scouting can be used to evaluate potential development directions of a company on a strategic level and to identify possible solutions for short-term problems on the operative level. Further information on our business setting can be found in [41].

Professional technology scouts are often required to work together and update their knowledge about the domains they are responsible for. Hence, we consider technology scouting as an instance of professional information seeking with the need to investigate, update and extend existing search tasks. The scouting task is demanding with respect to both domain knowledge and search expertise. Therefore, some companies even specialize in technology scouting and offer extensive services to their customers. The product of such a service can be a comprehensive written report about all relevant entities for a given problem scenario, a detailed description of expert researchers that work in the field and suppliers that offer relevant solutions. However, especially larger companies employ experts and even smaller departments that are responsible for innovation management and technology scouting themselves. For our professional information seeking use case we will consider both, the specialized service providers and the scouting departments within an organization

With respect to the actual information seeking task one can think of technology scouting as consisting of four phases: planning, exploration, collection, and summarization. These phases are not necessarily sequential and searchers may jump between the phases several times. In the following, we briefly describe these phases in more detail. They are also shown as vertical boxes in Fig. 3. The figure shows two executions of a scouting task at different points in time leading to an initial product and an updated product later.

Planning Phase: To plan a search task takes into account the business environment in which it is carried out. Planning necessarily comprises of search-related actions like defining the general search goals, identifying relevant topics, sources to investigate and eventually the needed information. In addition it includes actions of sharing task specifics within a community to benefit from others' expertise and scheduling necessary actions in the light of other work tasks. Planning also includes specifying the product to be created and dividing the work among collaborating searchers in a group. While planning a scouting task, the members of a single department or multiple departments of a company can be affected. The latter is the case when the addressed topics require experts from different domains to participate. For example, a scouting task dealing with automation technologies in the area of human-robot-collaboration may require experts from engineering, psychology and computer science. These planning tasks are especially challenging because of the additional coordination effort for the experts to work together effectively.

Exploration Phase: The aim of the exploration phase is to find relevant information sources that are needed to accomplish the scouting task. The amount of information that is needed depends on the task objectives and the desired product. The exploration phase is influenced by the available sources and the ease to access them. As a result of the exploration phase resources (documents) are discovered that contain information such as text, images or tables about the

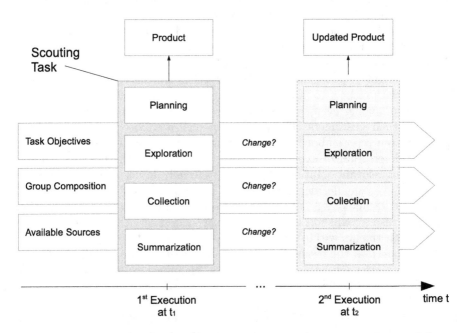

Fig. 3. A scouting task with a longer-lasting scope and two executions at different points in time and contextual variables like task objectives, group composition, and available sources that affect these executions. The contextual variables of one execution are not necessarily identical to those of another. Changes in these variables pose additional challenges on the scouting task.

search topic. The actual exploration is performed, e. g., by issuing search queries to a search engine and browsing the resulting resources.

Collection Phase: Collecting relevant content from a source document is the task of identifying those passages/entities within the text that are relevant for the search task. The challenge of extracting the "right" information from a source document is twofold. It requires a good understanding of the search task and its objectives and also a good background knowledge of the search topic to estimate which information contributes to the task.

Summarization Phase: In the summarization phase the searcher finally accumulates all the gathered information and creates the product, e. g., as a written report or as a standardized presentation. Sometimes, especially when the scouting is carried out as part of a routine technology scanning process no such report may be required. In such cases, the collection of retrieved documents may be the only result of the task.

An important aspect of technology search and professional search in general is environmental change. Environmental change addresses the time dimension of a scouting task. One time-related property of the task is its duration. Duration describes the elapsed time between planning the execution of a search task and creating the (intermediate) product. Since the objectives of a technology task may not be fully satisfied when the product is created, there is another property that describes how long the objectives of a search task are valid. This property we call scope of a scouting task. The scope is the time interval from starting a search task to finally arriving at a product that sufficiently answers all the initial questions. If the objectives of the task can be satisfied in a single run/execution, then duration and scope are equal. Essentially, the scope of a search task can last over weeks, months and in rare occasions even years, so the environmental conditions may change from one execution to another. These effects need to be taken into account when designing tools that seek to support the process. We summarize some of such conditions in the following. They are also shown in horizontal boxes in Fig. 3.

– *Technological developments and breakthroughs:* Technological developments are one of the reasons why topics need to be scouted repeatedly over time. Information about developments is published (e. g., as news articles or patents) and becomes available for technology scouts to be discovered. This creates a constant information stream that technology scouts need to filter, explore and evaluate for innovative domain-related developments they can use in their businesses.
– *Workforce fluctuation:* Workforce fluctuation refers to the fact that the group composition of a scouting task may change over time. Some participants may leave the department or take on other responsibilities. Then, some important insights in the scouting process, including already gathered information and specifics about the objectives of the task, may be lost. New members joining the group may find it difficult to understand the current status of a scouting task and to determine what their contributions can be.

– *Task updates:* Sometimes the objectives of a scouting task need to be adjusted over time, e. g., when new environmental or business conditions alter the domain in question which could not be anticipated. This is especially the case with disruptive innovations. Then, task specifics like the addressed topics or the desired output have to be updated, often resulting in further executions of the search task.

4.2   User Survey

In order to get a better understanding of the real-life application of technology scouting we conducted a small survey research in a technology management department of a large automotive company. Although, our main focus was to investigate how collaboration in context of a scouting task is currently achieved and how it can be improved, we also addressed environmental circumstances in which technology scouting is performed in general. We have designed our study in terms of statements that had to be answered by the participants using a Likert scale. A set of items (statements) was provided and the participants had to rate whether they either "strongly agree", "partially agree", "partially disagree", "strongly disagree" or that they are "undecided" towards this statement. It was only allowed to chose one option. The answers were collected anonymously. Furthermore, we included some open questions. Altogether, the questionnaire included 45 statements and five questions. The survey was conducted between December 2014 and January 2015 and was answered by nine experts within the department. One expert was female. All participants know each other personally. Seven participants were between 40 and 55 years old and two PhD students were betwen 25 and 30 years old. Most of the participants stated that they are apt to try new technologies privately. That means they may have an affinity towards technologies in general and may be more open-minded. They also consider themselves experienced with search engines. Five participants have been in the technology scouting job for more than 15 years, one participant less than 10 years and three less than 5 years. The majority of the participants had to gather information frequently during the last two years.

In the following, we first discuss the results of our study in more detail. A summary of the main findings – in form of major survey statements and answers - is given at the end of this section in Table 1.

Six participants consider a technology search as particularly challenging. When they were asked for reasons, one participant answered that technology search often concerns novel topics for which information is often not largely available. Two participants add that often required information is not easily (or freely) accessible. One participant specifically points out the lack of trust in the correctness of information provided from some sources. For example, facts provided on the World Wide Web are said to be not always right. Another participant highlights the circumstance that collected information sometimes need to be treated with confidentiality. For this, one has to consider that technology scouting often includes gathering information from internal sources of an organization. Another statement was that technology search tasks are subjective and every person values information differently. Thus each technology scout involves a "subjective filter" to the task. The volume of available information related to a specific topic also influences the differentiation between relevant and non-relevant information and makes the scouting more intricate. Another participant mentioned an example, were he/she had a concrete application of an investigated technology in a business setting in mind and said that it is "sometimes unclear what information the colleagues from operative business units consider helpful."

When asked for the technology topics the participants are responsible for, eight of nine strongly agree that new developments occur regularly. Seven of the participants stated that there are topics for which they want to continue an existing search task. This supports our hypotheses that novel information is published repeatedly and search tasks need to be updated occasionally. The majority also knows what topics their colleagues are interested in. Interestingly, six participants said that it is easy for them to continue a search task they started more than a week earlier. That is surprising because it contradicts our initial experience when discussing the topic of extensibility of search tasks with the participants prior to the survey. A possible explanation is that it is not clear what continuing a search task actually means. Six participants agreed that a colleague should be able to continue their search task where they stopped. Interestingly, five disagreed strongly that they are currently able to continue the researches of their colleagues which hints at a lack in support in the used tools. The exchange of information among the participants is valued highly by seven of them. The exchange with colleagues from other departments is equally important (seven of nine agreed strongly).

When it comes to planning a search task five participants state that they typically know what information they have to collect at the beginning of a search task, four of them are undecided. So one can assume that there is usually a particular problem that needs to be addressed. Asked how they value the ability to work together in planning their search tasks the answers are diverse. Four of them would like to plan search tasks together with others, three disagree and two are undecided. We also asked them to outline when they would work together with others in the planning phase. One major reason to work together is when they deal with interdisciplinary problems or domains where experts with different backgrounds have to make contributions. Another reason is when the same topic is interesting to multiple experts and synergies can be lifted. Another participant refers to social aspects of the collaboration. Some experts have connections to relevant people in the domain and should, therefore, be included in the search task. That is, collaboration is desirable if expert networks can be used. Another participant points out that he/she would work together with others if the process was efficiently implemented. One participant states that collaboration in the planning phase is desirable to split a search task into disjunct parts and reduce the risk of redundant work. Currently, collaboration in the planning phase is very limited. Only one participant works together with colleagues when planning a search task. However, six of them work together with their superior.

Table 1. Summary of major survey statements and answers.

Summary of survey statements and answers concerning...	
... planning	**... exploration**
– Currently, collaboration only as consultations with superior. – Actual wish to work together in the planning phase is not clearly stated. – Reasons for collaboration: interdisciplinary domains, mutual interest, and redundancy reduction.	– The current degree of collaboration is very limited. – However, the majority would like to work together in their search tasks more often in the future. – Reasons for collaboration: quick evaluation from different perspectives, reduction of individual effort.
... collection	**... summarization**
– Accessing the results of previous search tasks is very important. – Colleagues should be able to access the collectively gathered information of a group. – However, this is currently not possible.	– Currently, no collaboration among colleagues in the summarization phase. – Relationships between contents of different search tasks are not visible for the participants, but they are desired.

In the exploration phase of a search task five of the participants do not feel very good supported today. The degree of collaboration between the participants is again rather limited. Only one of them states that he/she is working together with colleagues of the same department while three say they work together with experts from other departments. From subsequent interviews we know that these collaborations are often through telephone calls or emails. Six participants say they would like to work together in their search tasks more often.

If they find interesting documents during exploration three participants say they file away this document always, five make this often and one rarely. Two of them always create an accumulative document where they store the specific facts that have been interesting to them. Four of them do this often and three rarely. Sharing this information within the team is also always done by two and regularly by four. Some of the reasons for working together in the exploration or collection phases were described as follows. One participant states that he/she would work together with others if he/she needs the collected information to be quickly evaluated from different perspectives. Another writes that working together is desirable to reduce the individual effort. He/she adds that the co-searchers should use the same "standards for the search task" to allow for an exchange of information after the task is completed. Another mentions that the division of labour should be clear. The same participant as before says that tools should make the collaboration very efficient. Accessing the results of their previous search tasks is important for eight of the participants. Almost all of the participants say that their colleagues should be able to access the information they gather in a search task. However, six of them disagree that they actual can access the results of their colleagues'.

Collaboration among colleagues in the summarization phase of a search task is currently regarded as non-existent, as well. None of the participants work together with their colleagues when it comes to preparing the results. Four of them say they would like to increase collaboration in the future while four are undecided. Most participants do not consider it easy for them to see relationships between the results of different search tasks in their department. So it comes as no surprise that four participants think it would help them if they could relate contents or results from one search task with those of others.

5   Professional Information Seeking Support for Technology Scouting

Our approach to support technology scouting in an organization is guided by the insights gained in the survey described in the previous section and it is mainly twofold: (I) make exploratory search more traceable and accessible for a group of experts across search sessions, and (II) offer an environment which allows creative interaction with collected information. Taking the cost factors described in Sect. 3.2 into account we try to increase a user's motivation to adopt to the new system by adhering to three design principles:

Principle 1: Create an independent *collaboration layer* that can be used in conjunction with any (standard) solitary web-search tool. Integrate this additional layer seamlessly into the user's web-search infrastructure to be as little intrusive to the user's accustomed search environment as possible.

Principle 2: Automatically collect browser interaction data of each user and store it on a central server database. Leverage this data to make sharing search-related data in a group easier.

Principle 3: Lastly, allow experts to be able to personalize the outcome of a collaborative search task, e. g., by creating personalized views for the data they collect in a search task.

5.1   Traceable Collaborative Search

When addressing traceability in a (collaborative) search task, our general approach is to treat exploratory search like an orienteering hike. In an orienteering hike participants use maps and other tools to navigate in previously unfamiliar terrain to find special points of interest within a given time. In exploratory search points of interest are resources that contain information that (partially) answer an information need. One of the main differences between orienteering and exploratory search is that in orienteering the maps of the terrain are often provided upfront to help navigation, whereas maps of the information space typically do not exist in exploratory search. Thus, similar to the maps in orienteering our approach is to provide a visual guide for exploratory search activity by creating a map of the explored information space. In particular, the members of a group should be able to trace what part of the information space they have explored, including what directions they took, where they found relevant information, and how they arrived there. With the help of a special-tailored browser extension we collect data about each user's individual exploration progress, e. g., the visited websites. Since the data is collected during search on-the-fly we are able to visualize this progress without further user interaction.

The general design of the map is shown in Fig. 4a and b. The map lays out visited websites of a group of searchers as tiles in 2-dimensional space. The tiles are organized as a horizontal tree where the root is on the left-hand side, so that exploration paths can be read from left to right. We have chosen a tree visualization because it provides a definite start (root) and end (leaf) for each path the searchers take. The structure of the tree is the result of how the searchers explore the information space. Unfortunately, it is beyond the scope of this paper to provide a detailed description about how the structure is created. Basically, the browser extension collects browser interaction data to determine how a user moves from website to website. It then processes this data to create the corresponding tree. The server is able to process the data of multiple searchers and create a single tree representation of it.

A concrete implementation of the map, which we call a Search Map [40], is shown in Fig. 5. There are additional interaction features we have implemented into the Search Map. For example, it is possible to zoom in and out of the map to either receive a general idea of what paths have been taken in general or examine the details of a path. When zoomed out the tiles shrink gradually and some of the shown information within a tile is omitted. Since a Search Map can become large quickly, especially in a collaborative context, it is also possible to fold/unfold or hide exploration paths on demand, e. g., by filtering classes of actions like queries, documents, or snippets, or by issuing meta search queries that highlight

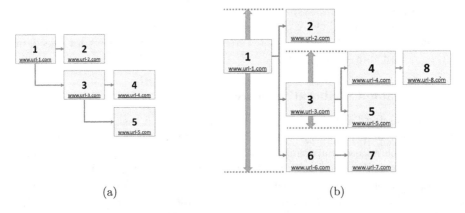

(a)   (b)

Fig. 4. Conceptual design of a Search Map as a dynamic horizontal tree displaying (a) five and (b) eight visited websites. Exploration paths can be read from left to right. Violet arrows in (b) indicate how tiles move up and down to remain visible on the vertical axis when the Search Map is scrolled up/down. (Color figure online)

parts of the map that match these queries. Additional interactions with the map encompass user annotations, like comments or symbols, that can be pinned on the map to communicate (meta) information concerning the exploration. Such meta information can be, for instance, a hint on a dead-end in a search path or the need for future updates. A user study is still needed to confirm the usefulness of these interactions and the Search Map in general. However, we expect that especially the annotations are helpful when tasks have to be updated and searchers want to communicate what future search sessions could focus on. For instance, they can leave messages on the map indicating how to continue a direction in the future.

Also, while moving the Search Map (up and down or left and right), a special layout algorithm automatically adjusts the placement of the tiles so that tiles of a search path are moved up and down on the vertical axis to remain visible. Violet arrows in Fig. 4b illustrate this movement. If the map is moved downwards the tiles move down, too, and upwards respectively. Some of the tiles represent normal websites (1). Other tiles show search engine results pages which are indicated by the issued query terms[1] (2). These query terms are automatically extracted from the website URL of a search engine. So far, three major search engines are supported: Google, Bing, and Yahoo. Again other tiles show extracted snippets from websites (3). These snippets are extracted manually by a user with the help of interaction features provided by the browser extension. Snippets contain information relevant for the search topic. We distinguish two types of snippets. Searchers can extract sentences or images from resources. They can also extract

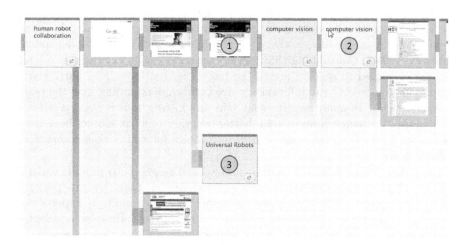

Fig. 5. An implementation of a Search Map visualizing the explored landscape of a group of searchers. The Search Map displays user actions like visiting a website, issuing a search query, and extracting snippets from a website as tiles in a horizontal tree.

---

[1] What search engine is used does not affect the visualization of the Search Map, so long as the query can be determined by our browser extension. Thus, even Intranet search engines of companies can be incorporated in the map.

keywords from a resource which are often concepts or entities that relate to the search topic. For example, in the automotive scenario the concepts can be product and production technologies, suppliers, research institutes, development projects, challenges, or people. By displaying these keywords, facts, or images as tiles on the map, we seek to make it easier for the group to understand the outcome of a path. If keywords are extracted they are also used as input to the creative sensemaking interface, which is described in the next section.

As an instance of the collaboration layer the idea is to interfere as little with solitary information search tools as possible. So the Search Map can be faded over any active website in a browser window using a hotkey or a button on a browser toolbar, but remains invisible otherwise. So, whenever individual searchers want to know what the current progress of the collaborative search is (or of their solitary one for that matter), they can investigate the Search Map. Personalizing the outcome of the search task is achieved by creating individual views of the Search Map and reorganizing the tiles according to personal needs. Therefore, searchers can create different views for a Search Map of the same search task. Each view uses the same data about the exploratory behaviour of the group. Reorganizing tiles within a view using "drag and drop"-mechanics simply creates a custom interpretation of this data. So views are essentially "subversions" of the original Search Map that automatically merge newly added tiles according to the changes that have been made in the view. This way, it is possible for individuals to organize the map according to contents and topics, e.g., rather than on the actual search behaviour. By visualizing the joint search strategy of a team with the help of a Search Map we enable individuals to trace their search progress and be more aware of how they explore the information space together. We specifically want to encourage and empower parallel and divergent search strategies in a collaborative context while leaving room for independent strategies, as well. Considering that search tasks need to be extended at a later time, this is aimed to quickly access the resources that have been particularly helpful when answering the information need and understanding how the team discovered them. Domain experts that join an existing search task at a later time can use the Search Map to get a better overview of what sources have been explored and pick up loose ends or drill into topics for which no answers were available before, for example.

The advantage of a Search Map in professional search is to provide experts with a tool to more easily continue a previous search task, i.e., to perform task-updates, when exploring a previous map. Also, since multiple experts can contribute to the same Search Map it is easier for them to share related websites or contents, reducing the need to write additional E-Mails or chat messages.

5.2 Creativity-Focused Sensemaking

As outlined in Sect. 3.1 sensemaking in professional search often goes along with generating solutions to a given (domain-related) problem within a group of experts. There are some major challenges that arise when designing a search user interface to support this creative process: The interface should provide

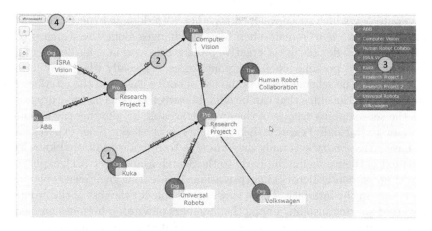

Fig. 6. An implementation of a topic graph. The mind map-like design of the interface is aimed at creatively interacting with collected information of a search task. Labelled nodes (1) are entities which are linked to each other by directed, labelled edges (2). To the right is an editable list of all available entities (3) in the graph. Tabs (4) are used to create personalized views for a search task.

interaction capabilities so that the group can express and discuss their (individual) concepts and merge these into a coherent whole; the interface should be based on a visualization that allows each individual searcher to (1) contribute their view, and (2) draw their own conclusions when the task is completed. Our general idea is to extend the collaborative layer created by the interface described in the previous section by elements supporting creative sensemaking and use of gathered information of the search task.

For the design of our creative sensemaking interface we lend some ideas from collaborative learning research. In collaborative learning mind maps, also called concept maps, have been reported to show good results when learners work together in a meaning-making and meaning-negotiation task (e. g., [4]). Therefore, the interface is designed like a mind mapping interface that we integrate into the collaboration layer. This interface can be used by searchers to organize and share their understanding of the search topic graphically and iteratively refine their individual and group's view during search. This is particularly helpful in an exploratory setting where this understanding develops over time and is seldom very elaborate at the beginning. It also offers the opportunity to evolve the mind map with each new execution of a search task. A simple example of such an interface is shown in Fig. 6. We call this example a topic graph because it is a graph-based representation of the group's view about the search topic [42]. Nodes of the topic graph represent domain entities of a search topic and edges represent relationships between these entities. The entities are either extracted during exploration (see Sect. 5.1) or added manually. Typically, mind maps do not possess any limitation concerning the use of entity classes or relationship types. The topic graph, however, is based on a flexible schema that provides (some) structure and semantics. Although, this schema is originally derived from a domain ontology which was developed together with domain experts, the central idea of the schema is to remain open towards changes along the search process and, thus, be more flexible in the creative process it is used in. This degree of flexibility is often not possible when using ontologies, especially when they become large/complex. The schema restricts the use of entity classes in the interface and the available relationships that can be added between them. The topic graph also makes the sensemaking results of the group traceable by allowing each member of the team to (formally) express their thoughts on the topic. Since experts sometimes have different backgrounds they are able to provide additional knowledge and context of their domain. Similarly to the Search Maps (Sect. 5.1), experts are able to express (contradictory) interpretations by creating their own topic graph views as tabs in the interface. These views are visible for the rest of the group, as well, so that sharing insights among the members of a group becomes an option. The topic graphs are physically stored in a dedicated graph database and made available for co-searchers in a group to explore during their search tasks. We elaborate more on the possibilities of active, explicit collaboration in [42]. Centrally storing the sensemaking data of all search tasks also allows for interesting postprocessing procedures. For example, analysing the structure and semantics of all topic graphs can lead to helpful recommendations in future search tasks that deal with similar topics. This kind of implicit collaboration can be further augmented by facilitating the information about the exploratory actions underlying a topic graph which are stored in the corresponding Search Maps.

5.3   Conclusion

In practice, when working with the two interfaces presented above, Search Maps and topic graphs are aimed to complement each other. Topic graphs help to gain an overall understanding of the search topic by looking at the mind maplike representation of domain-related information. When members of a group identifies an entity or a relation of interest they can use the Search Map to investigate the exploratory activities that led to its discovery. In a professional setting we believe this makes it easier to address complex search tasks more completely and synergies can be leveraged more effectively. For example, sparse information spaces can be explored more systematically even if new information becomes available at a fast pace. Especially in situations where new information may render previously collected data invalid, working with Search Maps and topic graphs may help to understand and interpret changes across search tasks.

6   Summary

Domain experts often perform professional information seeking tasks as part of their daily work. Designing adequate computer support is challenging, especially due to the often collaborative nature of these tasks, which demands for specialized interaction features. Experts typically have to solve an underlying domain problem using the information they gather together as a group. Solving these problems requires extensive exploratory search, collaborative sensemaking and repeated updates as new information becomes available. In order to tackle these challenges we highlighted two aspects of a collaborative search task that are still rarely addressed: traceability and creative sensemaking. Traceability describes a group's ability to understand the structure, semantics, and relevance of their collaborative information seeking behaviour. Creative sensemaking describes the group's ability to solve a shared domain problem together by reorganizing newly acquired information into a coherent whole that satisfies their underlying information need. We outlined how these aspects blend into the collaborative search process with the help of an extended model of collaborative information seeking that we built based on Wilson's earlier model. Although, we present user interface prototypes that support traceability and creative sensemaking in a collaborative search task, much of the challenges in professional information seeking still remain. Especially, for the design of future search systems it is important to investigate the dynamics and demands of the professional setting in more detail. Search systems that allow a lean participation of group members and at the same time maintain much of their individual experience, will likely advance and may overthrow how we search together in a professional environment.

References

1. Anderson, L.W., Krathwohl, D.R., Airasian, P.W., Cruikshank, K.A., Mayer, R.E., Pintrich, P.R., Raths, J., Wittrock, M.C.: A Taxonomy for Learning, Teaching, and Assessing: A Revision of Bloom's Taxonomy of Educational Objectives, 2nd edn. Allyn & Bacon, Boston (2001)
2. Aula, A., Russell, D.M.: Complex and exploratory web search. In: Information Seeking Support Systems (2008)
3. Azzopardi, L., Pickens, J., Sakai, T., Soulier, L., Tamine, L.: ECol 2015: first international workshop on the evaluation on collaborative information seeking and retrieval. In: Proceedings of the 24th ACM International Conference on Information and Knowledge Management, CIKM 2015, pp. 1943–1944. ACM, New York (2015)
4. Basque, J., Pudelko, B.: Intersubjective meaning-making in dyads using object-typed concept mapping. In: Torres, P.L., Marriott, R.D.C.V. (eds.) Handbook of Research on Collaborative Learning Using Concept Mapping, pp. 180–206. IGI Global, Hershey (2010). Chap. 10
5. Belkin, N.J., Oddy, R.N., Brooks, H.M.: ASK for information retrieval: part I. Background and theory. J. Doc. **38**(2), 61–71 (1982)
6. Bergamaschi, S., Ferro, N., Guerra, F., Silvello, G.: Keyword-based search over databases: a roadmap for a reference architecture paired with an evaluation framework. In: Nguyen, N.T., Kowalczyk, R., Rupino da Cunha, P. (eds.) Transactions on Computational Collective Intelligence XXI. LNCS, vol. 9630, pp. 1–20. Springer, Heidelberg (2016). doi:10.1007/978-3-662-49521-6_1
7. Byström, K., Järvelin, K.: Task complexity affects information seeking and use. Inf. Process. Manage. **31**(2), 191–213 (1995)
8. Capra, R., Chen, A.T., McArthur, E., Davis, N.: Searcher actions and strategies in asynchronous collaborative search. In: Proceedings of 76th ASIS&T Annual Meeting: Beyond the Cloud: Rethinking Information Boundaries, pp. 75:1–75:10 (2013)

9. Capra, R., Marchionini, G., Velasco-Martin, J., Muller, K.: Tools-at-hand and learning in multi-session, collaborative search. In: Proceedings of SIGCHI Conference on Human Factors in Computing Systems, pp. 951–960. ACM (2010)

10. Cole, M.J., Hendahewa, C., Belkin, N.J., Shah, C.: User activity patterns during information search. ACM Trans. Inform. Syst. (TOIS) **33**(1), 1 (2015)

11. Ellis, D.: A behavioral approach to information retrieval system design. J. Doc. **45**(3), 171–212 (1989)

12. Ellis, D., Cox, D., Hall, K.: A comparison of the information seeking patterns of researchers in the physical and social sciences. J. Doc. **49**(4), 356–369 (1993)

13. Ellis, D., Haugan, M.: Modelling the information seeking patterns of engineers and research scientists in an industrial environment. J. Doc. **53**(4), 384–403 (1997)

14. Evans, B.M., Chi, E.H.: Towards a model of understanding social search. In: Proceedings of ACM Conference on Computer Supported Cooperative Work, pp. 485–494. ACM (2008)

15. Gäde, M., Hall, M., Huurdeman, H., Kamps, J., Koolen, M., Skov, M., Toms, E., Walsh, D.: Supporting complex search tasks. In: Hanbury, A., Kazai, G., Rauber, A., Fuhr, N. (eds.) ECIR 2015. LNCS, vol. 9022, pp. 841–844. Springer, Cham (2015). doi:10.1007/978-3-319-16354-3_99

16. Georghiou, L.: The Handbook of Technology Foresight: Concepts and Practice. Edward Elgar, Cheltenham (2008)

17. Golovchinsky, G., Qvarfordt, P., Pickens, J.: Collaborative information seeking. Computer **42**(3), 47–51 (2009)

18. Gossen, T., Nitsche, M., Haun, S., Nürnberger, A.: Data exploration for bisociative knowledge discovery: a brief overview of tools and evaluation methods. In: Berthold, M.R. (ed.) Bisociative Knowledge Discovery. LNCS (LNAI), vol. 7250, pp. 287–300. Springer, Heidelberg (2012). doi:10.1007/978-3-642-31830-6_20

19. Gossen, T., Bade, K., Nürnberger, A.: A comparative study of collaborative and individual web search for a social planning task. In: Proceedings of LWA Workshop (2011)

20. Hearst, M.A.: What's missing from collaborative search? Computer **47**(3), 58–61 (2014)

21. Hembrooke, H.A., Granka, L.A., Gay, G.K., Liddy, E.D.: The effects of expertise and feedback on search term selection and subsequent learning: research articles. J. Am. Soc. Inf. Sci. Technol. **56**(8), 861–871 (2005)

22. Kelly, R., Payne, S.J.: Collaborative web search in context: a study of tool use in everyday tasks. In: Proceedings of the 17th ACM Conference on Computer Supported Cooperative Work and Social Computing, CSCW 2014, pp. 807–819. ACM, New York (2014)

23. Knight, S.A., Spink, A.: Toward a web search information behavior model. In: Spink, A., Zimmer, M. (eds.) Web Search, Information Science and Knowledge Management, vol. 14, pp. 209–234. Springer, Heidelberg (2008)

24. Kotov, A., Bennett, P.N., White, R.W., Dumais, S.T., Teevan, J.: Modeling and analysis of cross-session search tasks. In: Proceedings of the 34th International ACM SIGIR Conference on Research and Development in Information Retrieval, pp. 5–14. ACM (2011)

25. Kuhlthau, C.C.: Inside the search process: Information seeking from the user's perspective. J. Am. Soc. Inf. Sci. **42**(5), 361–371 (1991)

26. Kuhlthau, C.C.: Seeking Meaning: A Process Approach to Library and Information Services. Ablex Publishing, Norwood (1994)

27. Marchionini, G.: Exploratory search: from finding to understanding. Commun. ACM **49**(4), 41–46 (2006)

28. McAfee, A., Brynjolfsson, E.: Big data: the management revolution. Harvard Bus. Rev. **90**, 60–68 (2012)
29. Morris, M.R.: Interfaces for collaborative exploratory web search: motivations and directions for multi-user designs. In: CHI 2007 Workshop on Exploratory Search and HCI (2007)
30. Morris, M.R.: Collaborating alone and together: investigating persistent and multi-user web search activities. Technical report MSR-TR-2007-11, Microsoft Research (2007)
31. Morris, M.R., Teevan, J., Bush, S.: Enhancing collaborative web search with personalization: groupization, smart splitting, and group hit-highlighting. In: Proceedings of ACM Conference on Computer Supported Cooperative Work, pp. 481–484. ACM (2008)
32. Nürnberger, A., Stange, D., Kotzyba, M.: Professional collaborative information seeking: on traceability and creative sensemaking. In: Cardoso, J., Guerra, F., Houben, G.-J., Pinto, A.M., Velegrakis, Y. (eds.) KEYSTONE 2015. LNCS, vol. 9398, pp. 1–16. Springer, Cham (2015). doi:10.1007/978-3-319-27932-9_1
33. Poltrock, S.E., Grudin, J., Dumais, S.T., Fidel, R., Bruce, H., Pejtersen, A.M.: Information seeking and sharing in design teams. In: Schmidt, K., Pendergast, M., Tremaine, M., Simone, C. (eds.) GROUP, pp. 239–247. ACM (2003)
34. Reddy, M.C., Jansen, B.J.: A model for understanding collaborative information behavior in context: a study of two healthcare teams. Inf. Process. Manage. **44**(1), 256–273 (2008)
35. Russell, D.M., Stefik, M.J., Pirolli, P., Card, S.K.: The cost structure of sensemaking. In: Proceedings of INTERACT 1993 and CHI 1993 Conference on Human Factors in Computing Systems, pp. 269–276. ACM (1993)
36. Shah, C.: Collaborative information seeking: a literature review. In: 2009 Workshop on Collaborative Information Behavior (2009)
37. Shah, C.: Collaborative Information Seeking - The Art and Science of Making the Whole Greater than the Sum of All. Springer, Heidelberg (2012)
38. Shah, C.: Collaborative information seeking. J. Assoc. Inf. Sci. Technol. **65**(2), 215–236 (2014)
39. Shah, C., Capra, R., Hansen, P.: Workshop on social and collaborative information seeking (SCIS). SIGIR Forum **49**(2), 117–122 (2016)
40. Stange, D., Nürnberger, A.: Search maps: enhancing traceability and overview in collaborative information seeking. In: Rijke, M., Kenter, T., Vries, A.P., Zhai, C.X., Jong, F., Radinsky, K., Hofmann, K. (eds.) ECIR 2014. LNCS, vol. 8416, pp. 763–766. Springer, Cham (2014). doi:10.1007/978-3-319-06028-6_91
41. Stange, D., Nürnberger, A.: Collaborative knowledge acquisition and exploration in technology search. In: Proceedings of the Professional Knowledge Management Conference (ProWM), ProWM 2015, pp. 843–849 (2015)
42. Stange, D., Nürnberger, A.: When experts collaborate: sharing search and domain expertise within an organization. In: Proceedings of the 15th International Conference on Knowledge Technologies and Data-Driven Business, i-KNOW 2015, pp. 45:1–45:4. ACM, New York (2015)
43. White, R.W., Dumais, S.T., Teevan, J.: Characterizing the influence of domain expertise on web search behavior. In: Proceedings of the Second ACM International Conference on Web Search and Data Mining, pp. 132–141. ACM (2009)
44. Wilson, T.D.: On user studies and information needs. J. Doc. **37**(1), 3–15 (1981)
45. Wilson, T.D.: Models in information behaviour research. J. Doc. **55**(3), 249–270 (1999)

Exploiting Linguistic Analysis on URLs for Recommending Web Pages: A Comparative Study

Sara Cadegnani[1], Francesco Guerra[1(✉)], Sergio Ilarri[2],
María del Carmen Rodríguez-Hernández[2], Raquel Trillo-Lado[2],
Yannis Velegrakis[3], and Raquel Amaro[4]

[1] Università di Modena e Reggio Emilia, Modena, Italy
{sara.cadegnani,francesco.guerra}@unimore.it
[2] University of Zaragoza, Zaragoza, Spain
{silarri,raqueltl}@unizar.es, mary0485@gmail.com
[3] University of Trento, Trento, Italy
velgias@disi.unitn.eu
[4] Universidade Nova de Lisboa, Lisbon, Portugal
raquelamaro@fcsh.unl.pt

Abstract. Nowadays, citizens require high level quality information from public institutions in order to guarantee their transparency. Institutional websites of governmental and public bodies must publish and keep updated a large amount of information stored in thousands of web pages in order to satisfy the demands of their users. Due to the amount of information, the "search form", which is typically available in most such websites, is proven limited to support the users, since it requires them to explicitly express their information needs through keywords. The sites are also affected by the so-called "long tail" phenomenon, a phenomenon that is typically observed in e-commerce portals. The phenomenon is the one in which not all the pages are considered highly important and as a consequence, users searching for information located in pages that are not condiered important are having a hard time locating these pages.

The development of a recommender system than can guess the next best page that a user wouild like to see in the web site has gained a lot of attention. Complex models and approaches have been proposed for recommending web pages to individual users. These approached typically require personal preferences and other kinds of user information in order to make successful predictions.

In this paper, we analyze and compare three different approaches to leverage information embedded in the structure of web sites and the logs of their web servers to improve the effectiveness of web page recommendation. Our proposals exploit the context of the users' navigations, i.e., their current sessions when surfing a specific web site. These approaches do not require either information about the personal preferences of the users to be stored and processed, or complex structures to be created and maintained. They can be easily incorporated to current large websites to facilitate the users' navigation experience. Last but not least, the paper reports some comparative experiments using a real-world website to analyze the performance of the proposed approaches.

© Springer International Publishing AG 2017
N.T. Nguyen et al. (Eds.): TCCI XXVI, LNCS 10190, pp. 26–45, 2017.
DOI: 10.1007/978-3-319-59268-8_2

1   Introduction

A great deal of of websites, in particular websites of Public Administration institutions and govermental bodies, contain a large amount of pages with a lots of information. The content of this kind of websites is usually very wide and diverse, as it is targeting a broad group of diverse users. Moreover, these institutions are frequently the owners and the reference authorities of most of the content offered in their web pages (i.e., they are not simple information aggregators, but they are the providers of authoritative information). Therefore, a huge amount of visitors is interested in exploring and analyzing the information published on them. As an example, the ec.europa.eu and europa.eu websites, managed by the European Commission, have been visited by more than $520M$ people in the last year[1].

The websites of these institutions offering large amounts of data are typically organized in different thematic categories and nested sections that generally form large trees with a high height (e.g., the previously cited website is organized in six sections: "The Commission and its Priorities", "About the European Commission", "Life, work and travel in the EU", etc.). Nevertheless, users usually consider the retrieval of useful information a difficult task since the way in which the information is organized (i.e., the conceptualization of the website) can differ from what they expect when they are surfacing it, and unfrequent information demands usually require them to spend a lot of time in order to locate the information they need. So, some techniques and best practices for the design these websites have been proposed and experimented along the time. In some websites, for example, the information is grouped according to the topic. In other websites, a small set of different profiles (types of users) are defined and users are explicitly asked to choose one of those roles to surface the websites (e.g., in a university website, users can be asked to declare if they are students, faculty members, or companies, and according to this and the information provided when they enter in sections of the website, the information is structured in different ways). However, the "long tail" phenomenon[2] also affects the task of searching information in this kind of websites, where there are thousands of pages that can be accessed any time, independently of their publication date.

Different approaches and techniques have been proposed to improve users' experience navigating large websites. One of the solutions typically adopted is to include a search form in the header of the web pages to allow users to express their information needs by mean of keyword queries. Another approach to support users is to provide users with a little frame or area in the web page (or a special web page) where a list of "suggested links" is shown. The main disadvantage of the first approach is that it requires to maintain updated a complex indexed structure which must change when the web pages are modified (additions, removals, updates of content, etc.). Even if the data to search is stored in a

---

[1] http://ec.europa.eu/ipg/services/statistics/performance_en.htm, statistics computed on June 1st, 2015.

[2] http://www.wired.com/2004/10/tail/.

structured database, the issue remains since keyword queries against databases are not easily solvable [3,4]. Besides, it requires that users explicit through keywords their information needs, which could be difficult for some users. Moreover, there exists a semantic gap between the users' information needs and the queries submitted to the search system. With respect to the second option, two trends have been identified: (1) showing the same content to all the users visiting the website at a specific moment, and (2) considering the profile of each user to offer him/her a personalized list of suggested links. Showing all users the same recommendations cannot be appropriate, as this type of websites are oriented to a wide heterogeneous public, and what is interesting for a visitor can be useless for another. On the other hand, maintaining profiles of users implies that the users should be registered in the website, and profiled with respect their interest. This also leads to the need (1) to take into account complex and reliable procedures to securely maintain their personal information while respecting their privacy and legal issues, and (2) to effectively profile the users on the basis of the (few) personal data available.

In this paper, we analyze and compare three different approaches to create a dynamic list of "suggested links to web pages of the website" which consider information embedded in the structure of the website and the logs of their web servers. In particular, our proposals for recommender systems take into account:

- *The web pages that the user is visiting in the current session.* The recommendation system works in real time and dynamically updates the links to propose by taking into account the pages he/she is navigating. Moreover, the suggested links are updated after new pages are visited in a specific session.
- *Navigational paths (routes) of previous users.* By analyzing the logs of the web servers of the website, we can discover the next pages visited by other users when they were in the same page as the current user. In particular, we consider that the users' navigation "sessions" extracted from the logs are sets of pages related to each other that satisfy the same information need. In fact, we assume that in a session the user is looking for something to satisfy a specific information need and that the session contains all the pages required for satisfying that need. In this way, the historical sessions can play the role of "suggestion spaces", as they include pages considered relevant in the same "context".
- *The website structure.* The structure of a website follows a conceptual taxonomy that is exploited for the recommendation, by suggesting more specific or more general web pages than the current one.
- *Lexical and semantic knowledge about the pages.* The content of the pages is used in order to suggest pages with a similar content. The extraction of keywords/topics representing the content can be a huge and complex task for some websites. For this reason, we tried to exploit the URL as a means for approximating the content of the pages. This idea is based on the observation that in some particular websites the URLs are highly explicative in the sense that they contain a lot of textual information about the pages and the categories the pages belong to. If this is the case for the website under analysis, we

can exploit this information in order to make suggestions. It should be noted that the use of descriptive URLs is a usual recommendation for SEO (Search Engine Optimization); moreover, thanks to the use of descriptive URLs, end users can anticipate what they can expect from a web page.

In this paper (extended version, with new experiments and discussion, of [5]), we analyze and compare three methods to make the recommendations: (1) No History method (NoHi), (2) My Own History method (MOHi), and (3) Collective History method (CoHi). The first method only considers the website structure and lexical and semantic knowledge of the pages. The second method additionally considers the information related to the pages that the user is visiting in the current session. Finally, the Collective History Method considers the same information as the two previous methods as well as navigational paths (routes) followed by previous visitors of the website. Besides, the performance of the different methods is analyzed under different configurations, which represent different contexts, by means of a wide set of experiments and considering the website of the Comune di Modena in Italy (http://www.comune.modena.it).

The remainder of this paper is structured as follows. Firstly, some related work is studied and analyzed in Sect. 2. Secondly, the different proposals to recommend web pages in large web sites are described and analyzed in Sect. 3. After that, in Sect. 4 the results of a set of experiments to evaluate the performance of the approaches are described. Finally, some conclusions and future work lines are presented in Sect. 5.

2   Related Work

Some works tackle the problem of web page recommendation in a general context, aiming at providing the user with interesting web pages that could fit his/her interests (e.g., [1,2,21,25]). For example, [1,2] propose the use of a multiagent system to search interesting articles in the Web in order to compose a personalized newspaper. In [21,25], the idea is to estimate the suitability of a web page for a user based on its relevance according to the tags provided by similar users to annotate that page. The previous works do not explicitly consider the notion of user session, as their goal is just to recommend web pages to a user independently of his/her current navigation behavior within a specific web site, i.e., the current context of the user.

Other approaches, such as [7,9,12,24], explicitly exploit user sessions and therefore are closer in spirit to our proposals. The SurfLen system [9] suggests interesting web pages to users based on the sets of URLs that are read together by many users and on the similarity between users (users that read a significant number of similar pages). The proposal described in [12] tackles the recommendation problem within a single e-commerce website and proposes an approach to recommend product pages (corresponding to product records in the website database) as well as other web pages (news about the company, product reviews, advises, etc.); although the recommendation is based only on the web page that the user is currently visiting and not directly on the previous web pages visited by that user, user historical sessions are also exploited to extract information regarding the pages which are visited together (in one session). The approach presented in [7] is based on clustering user sessions and computing a similarity between user sessions in order to recommend three different pages that the user has not visited (a hit is considered if any of the three recommended pages is the next request of the user); the similarity between two user sessions is computed by considering the order of pages, the distance between identical pages, and the time spent on the pages. Another interesting proposal is introduced in [19], where the recommendation system is based on an ad-hoc ontology describing the website and on web usage information. The recommendation model PIGEON (PersonalIzed web paGe rEcommendatiON) [24] exploits collaborative filtering and a topic-aware Markov model to personalize web page recommendations: the recommendations are not just based on the sequence of pages visited but also on the interests of the users and the topics of the web pages. A web page recommendation system is also proposed in [6], but that proposal focuses exclusively on the domain of movies. Movie web pages are clustered by using a weighted k-means clustering algorithm, where pages visited by many users are given higher weights (more importance in the clustering). To recommend new movie web pages to a user, the current active navigation session of the user (web pages that he/she has recently visited) is compared (by using a similarity measure) with the clusters of the movie web pages previously obtained.

There are also some proposals that generalize the problem of web page recommendation to that of web personalization (e.g., see [8,18]). The goal of web personalization is rather to compute a collection of relevant objects of different types to recommend [18], such as URLs, ads, texts, and products, and compose customized web pages. So, a website can be personalized by adapting its content and/or structure: adding new links, highlighting existing links, or creating new pages [8]. Interesting surveys on web mining for web personalization are also presented in [8,13]. However, this kind of approaches require users to be registered in the web site and they need to create and maintain profiles for the different users.

As compared to the previous works, we aim at solving the problem of next URL recommendation within a single web site by exploiting only a limited amount of information available in previous historical user logs. For example, we do not assume that information about the times spent by the users at each URL is available, which may be important to determine the actual interest of a web page (e.g., see [15,22]). Similarly, we do not assume that users can be identified (i.e., they are anonymous), and so it is not possible to extract user profiles. Instead, we propose several methods that require a minimum amount of information and evaluate and compare them in a real context. The methods proposed are also lightweight in the sense that they do not require a heavy (pre-) processing such as semantic extraction from the contents of web pages or the creation and maintenance of indexed structures such as inverted indexes on the content of the web pages.

Finally, a number of other approaches are based the knowledge extracted from URLs. Among them, in [23] the authors applied named entity recognition techniques to URLs with the aim of effectively annotating the contents of the webpages and in [10], websites are clustered on the basis of their URLs.

3   Study of Techniques for Recommending Web Pages

The goal of the recommendation approaches proposed in this paper is to provide the user with a ranked list of suggested URLs (available within a potentially-large website) by considering the context of the user (e.g., the URLs that he/she is currently visiting), structural information about the website, and statistical information available on the logs of the web servers where the site is located. The goal of the application is to recommend pages where the content is similar/related to the content offered by the web page that users are viewing at a specific moment. We assume that users behave rationally and that the exploration performed by them has a purpose (i.e., they are looking for information on a specific topic).

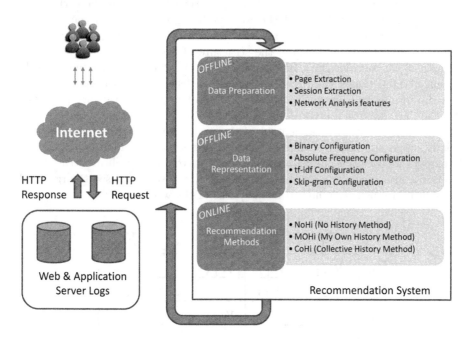

Fig. 1. Functional architecture.

In this section, firstly, models and structures to represent the context of the user, and the content and structure of the website, are presented. After that, three proposed methods (No History Method – NoHi, My Own History Method –

MOHi, and Collective History Method – CoHi) to perform the recommendation are described in detail.

The methods have been implemented in prototypes and evaluated in a real scenario. All the prototypes are built according to the same functional architecture, shown in Fig. 1, where the recommending task is divided into three steps. The first two steps are executed offline and consist in extracting the information about the visited pages in the users' sessions and their representations with proper matrices. We developed and compared four possible techniques (three based on sparse vectors, one on dense vectors) for representing the users' navigation paths in the website as described in Sect. 3.1. In the third step, these different models and structures are used by three methods, as introduced in Sect. 3.2, to generate recommendations.

3.1   Representation of the User Context and the Website

We modeled the users' interactions with the website by adopting and experimenting both sparse and continuous representations of the navigation paths. In particular, by taking as inspiration different classic Information Retrieval (IR) models, we proposed three "bag-of-word" matrix adaptations where the rows represent the different URLs of the website being explored and the columns the vocabulary of those URLs (i.e., all the words that appear in the set of URLs) to model the content and the structure of the website (see Fig. 2). For example, if we consider the URL http://europa.eu/youreurope/citizens/travel/passenger-rights/index_en.htm of the official website of the European Union, then the terms "your europe", "citizens", "travel", "passenger rights", "index" and "en" are part of the vocabulary of the URLs of the website. In this way, the semantic and the lexical content of the web pages is indirectly considered, as it is supposed that the name of the web pages is not random and that the developers follow some kind of convention. Moreover, the website structure is also taken into account, as the categories and nested sections used to organized the website are usually reflected in the paths of the web pages.

	F_1	F_2	F_3	...	F_m
P_1	W_{11}	W_{12}	W_{13}	...	W_{1m}
P_2	W_{21}	W_{22}	W_{23}	...	W_{2m}
P_3	W_{31}	W_{32}	W_{33}	...	W_{3m}
...	...	...	...	...	...
P_n	W_{n1}	W_{n2}	W_{n3}	...	W_{nm}

Fig. 2. Matrix represention of a website.

The user's context is modeled by the vector that represents the web page that he/she is currently visualizing, thus this vector is equal to the row corresponding to the URL of the web page in the matrix representing the website.

To give a value to the different components of the vector representing the user context and the matrix representing the website, classic IR models are considered again as inspiration and the following configurations were analyzed:

- Binary configuration. This configuration is inspired by the Boolean IR model. Thus, each element in the matrix (or vector) indicates whether the URL considered (the row of the matrix or the vector representing the user context) contains (value 1) or does not contain (value 0) the keyword (the term) corresponding to the column of the matrix.
- Absolute-frequency configuration. This configuration is inspired by the first Vector Space IR models. Thus, each element in the matrix (or vector) indicates how many times the keyword corresponding to the column of the matrix appears in the URL considered (the row of the matrix or the vector representing the user context), i.e., the absolute frequency (or raw frequency) of the term in the URL. For example, if we consider the URL http://www.keystone-cost.eu/meeting/spring-wg-meeting-2015/ and the keyword "meeting" then the value of the element corresponding to the column of the term "meeting" is 2. The absolute frequency of a term i in a URL j is represented by $f_{i,\,j}$. So, in this case
  $$f_{meeting,\ www.keystone-cost.eu/meeting/spring-wg-meeting-2015/} = 2$$
- TF_IDF configuration. This configuration is inspired by more modern Vector Space IR models, where the length of the documents and the content of the corpus analyzed are considered. Thus, in this case, the length of the URLs and the vocabulary of the set of URLs of the website are considered to define the value of each element of the matrix. In more detail, each element in the matrix (or in each vector) is the product of the relative *Term Frequency* (*TF*) of the keyword corresponding to the column of the matrix in the URL considered (the row of the matrix) and the corresponding *Inverse Document Frequency* (*IDF*), i.e., the number of URLs in which that keyword appears. In more detail, $w_{ij} = TF_{ij} * IDF_i$ where

$$TF_{ij} = \frac{f_{i,\,j}}{maximum(f_{i,\,j})} \tag{1}$$

$$IDF_i = \log N/n_i \tag{2}$$

where N is the number of URLs of the website and n_i is the number of URLs where the term i appears.

The previously introduced matrices are both high dimensional (the number of columns is equal to the number of terms existing in the URLs of the website, and the number of rows is equal to the number of web pages available on the website) and sparse (typically, the URL of a web page only contains a limited number of terms of the vocabulary considered as columns), thus only few entries assume values different from zero. An alternative is to use short, dense vectors/matrices (of length 50–2000 columns) that can be efficiently and effectively computed with machine learning techniques. The development of techniques for using dense matrices in NLP for representing words and documents has recently become popular thanks to works published in [14, 16], where a neural network-based model is exploited for building dense and concise word representations in a vector space. Two architectures have been proposed: the CBOW (i.e., continuous bag-of-words) architecture that builds a model that is able to predict the current word based on a context with a parametric dimension, and the Skip-gram model which can support the predictions of surrounding words given the current word. Furthemore, as shown in [17], it was found that similarity of word representations adopting Skip-gram and C-BOW models goes beyond simple syntactic regularities. Using a word offset technique where simple algebraic operations are performed on the word vectors, it was shown for example that vector("King") - vector("Man") + vector("Woman") results in a vector that is the closest to the vector representation of the word Queen. These regularities can be exploited in our scenario for building meaningful and summarized representations of all the pages visited during a session. In this paper, we selected to adopt a Skip-gram model to represent sessions and URLs and our prototypes relies on the gensim[3] library, which provides an implementation of the model in Python. The library requires the model to be trained through "sentences" and generates a dense matrix representing the words used in them. In our scenario, we consider user sessions as sentences and pages browsed in the sessions as words. The result is a model where rows are the URLs of the webpages and columns describing features are exploited for predicting the pages interesting for a user. The Skip-gram model allows also the users to set a number of parameters. We experimented the recommending system with models having different dimensions, trained taken into account contexts with different sizes, and URLs occurring in a predefined number of sessions at least. The results of our experiments are shown in Sect. 4.

3.2   Methods

Three methods proposed to perform web page recommendation in large web sites are described and compared in the following:

- *No History method (NoHi)*. In this method, only the current user context is considered, i.e., this method takes into account the information of the web page that the user is currently visualizing to make the recommendation but it does not consider the previous pages that the user has already visited in his/her current session. Thus, the pages recommended to the user are selected by computing the similarity between his/her current state represented by the vector of the URL of the web page visualized and the remaining URLs of the website (the rows of the matrix representing the website in Fig. 2). The most similar URLs to the current user's state are recommended by using as measurement the cosine similarity. According to the literature, this method can be classified as a "content-based recommender system".

---

[3] https://radimrehurek.com/gensim/.

$$\mathbf{S_{k_{history}}} = \begin{array}{l} \mathbf{P_1} \left[w_{11} \quad w_{12} \quad w_{13} \quad \ldots \quad w_{1m} \right] \oplus \\ \mathbf{P_2} \left[w_{21} \quad w_{22} \quad w_{23} \quad \ldots \quad w_{2m} \right] \oplus \\ \qquad\qquad\qquad \ldots \qquad\qquad\qquad\quad \oplus \\ \mathbf{P_k} \left[w_{k1} \quad w_{k2} \quad w_{k3} \quad \ldots \quad w_{km} \right] \end{array}$$

Fig. 3. User historical context.

- *My Own History method (MOHi).* In this method, the current web page visited by the user and also the web pages visited in his/her current session (i.e., his/her history) are considered to make the recommendation. Furthemore, the number of pages previously visited taken into account can be limited to a certain number $K_{history}$, which is a configuration parameter of the system. In this case, the user context is modeled as the result of an aggregate function of the already-visited web pages. In this proposal, we adopted two ways for representing the web pages visited in a session: (1) we approximated a session as the sum of the vectors representing its constituent web pages for evaluating recommending systems based on "sparse" representations; and (2) we considered the webpages in each session as a cluster of vectors and the resulting "centroid" as the vector describing the session for evaluating recommending systems based on "dense" vector representations. Nevertheless, any other aggregate function such as a weighted sum (see Fig. 3) could be used. The recommendation is performed in a way similar to the previous method (NoHi). Thus, the aggregated vector is compared with the URLs of the website (the rows of the matrix representing the website in Fig. 2) and the most similar URLs are recommended. This method can also be classified as a "content-based recommender system".

- *Collective History method (CoHi).* In this method, the history of the user in the current session is also considered. The history is modeled as a list where the items are the different URLs corresponding to the pages that the user has visited. Moreover, this method uses the previous sessions of other users to recommend the web pages. The sessions of the other users are built by extracting information from the logs of the web server of the website and by considering the following rules:

  • A session lasts at most 30 min.
  • A session has to have at least 5 items (i.e., the user has to have visited at least 5 web pages of the website in a session).

In more detail, matrixes where rows represent the different sessions of the previous users of the website and columns represent the vocabulary of the URLs of the website are built in an analogous way to the previous methods (NoHi method and MOHi method). Aggregated vectors containing all the keywords of the URLs visited during the sessions of the users are built. Those aggregated vectors are built by a simple addition of all the weights of the vectors corresponding to the URLs of the resources visited during the session.

Nevertheless, a weighted sum where for example, the URLs visited initially have less importance than the URLs visited at the end of the session could be applied. After that, the list that models the current session of the user is compared with the sessions of previous users and the top-k similar sessions are retrieved according to the cosine distance. Now, for suggesting the web pages from the top-k sessions we adopt a voting system based on a simple heuristic rule. In particular, we extract all the pages from the sessions and we weigh them according to the position of the session. The rule we follow is that the pages extracted from the top-1 session are weighted k times more than the ones in the k-th session retrieved. The weights in the web pages are then added up, thus generating their rank. Since it exploits the knowledge provided by the navigation of other users, this method can be classified as an "item-based collaborative filtering" recommendation system.

Each method has been implemented to work with the different data configurations described previously. Note that, as shown in Fig. 4, the CoHi method is not applicable to the skip-gram configuration.

	NoHi	MOHi	CoHi
Binary Configuration	X	X	X
Absolute Frequency Configuration	X	X	X
tf-idf Configuration	X	X	X
Skip-gram Configuration	X	X	N.A.

Fig. 4. Approaches developed and compared in the paper.

4 Experimental Evaluation

In this section, we present the experimental evaluation performed to evaluate the proposed methods for web page recommendation. Firstly, in Sect. 4.1, we focus on the dataset used. Then, in Sect. 4.2, we describe the experimental settings. Finally, the results of the experimental evaluation are presented and analyzed in Sect. 4.3.

4.1 Dataset

The "Comune di Modena" Town Hall website[4] has been used in our experiments. It is the official website of an Italian city, having a population of about 200000 citizens. The website visitors are mainly citizens looking for information about

---

[4] http://www.comune.modena.it.

institutional services (schools, healthcare, labour and free time), local companies that want to know details about local regulations, and tourists interested in information about monuments, cultural events, accommodations and food. To understand the main features of the dataset, we performed two complementary analyses: first, we analyzed the website structure to evaluate the main features of the dataset independently of its actual exploitation by the users; and second, we evaluated the users' behaviors in 2014 by analyzing the logs of the accesses. For achieving the first task, a crawler has been built and adapted for extracting some specific metadata (URL, outgoing links, creation date, etc.) describing the pages. A graph where the web pages are nodes and the links between them are direct edges has been built. The graph representation allowed us to apply a number of simple statistical and network analysis to obtain some details about the website. The results we obtained show that this is a large website composed of more than 13000 pages, classified into more than 30 thematic areas. The average in-degree and out-degree of the pages (i.e., the average number of incoming and outgoing links) is around 13 (the links in the headers and footers have not been computed). This value shows that pages are largely interconnected with each other. Despite the large number of pages, the diameter of the graph is small (8), which means that in the worst case a page can reach another page following a path that crosses 8 other pages. The average path length is 4.57. The modularity of the graph is 0.812. This is a high value that shows that the pages in the website are strongly connected in modules which are poorly coupled with each other. According to this value, the website seems to be well designed with a fixed structure and the information classified in defined sections. Finally, the average clustering coefficient (AAC) is 0.296. This values shows that the graph nodes are not highly connected (a graph completely connected has ACC equal to 1). This value seems to show a countertrend with respect to the other measures that show strong connection levels. As reported by the modularity value, this AAC low degree is normal, since the website is organized in strongly connected modules loosely coupled with each other, and it contains thousands of pages only hierarchically connected.

This analysis was complemented by the analysis of the logs showing the real website usage by the users. In 2014, the number of sessions[5] computed was more than 2.5 millions. The average length of the session is 2.95 pages. Around 10000 pages (72.29% of the overall number of pages) have been visited by at least one visitor in 2014. Only 2809 sessions (0.11% of the overall number of sessions) include in their page the "search engine page" or do not follow the direct links provided in their pages. This demonstrates the quality of the structural design of the website.

4.2 Experimental Settings

In our experiments, we considered the logs from the website limiting our focus on sessions composed of at least 5 pages. The sessions satisfying this requirement

---

[5] As described in Sect. 3.2, a session includes the pages which are visited by the same user, i.e., the same IP address and User-Agent, in 30 min.

are 303693, 11% of the overall amount. The average length of these sessions is 7.5 pages.

The methods based on sparse matrices have been experimented with a vocabulary of terms built by stemming the words (we adopted the usual Porter stemming algorithm) extracted from the URLs. The vocabulary is composed of 5437 terms representing single words. For improving the accuracy, we added 23555 terms to the previous set, by joining each two consecutive words in the URLs. The methods based on dense vectors have been experimented with a large number of parameter settings, to obtain matrices with different dimensions (50, 100, 250, 500, 1000, and 2000 features), trained taken into account contexts composed of 3 and 6 words, and for words occurring in at least 1 and 10 sessions.

For evaluating the predictions, we divided the pages of a session in two parts: we considered the first two thirds of the web pages in a session as representing the current user's navigation path (we called these pages as the *set of navigation history*), and the remaining one third as the ground truth, i.e., the *set of correct results*. Therefore, our approaches take for each session the set of navigation history as input and provide a recommended page. Only if the page is in set of correct results the result is considered as good.

The following configurations are also considered to decide the types of web pages that can be recommended:

- **No_Exclusion**. This is the general case where URLs that the user has already visited in the current session can also be suggested. Notice that, in this case, the URL where the user is in a specific moment can be also suggested, i.e., the suggestion in this case would be to stay in the same page and not to navigate to another one.
- **Exclusion**. URLs that the user has already visited in the current session cannot be suggested. In this way, the recommendation of staying in the same page is avoided. Moreover, with this configuration, navigating to a previously visited page or the home page of the website is never recommended, despite the fact that coming back to a specific web page already visited during a session is a typical pattern of the behavior of web users.
- **Sub_No_Exclusion**. The difference between this configuration and the one called Exclusion is that we consider only the sessions with no repeated web pages in the set of navigation history. This reduces the number of sessions used in the experiments to 107000. In this configuration, we aim at comparing the performance of our proposal with the one of a typical recommending system. These systems usually do not to recommend items already known/owned by the users. Nevertheless, in the context of websites it is normal that people navigate the same pages multiple times. For this reason in this configuration we consider only cases where in the navigation history there are no pages visited several times in the same sessions. The same constraint is not applied in the set of correct results where we can find pages which are also part of the navigation history (pages already visited).

– **Sub_With_Exclusion.** The difference between this configuration and the one called Sub_No_Exclusion is that here we remove sessions containing repeated web pages independently of their position in the session. In this case, we aim at perfectly simulating the behavior of a typical recommending system.

Note that, for the creation of the matrixes we did not exploited all the logs provided by the web server. Actually, logs have been split into two groups: the first one consists of two thirds of the pages and is used as a training set (i.e., they are used to create the matrices), and the remaining 1/3 of the data is used as a test set (i.e., they provide the sessions used to evaluate the performance of the method). In our experiments, the logs of the 20 first days of each month are considered as training sets while the logs of the last 10 days of each month are considered as test sets.

4.3   Results of the Experiments

Table 1 shows the accuracy of our three approaches based on sparse representations and computed according to the experimental setting defined in the previous section. In particular, Table 1(a) shows the accuracy obtained by the NoHi method, Table 1(b) the accuracy of the MOHi method and finally Table 1(b) the accuracy of CoHi method. Each column of the tables represents one of the configurations introduced in Sect. 3.1 for weighting the matrix that represents the pages visited by the users. In particular, the results applying absolute-frequency, binary, and TF_IDF configurations are shown, in the first, second and third column, respectively.

Table 1. Accuracy achieved in the experiments with sparse representations.

(a) Accuracy on the NoHi method

Configuration	Abs. Freq	Binary	tf_idf
No_Exclusion	0.204	0.21	0.218
Exclusion	0.125	0.130	0.133
Sub_No_Exclusion	0.235	0.243	0.256
Sub_With_Exclusion	0.242	0.252	0.264

(b) Accuracy on the MOHi method

Configuration	Abs. Freq	Binary	tf_idf
No_Exclusion	0.397	0.417	0.467
Exclusion	0.095	0.101	0.101
Sub_No_Exclusion	0.178	0.186	0.194
Sub_With_Exclusion	0.172	0.186	0.188

(c) Accuracy on the CoHi method

Configuration	Abs. Freq	Binary	tf_idf
No_Exclusion	0.584	0.587	0.595
Exclusion	0.192	0.194	0.203
Sub_No_Exclusion	0.310	0.314	0.332
Sub_With_Exclusion	0.360	0.363	0.384

The experiments show that the accuracy of the methods NoHi and MOHi is only partially satisfactory. Moreover, the MOHi approaches suffer from some

Table 2. Accuracy achieved in the experiments with dense representations.

(a) Accuracy on the NoHi method

Num Features	Context	Min Word	Accuracy
50	3	1	0.284
50	6	1	0.293
50	3	10	0.287
50	6	10	0.286
100	3	1	0.285
100	6	1	0.302
100	3	10	0.285
100	6	10	0.287
250	3	1	0.284
250	6	1	0.284
250	3	10	0.294
250	6	10	0.284
500	3	1	0.279
500	6	1	0.283
500	3	10	0.284
500	6	10	0.277
1000	3	1	0.281
1000	6	1	0.286
1000	3	10	0.282
1000	6	10	0.283
2000	3	1	0.281
2000	6	1	0.278
2000	3	10	0.293
2000	6	10	0.281

(b) Accuracy on the MOHi method

Num Features	Context	Min Word	Accuracy
50	3	1	0.387
50	6	1	0.390
50	3	10	0.379
50	6	10	0.389
100	3	1	0.402
100	6	1	0.410
100	3	10	0.398
100	6	10	0.400
250	3	1	0.400
250	6	1	0.407
250	3	10	0.398
250	6	10	0.405
500	3	1	0.404
500	6	1	0.408
500	3	10	0.395
500	6	10	0.404
1000	3	1	0.403
1000	6	1	0.407
1000	3	10	0.394
1000	6	10	0.404
2000	3	1	0.397
2000	6	1	0.406
2000	3	10	0.396
2000	6	10	0.406

noise except in the *No_Exclusion* configuration generated by the user history. Conversely, the accuracy obtained by the application of the CoHi method is good enough for testing the approach in a real environment and is in line with most of the existing recommender systems evaluated in the literature. Moreover, an analysis of the users' sessions show that users typically visit the same pages several times, thus the better results obtained with the No_Exclusion settings. Finally, the experiments in scenarios where both training and testing sessions do not contain repeated visit to the same pages in the same session do not show high accuracy due to the reduced number of instances found in the logs.

Table 2 shows the results obtained evaluating the different settings of the dense representations of URLs. Note that only the outcomes achieved for the *No_Exclusion* configuration (the most general one) and related to the NoHi and CoHi methods (the only techniques applicable to dense matrices) have been reported.

The approaches exploiting dense representations and in particular the ones based on the MOHi methods obtain accuracy values about 40% thus demonstrating effectiveness and performance in line with most of the existing recommender systems. The results show that the accuracy value is not really dependent on the selected parameters: low dimensional dense representations obtain accuracy results close to the ones obtained with higher dimensional matrices and also high dimensional sparse matrices. This is an interesting result, since it makes the approaches based on dense representation usable more efficiently in real world scenarios, where time performance and reduced computational power can limit the usability of high dimensional vectors.

Finally, we can observe that evaluating a recommender system against logs is unfair. Doing it, we assume that the interesting pages for the users are only the ones that they have really visited. This is not always true, since the suggestions performed by the system can "alter" and "drive" the users' interests. Moreover, some users could have not found the information that they needed. In other words, it would be similar to evaluating a recommender system that suggests products in an e-commerce system based only on the actual purchases made by the users. Other products (web pages in our case) can also be interesting for the users (and potentially suggested by our approaches), even if they did not generate a real purchase (a visit in our case) in the historical data available. Therefore, the results shown in Tables 1 and 2 represent the evaluation in the worst possible scenario.

4.4 Using Statistical and Network Analysis for Improving the Accuracy

All the methods proposed recommends and ranks the interesting web pages on the basis of their context, i.e., the pages (the last one or the complete set) visited in the current session. Statistical analysis on the web server logs and structural analysis provided by network analysis applied to the structure of the website can be applied for improving the accuracy of results.

In this work, we have decided to use additional information in a post-process phase where the pages recommended by the methods are filtered and ranked after. In particular, in this phase we experimented the following measures:

- *Number of visitor per page*: the measure, i.e., the overall amount of times the page has been visited by the users, represents the popularity degree of the page.
- *Page Rank*: this measure indirectly shows the popularity degree of a page at the structural level and estimates the importance of a page on the basis of its neighbors.
- *Betweenness*: the measure computes the importance of a node in a network on the bases of the number of the shortest paths passing through it. This is a measure of the ability of a page to connect other pages, i.e., to be a "central point" in the network.
- *Degree*: the measure shows for each page the number of in-going and out-going links, i.e. the strenght of the connection of a page with the rest of the site. It provides a direct indication on the importance of the page with respect to the structure of the overall site.

Table 3. Accuracy achieved in the experiments with sparse representations and the application of a filter.

(a) Accuracy on the NoHi method and tf-idf configuration

Configuration	Vis.	P.R.	Betw	Dgr.
No_Exclusion	0.261	0.211	0.2	0.2
Exclusion	0.154	0.11	0.107	0.11
Sub_No_Excl	0.303	0.23	0.212	0.212
Sub_With_Excl	0.313	0.236	0.218	0.221

(b) Accuracy on the MOHi method and tf-idf configuration

Configuration	Vis.	P.R.	Betw	Dgr.
No_Exclusion	0.454	0.361	0.36	0.357
Exclusion	0.144	0.1	0.097	0.1
Sub_No_Excl.	0.25	0.159	0.157	0.163
Sub_With_Excl.	0.276	0.186	0.185	0.19

(c) Accuracy on the CoHi method and tf-idf configuration

Configuration	Vis.	P.R.	Betw	Dgr.
No_Exclusion	0.487	0.449	0.456	0.451
Exclusion	0.16	0.137	0.142	0.14
Sub_No_Excl	0.263	0.222	0.227	0.223
Sub_With_Excl	0.386	0.264	0.272	0.27

Table 3 shows the accuracy obtained after the application of the filter on the tf-idf configuration (the one where best results have been achieved as reported in Table 1). The accuracy values do not improve in all the scenarios: typically better results are achieved by ranking the results according to the number of visited pages and the Page Rank. Similar values have been experimented considering approaches based on dense representations of the URLs.

4.5 Further Improvements Using Lexical and Semantic Analysis

One possible direction to improve recommendation systems is to further explore the lexical and semantic information provided by URLs constituents. This approach considers available lexical resources, such as WordNet, that encodes specific and tagged relations between lexical units. Note, however, that the productivity and efficiency of this approach are directly related to the number of units and relations in these resources, as well as encoding options concerning sense specification and delimitation (granularity issues [20]). From the available semantic relations in these resources, the ones serving our purposes are the following:

- Synonymy. Although absolute synonymy is a rare phenomenon in natural languages, the fact is that not always users are completely aware of the actual and/or specialized word that is used in a given context. For example, in the considered website the following terms are synonyms *avviso avvertenza; avviso annuncio annunzio comunicazione* (i.e., advertisement).
- Meronymy/holonymy. The relation part-whole is quite relevant in the organization of information/concepts (see [11]). In many cases, meronymy relations provide the conceptual line for the organization of the information, replacing

subtyping relations. For example, in the considered website we found that relationships in *comune giunta* (Municipality - Council); *faculty university*.

- Hyponymy/hyperonymy. Given the fact that hyponymy/hyperonymy relations are the typical hierarchical relations for information organization, and thus reflected on the URL constituents, using subtyping relations for recommendation purposes is likely to return redundant or non-relevant nodes, since hyperonym nodes are expected to be part of the path reflected in the URL. For example the URL http://www.comune.modena.it/tributi/ imu-imposta-municipale-propria refers to a local tax (imu) which is part of the section "tax office" (tributi).
- Co-hyponymy. Co-hyponyms are sets of words that share a direct hyperonym and that refer to related concepts and, thus, are relevant for recommendation purposes. For example the terms *scuola publica - scuola privata - scuola serale - accademia* describes different kinds of schools.

These relations can be used differently to test and further improve the different recommendation methods considered. For instance, identifying co-hyponymy relations between pages in MOHi and CoHi methods can be used to refine recommendations and avoid redundant pages; synonymy relations can be used to merge columns in the different matrixes, reducing the second dimension of the matrixes and contributing to increasing the systems speed. This direction assumes shallow processing tasks and can be improved by Part-of-Speech tagging, since lexical resources consider this information and it can be of great use for disambiguation tasks. Besides, the combination of Part-of-Speech info and stemming with the semantic information in these type of resources can also lead to identify and morphologically related words, as in http://comune.modena.it/ aree-tematiche/lavoro-e-formazione and *. . ./lavoro-e-impresa/opportunita-di-lavoro/cercare-lavoro-nel-settore-pubblico/lavorare-per-luniversita/* (URLs referring to the employment sector where "lavoro" means "work" –noun and "lavorare" means "to work" –verb), further exploring the linguistic analysis on URLs.

5   Conclusions and Future Work

In this work, we have introduced two content-based recommendation systems (the NoHi and MOHi methods) to suggest web pages to users in large web sites. These methods base their recommendations on the structure of the URLs of the web site. In particular, they take into account the keywords included in the URLs of the web site. Moreover, we have also presented the CoHi method, that we can consider as a hybrid approach between two types of recommendation systems: content-based recommendation and item-based collaborative filtering. This last approach does not only consider the structure of the URLs, but it also considers information provided by previous users (in particular, the sessions of previous users).

The evaluation of the accuracy of the methods in a real scenario provided by the analysis of the logs of the web servers of the "Comune di Modena" web site shows that the approaches, in particular the last one, achieve a good performance level. Along this work, we have assumed that if a user visits a page, he/she is interested in the content of that page in the web site. However, it is possible that a user visits a page for other reasons (the pages have been provided by a search engine but they do not satisfy the user information need, the user has clicked on a wrong link, etc.). So, analysis taking into account the amount of time the users spend in the pages will be considered to filter data from the logs used to train and valid the proposed methods.

Acknowledgement. The authors would like to acknowledge networking support by the ICT COST Action IC1302 KEYSTONE - Semantic keyword-based search on structured data sources (www.keystone-cost.eu). We also thank the support of the projects TIN2016-78011-C4-3-R (AEI/FEDER, UE), TIN2013-46238-C4-4-R, and DGA-FSE and the Rete Civica Mo-Net from the Comune di Modena for having provided the data exploited in this research.

References

1. Balabanović, M.: Learning to surf: multiagent systems for adaptive web page recommendation. Ph.D. thesis, Stanford University, May 1998
2. Balabanović, M., Shoham, Y.: Fab: content-based, collaborative recommendation. Commun. ACM **40**(3), 66–72 (1997)
3. Bergamaschi, S., Ferrari, D., Guerra, F., Simonini, G., Velegrakis, Y.: Providing insight into data source topics. J. Data Semant. **5**(4), 211–228 (2016)
4. Bergamaschi, S., Guerra, F., Interlandi, M., Lado, R.T., Velegrakis, Y.: Combining user and database perspective for solving keyword queries over relational databases. Inf. Syst. **55**, 1–19 (2016)
5. Cadegnani, S., Guerra, F., Ilarri, S., Carmen Rodríguez-Hernández, M., Trillo-Lado, R., Velegrakis, Y.: Recommending web pages using item-based collaborative filtering approaches. In: Cardoso, J., Guerra, F., Houben, G.-J., Pinto, A.M., Velegrakis, Y. (eds.) KEYSTONE 2015. LNCS, vol. 9398, pp. 17–29. Springer, Cham (2015). doi:10.1007/978-3-319-27932-9_2
6. Chanda, J., Annappa, B.: An improved web page recommendation system using partitioning and web usage mining. In: International Conference on Intelligent Information Processing, Security and Advanced Communication (IPAC 2015), pp. 80:1–80:6. ACM, New York (2015)
7. Gündüz, S., Özsu, M.T.: A web page prediction model based on click-stream tree representation of user behavior. In: Ninth ACM SIGKDD International Conference on Knowledge Discovery and Data Mining (KDD 2003), pp. 535–540. ACM 2003
8. Eirinaki, M., Vazirgiannis, M.: Web mining for web personalization. ACM Trans. Internet Technol. **3**(1), 1–27 (2003)
9. Fu, X., Budzik, J., Hammond, K.J.: Mining navigation history for recommendation. In: Fifth International Conference on Intelligent User Interfaces (IUI 2000), pp. 106–112. ACM (2000)
10. Hernández, I., Rivero, C.R., Ruiz, D., Corchuelo, R.: A statistical approach to URL-based web page clustering. In: Proceedings of the 21st International Conference on World Wide Web, WWW 2012 Companion, pp. 525–526. ACM, New York (2012)

11. Ittoo, A., Bouma, G., Maruster, L., Wortmann, H.: Extracting meronymy relationships from domain-specific, textual corporate databases. In: Hopfe, C.J., Rezgui, Y., Métais, E., Preece, A., Li, H. (eds.) NLDB 2010. LNCS, vol. 6177, pp. 48–59. Springer, Heidelberg (2010). doi:10.1007/978-3-642-13881-2_5
12. Kazienko, P., Kiewra, M.: Integration of relational databases and web site content for product and page recommendation. In: International Database Engineering and Applications Symposium (IDEAS 2004), pp. 111–116, July 2004
13. Kosala, R., Blockeel, H.: Web mining research: a survey. SIGKDD Explor. **2**(1), 1–15 (2000)
14. Le, Q.V., Mikolov, T.: Distributed representations of sentences and documents. CoRR, abs/1405.4053 (2014)
15. Lieberman, H.: Letizia: an agent that assists web browsing. In: 14th International Joint Conference on Artificial Intelligence (IJCAI 1995), vol. 1, pp. 924–929. Morgan Kaufmann (1995)
16. Mikolov, T., Chen, K., Corrado, G., Dean, J.: Efficient estimation of word representations in vector space. CoRR, abs/1301.3781 (2013)
17. Mikolov, T., Yih, W., Zweig, G.: Linguistic regularities in continuous space word representations. In: Vanderwende, L., III, H.D., Kirchhoff, K. (eds.) Human Language Technologies: Conference of the North American Chapter of the Association of Computational Linguistics, Proceedings, Westin Peachtree Plaza Hotel, Atlanta, Georgia, USA, 9–14 June 2013, pp. 746–751. The Association for Computational Linguistics (2013)
18. Mobasher, B., Cooley, R., Srivastava, J.: Automatic personalization based on web usage mining. Commun. ACM **43**(8), 142–151 (2000)
19. Nguyen, T.T.S., Lu, H., Lu, J.: Web-page recommendation based on web usage and domain knowledge. IEEE Trans. Knowl. Data Eng. **26**(10), 2574–2587 (2014)
20. Nirenburg, S., Raskin, V.: Supply-side and demand-side lexical semantics. In: Viegas, E. (ed.) Breadth and Depth of Semantic Lexicons. Text, Speech and Language Technology, vol. 10, pp. 283–298. Springer, Netherlands (1999)
21. Peng, J., Zeng, D.: Topic-based web page recommendation using tags. In: IEEE International Conference on Intelligence and Security Informatics (ISI 2009), pp. 269–271, June 2009
22. Shahabi, C., Zarkesh, A.M., Adibi, J., Shah, V.: Knowledge discovery from users web-page navigation. In: Seventh International Workshop on Research Issues in Data Engineering (RIDE 1997), pp. 20–29. IEEE Computer Society, April 1997
23. Souza, T., Demidova, E., Risse, T., Holzmann, H., Gossen, G., Szymanski, J.: Semantic URL Analytics to support efficient annotation of large scale web archives. In: Cardoso, J., Guerra, F., Houben, G.-J., Pinto, A.M., Velegrakis, Y. (eds.) KEYSTONE 2015. LNCS, vol. 9398, pp. 153–166. Springer, Cham (2015). doi:10.1007/978-3-319-27932-9_14
24. Yang, Q., Fan, J., Wang, J., Zhou, L.: Personalizing web page recommendation via collaborative filtering and topic-aware Markov model. In: 10th International Conference on Data Mining (ICDM 2010), pp. 1145–1150, December 2010
25. Zeng, D., Li, H.: How useful are tags? — An empirical analysis of collaborative tagging for web page recommendation. In: Yang, C.C., et al. (eds.) ISI 2008. LNCS, vol. 5075, pp. 320–330. Springer, Heidelberg (2008). doi:10.1007/978-3-540-69304-8_32

Large Scale Knowledge Matching with Balanced Efficiency-Effectiveness Using LSH Forest

Michael Cochez[1,2,3(✉)], Vagan Terziyan[3], and Vadim Ermolayev[4]

[1] Fraunhofer Institute for Applied Information Technology FIT,
Schloss Birlinghoven, 53754 Sankt Augustin, Germany
michael.cochez@fit.fraunhofer.de
[2] RWTH Aachen University, Informatik 5,
Templergraben 55, 52056 Aachen, Germany
[3] Faculty of Information Technology, University of Jyväskylä, P.O. Box 35 (Agora),
FI-40014 Jyväskylä, Finland
vagan.terziyan@jyu.fi
[4] Department of IT, Zaporozhye National University, 66, Zhukovskogo st.,
Zaporozhye 69063, Ukraine
vadim@ermolayev.com

Abstract. Evolving Knowledge Ecosystems were proposed to approach the Big Data challenge, following the hypothesis that knowledge evolves in a way similar to biological systems. Therefore, the inner working of the knowledge ecosystem can be spotted from natural evolution. An evolving knowledge ecosystem consists of Knowledge Organisms, which form a representation of the knowledge, and the environment in which they reside. The environment consists of contexts, which are composed of so-called knowledge tokens. These tokens are ontological fragments extracted from information tokens, in turn, which originate from the streams of information flowing into the ecosystem. In this article we investigate the use of LSH Forest (a self-tuning indexing schema based on locality-sensitive hashing) for solving the problem of placing new knowledge tokens in the right contexts of the environment. We argue and show experimentally that LSH Forest possesses required properties and could be used for large distributed set-ups. Further, we show experimentally that for our type of data minhashing works better than random hyperplane hashing. This paper is an extension of the paper "Balanced Large Scale Knowledge Matching Using LSH Forest" presented at the International Keystone Conference 2015.

Keywords: Evolving knowledge ecosystems · Locality-sensitive hashing · LSH Forest · Minhash · Random hyperplane hashing · Big data

1 Introduction

Semantic keyword search attempts to find results close to the intent of the user, i.e., it attempts to find out the meaning behind the keywords provided. Perhaps,

© Springer International Publishing AG 2017
N.T. Nguyen et al. (Eds.): TCCI XXVI, LNCS 10190, pp. 46–66, 2017.
DOI: 10.1007/978-3-319-59268-8_3

one of the biggest problems when attempting this is that the search system needs knowledge that is evolving in line with the world it serves. In other words, only if the search system has an up-to-date representation of the domain of interest of the user will it be possible to interpret the real world meaning of the keywords provided. However, this problem becomes very challenging given the wide range of possible search queries combined with the explosion in the volume of data available, its complexity, variety and rate of change.

Recently a conceptual approach to attack this challenging problem has been proposed [1]. The core of that proposal is the understanding that the mechanisms of knowledge evolution could be spotted from evolutionary biology. These mechanisms are enabled in an *Evolving Knowledge Ecosystem* (EKE) populated with *Knowledge Organisms* (KO). Individual KOs carry their fragments of knowledge—similarly to different people having their individual and potentially dissimilar perceptions and understanding of their environment. The population of KOs, like a human society, possesses the entire knowledge representation of the world, or more realistically—a subject domain. Information tokens flow into such an ecosystem, are further transformed into the knowledge tokens, and finally sown there. The KOs collect the available knowledge tokens and consume these as nutrition. Remarkably, the constitution of an EKE, allows natural scaling in a straightforward way. Indeed, the fragment of knowledge owned by an individual KO and the knowledge tokens consumed by KOs are small. Therefore, a well scalable method of sowing the knowledge tokens is under demand to complete a scalable knowledge feeding pipeline into the ecosystem.

This paper extends our earlier work [2] in which we reported on the implementation and evaluation of our knowledge token sowing solution based on the use of LSH Forest [3] using Jaccard distance. For this extended work we also experiment with angular distance. We demonstrate that: (i) the method scales very well for the volumes characteristic to big data processing scenarios, (ii) using random hyperplane hashing (RHH) for angular distance between knowledge tokens results in poor precision and recall, while (iii) Jaccard distance yields results with sufficiently good precision and recall. As a minor result we would like to highlight the f-RHH method which does not require more computations than standard RHH, but still improves the results. The rest of the paper is structured as follows. In Sect. 2 we sketch the concept of EKE and also explain how knowledge tokens are sown in the environments. Section 3 presents the basic formalism of Locality Sensitive hashing (LSH) and LSH Forest and introduces the distance metrics. Also our arguments for using LSH Forest as an appropriate method are given. Section 4 describes the settings for our computational experiments whose results are presented in Sect. 5. The paper is concluded and plans for future work are outlined in Sect. 6.

2   Big Knowledge—Evolving Knowledge Ecosystems

Humans make different decisions in similar situations, thus taking different courses in their lives. This is largely due to the differences in their knowledge.

So, the evolution of conscious beings noticeably depends on the knowledge they possess. On the other hand, making a choice triggers the emergence of new knowledge. Therefore, it is natural to assume that knowledge evolves because of the evolution of humans, their decision-making needs, their value systems, and the decisions made. Hence, knowledge evolves to support the intellectual activity of its owners, e.g., to interpret the information generated in event observations—handling the diversity and complexity of such information. Consequently, Ermolayev et al. [1] hypothesize that the mechanisms of knowledge evolution are very similar to (and could be spotted from) the mechanisms of the evolution of humans. Apart from the societal aspects, these are appropriately described using the metaphor of biological evolution.

A biological habitat is in fact an ecosystem that frames out and enables the evolution of individual organisms, including humans. Similarly, a knowledge ecosystem has to be introduced for enabling and managing the evolution of knowledge. As proposed in [1], such EKE should scale adequately to cope with realistic and increasing characteristics of data/information to be processed and balance the efficiency and effectiveness while extracting knowledge from information and triggering the changes in the available knowledge.

2.1   Efficiency Versus Effectiveness

Effectiveness and efficiency are the important keys for big data processing and for the big knowledge extraction. Extracting knowledge out of big data would be effective only if: (i) not a single important fact is left unattended (completeness); and (ii) these facts are faceted adequately for further inference (expressiveness and granularity). Efficiency in this context may be interpreted as the ratio of the utility of the result to the effort spent.

In big knowledge extraction, efficiency could be naturally mapped to timeliness. If a result is not timely the utility of the resulting knowledge will drop. Further, it is apparent that increasing effectiveness means incrementing the effort spent on extracting knowledge, which negatively affects efficiency. In other words, if we would like to make a deeper analysis of the data we will have a less efficient system.

Finding a solution, which is balanced regarding these clashes, is challenging. In this paper we use a highly scalable method to collect the increments of incoming knowledge using a 3F+3Co approach, which stand for Focusing, Filtering, and Forgetting + Contextualizing, Compressing, and Connecting (c.f. [1] and Sect. 3.2).

2.2   Evolving Knowledge Ecosystems

An environmental context for a KO could be thought of as its habitat. Such a context needs to provide nutrition that is "healthy" for particular KO species— i.e. matching their genome noticeably. The nutrition is provided by Knowledge Extraction and Contextualization functionality of the ecosystem [1] in a form of *knowledge tokens.* Hence, several and possibly overlapping environmental contexts need to be regarded in a hierarchy which corresponds to several subject domains of interest and a foundational knowledge layer. Environmental contexts are sowed with knowledge tokens that correspond to their subject domains. It is useful to limit the lifetime of a knowledge token in an environment – those which are not consumed dissolve finally when their lifetime ends. KOs use their perceptive ability to find and consume knowledge tokens for nutrition. Knowledge tokens that only partially match KOs' genome may cause both KO body and genome changes and are thought of as mutagens. Mutagens in fact deliver the information about the changes in the world to the environment. Knowledge tokens are extracted from the information tokens either in a stream window, or from the updates of the persistent data storage and further sown in the appropriate environmental context. The context for placing a newly coming knowledge token is chosen by the contextualization functionality. In this paper we present a scalable solution for sowing these knowledge tokens in the appropriate environmental contexts.

3   Locality-Sensitive Hashing

The algorithms for finding nearest neighbors in a dataset were advanced in the work by Indyk and Motwani, who presented the seminal work on Locality-sensitive hashing (LSH) [4]. They relaxed the notion of a nearest neighbor to that of an approximate one, allowing for a manageable error in the found neighbors. Thanks to this relaxation, they were able to design a method which can handle queries in sub-linear time. To use LSH, one has to create a database containing outcomes of specific hash functions. These hash functions have to be independent and likely to give the same outcome when hashed objects are similar and likely to give different outcomes when they are dissimilar. Once this database is built one can query for nearest neighbors of a given query point by hashing it with the same hash functions. The points returned as approximate near neighbors are the objects in the database which got hashed to the same buckets as the query point. [5] If false positives are not acceptable, one can still filter these points.

Formally, to apply LSH we construct a family $\mathcal{H}$ of hash functions which map from a space $\mathcal{D}$ to a universe $\mathcal{U}$.

Let $d_1 < d_2$ be distances according to a distance measure d on a space $\mathcal{D}$. The family $\mathcal{H}$ is (d_1, d_2, p_1, p_2)-sensitive if for any two points $p, q \in \mathcal{D}$ and $h \in \mathcal{H}$:

– if $d(p,q) \leq d_1$ then $\Pr[h(p) = h(q)] \geq p_1$
– if $d(p,q) \geq d_2$ then $\Pr[h(p) = h(q)] \leq p_2$

where $p1 > p2$.

Concrete examples of hash functions which have this property are introduced in Sect. 3.3. The probabilities p_1 and p_2 might be close to each other and hence only one function from $\mathcal{H}$ giving an equal result for two points might not be sufficient to trust that these points are similar. Amplification is used to remedy this problem. This is achieved by creating b functions g_j, each consisting of r hash functions chosen uniformly at random from $\mathcal{H}$. The function g_j is the concatenation of r independent basic hash functions. The symbols b and r stand for *bands* and *rows*. These terms come from the representation of data. One could collect all outcomes of the hash functions in a two-dimensional table. This table can be divided in b bands containing r rows each. (See also [6].) The concatenated hash function g_j maps points p and q to the same bucket if all hash functions it is constructed from hashes the points to the same buckets. If for any j, the function g_j maps p and q to the same bucket, p and q are considered close. The amplification creates a new locality sensitive family which is $\left(d_1, d_2, 1 - (1 - p_1{}^r)^b, 1 - (1 - p_2{}^r)^b \right)$ sensitive.

3.1   LSH Forest

The standard LSH algorithm is somewhat wasteful with regards to the amount of memory is uses. Objects always get hashed to a fixed length band, even if that is not strictly needed to decide whether points are approximate near neighbors. LSH Forest (introduced by Bawa et al. [3]) introduces variable length bands and stores the outcomes of the hashing in a prefix tree data structure.

The length of the band is reduced by only computing the hash functions if there is more than one point which is hashed to the same values. Put another way, in LSH the function g_j maps two points to the same bucket if all functions it is constructed from do so as well. LSH Forest potentially reduces the number of evaluations by only computing that much of g_j as needed to distinct between the different objects. Alternatively, one can view this as assigning a unique label with a dynamic length to each point. In the prefix tree the labels on the edges are the values of the sub-hash functions of g_j.

Hashing and quantization techniques have a limitation when considering very close points. If points are arbitrarily close to each other, then there is no number of hash functions which can tell them apart. This limitation applies to both traditional LSH and the Forest variant. Therefore, LSH assumes a minimum distance between any two points and LSH Forest defines a maximum label length equal to the maximum height of the tree (indicated as k_m).

3.2   Sowing Knowledge Tokens Using LSH Forest

The first requirement for knowledge token sowing is that similar tokens get sown close to each other. This is achieved by adding knowledge tokens to the forest. Similar ones will get placed such that they are more likely to show up when the trees are queried for such tokens. Further requirements come from the 3F+3Co [1] aspects. When using LSH Forest:

Focusing is achieved by avoiding deep analysis when there are no similar elements added to the trees.

Filtering is done by just not adding certain data to the tree.

Forgetting is achieved by removing data from the tree. Removal is supported by the Forest and is an efficient operation.

Contextualizing happens when different parts of the token are spread over the trees. A token may therefore belong to several contexts simultaneously.

Compressing the tree compresses data in two different ways. Firstly, it only stores the hashes computed from the original data and, secondly, common prefixes are not duplicated but re-used. Note that it is possible to store the actual data on a secondary storage and keep only the index in memory.

Connecting the Forest is a body which grows incrementally. Since representations of different tokens can reside together in disparate parts of the trees, they can be considered connected. However, the real connection of these parts will be the task of the KOs which will consume the knowledge tokens which are sown in a tree.

In the next section we will introduce our experiments. In the first experiment series we show that the Forest is able to fulfill the *focusing* requirement. The second one shows that the forest is able to aid the KO to *connect* concepts together. Finally, the last series shows that the data structure has desirable spacial and temporal properties, demonstrating that the tree is able to *compress* data meanwhile offering an appropriate efficiency—effectiveness trade-off.

3.3   Distance Metrics and Locality-Sensitive Hash Functions

In our previous work [2] we only used Jaccard distance to evaluate the use of LSH Forests. Typical metrics used in the literature for distance between textual documents are Jaccard and angular distance. In this work we will also use the later one and compare their performance.

The Jaccard distance is defined on sets A and B as $d\,(A, B) = 1 - sim\,(A, B)$. Here, sim (also referred to as the Jaccard similarity) is defined as the number of elements the sets have in common divided by the total number of elements in the sets (i.e., $sim\,(A, B) = \frac{|A \cap B|}{|A \cup B|}$). In the case of text documents the elements in the set are the words of the text (or are derived from the words in the text). The angular distance between texts is defined as the angle between vectors where each dimension encodes the frequency of a specific word (or derivation).

For example, if we have two texts $\hat{A} =$ "the cat sits on the table" and $\hat{B} =$ "the black cat sits with the other cats". Then, a preprocessing step could reduce these texts to "cat sit table" and "black cat sit cat" (removing common words and stemming, see also the next section). For the Jaccard distance, these texts will then be converted into sets $A = \{cat, sit, table\}$ and $B = \{black, sit, cat\}$ resulting in a Jaccard distance of $1 - \frac{2}{4} = 0.5$. For the angular distance we obtain vectors $A = [1, 1, 1, 0]$ and $B = [2, 1, 0, 1]$ where the dimensions encode the frequencies of the words cat, sit, table, and black, respectively. The resulting angular distance (the angle between A and B) is 0.785.

For both distance metrics Locality-Sensitive Hash functions are known. The LSH function family used for Jaccard distance is minhash from Broder [7]. The outcome of this hash function on a set is the lowest index (counting from 0) any of the elements in the set has in a permutation of the whole universe of elements. In our example from above with two documents the universe consists of only 4 words. One possible permutation is $[black, cat, sit, table]$ leading to an outcome of 1 for set A (the word in A with lowest index in the permutation is cat) and 0 for set B. The range of the outcome space is as large as the size of the universe. One could in principle first determine the size of the universe and then decide upon the permutations. However, measuring the size of the universe beforehand and performing actual permutations would be unpractical. Instead, we use a normal hash function to perform the permutation by mapping each original index to a target index. Hence, the outcome space is limited to the range of that hash function.

For the angular distance we use random hyperplane hashing (RHH) [8]. The core idea is to project the frequency vector onto a random vector. The result of the hash function is 1 if the projection is a positive multiple of the random vector and -1, otherwise. In practice this comes down to finding the sign of the dot product between the frequency vector and the random vector. Another way of looking at this is that we are deciding whether the vector in question is above or below[1] the hyperplane on which the random vector is a normal vector. An intuitive proof for the correctness of both minhash and RHH can be found from [6].

When using RHH the LSH Forest will place the element in the one subtree if the hash outcome is 1. On the contrary, an outcome of -1 will cause it to direct the element to the other subtree. However, sometimes this decision seems too harsh. If the projected vector is only a very small multiple of the random vector the element is very close to the hyperplane and the binary decision which is made could cause nearest neighbors to be hashed to different subtrees.

To alleviate this problem, we investigate a slightly different approach which we will call fuzzy random hyperplane hashing or f-RHH. Instead of only allowing a binary decision, the hash function can also report that it is unable to decide well enough on which side of the hyperplane the given vector is (i.e., the outcome of the projection is small). The result of the hashing can thus be 1, -1, or both. When the result is both, then we will place the element in both subtrees essentially ignoring the outcome of the hash function completely.

What we need to perform f-RHH is a way to decide whether a frequency vector is close to the hyperplane. Moreover, this method has to be efficiently implementable. A first attempt could be to compute the angle between the vector and the hyperplane. This is a feasible but relatively expensive computation (especially because it has to happen for all vector-hyperplane pairs). However, observe that the angle between the vector and the hyperplane is $\frac{\pi}{2} -$ 'the angle between the vector and the normal'. If we call the vector a and the normal n, then given an angle k^2, a will get assigned both hash outcomes if

---

[1] Above can be defined as on the same side as the normal vector; below is then the other side of the hyperplane.

[2] The maximumum angle between a vector and the hyperplane for a to be assigned both hash outcomes.

$$\frac{\pi}{2} - \widehat{an} = \frac{\pi}{2} - \arccos\left(\frac{a \cdot n}{\|a\|\|n\|}\right) < k$$

Which can be rewritten as:

$$\arcsin\left(\frac{a \cdot n}{\|a\|\|n\|}\right) < k$$

In this expression $\|n\|$ is essentially a positive constant[3] which we will call R. If we normalize the vector a before we compute the angle, the angle will remain the same. We will cal this normalized vector $\bar{a}$ where $\|\bar{a}\| = 1$. Using these facts, the previous expression can be rewritten as:

$$\arcsin\left(\frac{\bar{a} \cdot n}{R}\right) < k$$

Which can be rearranged to:

$$|\bar{a} \cdot n| < \sin(k) * R = C$$

What this expression tells us is that if the angle between a vector a and the hyperplane is smaller than k, then the absolute value of the dot product of the normalized vector $\bar{a}$ and the normal vector is smaller than a given constant number C.

This last expression can be implemented very efficiently. In fact, besides the normalization of each frequency vector (which has to happen only once), the dot product computation is exactly the same as what we would be computing anyway for the random hyperplane hashing.

To illustrate the effect of f-RHH, we present a two dimensional example in Fig. 1. The figure shows a random vector $\overrightarrow{n}$ and the hyperplane H on which $\overrightarrow{n}$ is a normal vector. The red shaded area contains all vectors for which the hash outcome will be negative. Conversely, vectors in the blue area will get the value $+1$ assigned. All vectors which are in the overlap between the red and blue are will get both values assigned; causing the hyperplane to not cut the space sharply in two. In other words, the hyperplane does not strictly subdivide the space into two subspaces. Instead it creates an overlapping boundary between the two subspaces in which points are in both of the subspaces at the same time.

One question which remains to be answered is the value of the constant C. In order to find a reasonable value, we ran several preliminary experiments and found that a reasonably well working value was 10^{14}. Note that our normal vector n has its components sampled from the range $[-2^{63}, 2^{63} - 1]$. We cautiously assume that this constant value is data and case dependent. Hence, this constant should not be taken as a general recommendation.

---

[3] The norm of a specific random vector, will be the same for all angle computations. Moreover, since this is a very high dimensional vector and each dimension of the vector is sampled from a uniform distribution, the expected norm of the random vectors is constant. In any case, the values are most likely different but will be in the same ballpark.

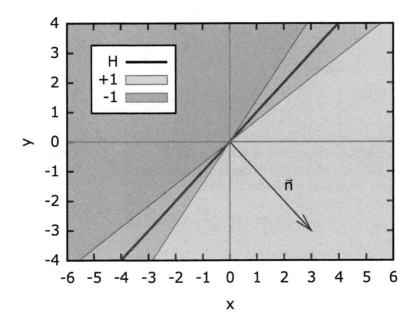

Fig. 1. An illustration of fuzzy random hyperplane hashing. Vectors which are in the area where −1 and 1 overlap have both hash outcomes at the same time. (Color figure online)

4   Evaluation

The experiments are designed so that we start from a fairly simple set-up and more complexity is added in each following experiment. In the first series of experiments, we feed knowledge tokens created from three different data sources into an LSH tree and present measure how they are spread over the tree. In the following series, we use two and later three data sources and measure how the LSH Forest classifies the tokens and how it is capable of connecting the knowledge tokens. In that same series we compare the performance of the different hash functions. Finally, in the third series we add dynamism to the experiment by sampling the knowledge tokens in different ways and measure how the memory usage and processing time evolve.

Finding a suitable dataset for the experiment is not obvious. What we need are small pieces of information (i.e., the knowledge tokens) about which we know how they should be connected (i.e., a gold standard). Further, the dataset should be sufficiently large to conduct the experiments. We solved this issue by selecting three large ontologies for which a so-called alignment [9] has been created. These particular ontologies are large and have a fairly simple structure. Further, by using only the labels of the ontology a reasonable alignment can be found [10]. Therefore, we extract the labels from these ontologies and use them as knowledge tokens. This is a relaxation of the knowledge token concept. In the earlier work [1] a knowledge token has an internal structure.

Datasets. The *Large Biomed Track* of the Ontology Alignment Evaluation initiative[4] is the source of the datasets used in our evaluation. The FMA ontology[5], which contains 78,989 classes is the first dataset. The FMA ontology only contains classes and non-hierarchical datatype properties, i.e., no object or datatype properties nor instances. Secondly, there is the NCI ontology[6] containing 66,724 classes, and finally a fragment of 122,464 classes of the SNOMED ontology[7]. The NCI ontology contains classes, non-hierarchical datatype and hierarchical object properties. The classes of all ontologies are structured in a tree using *owl:SubClassOf* relations. The UMLS-based reference alignments as prepared for OAEI[8] are used as a gold standard. From these reference alignments we only retain the equal correspondences, with the confidence levels set to one.

Preprocessing. We preprocess the ontologies by computing as many representations for each class as it has labels in the ontology. The preprocessing is very similar to the second strategy proposed in [10]. According to this strategy, for each label of each class, a set of strings is created as follows: the label is converted to lowercase and then split in strings using all the whitespace and punctuation marks as a delimiter. If this splitting created strings of 1 character, they are concatenated with the string that came before it. In addition to these steps, we also removed possessive suffixes from the substrings and removed the 20 most common English language words according to the Oxford English Dictionary[9]. This preprocessing results in 133628, 175698, and 122505 knowledge tokens, i.e., sets of strings for the FMA, NCI, and SNOMED ontology, respectively.

Implementation. The implementation of our evaluation code heavily uses parallelism to speed up the computation. From the description of the LSH algorithm, it can be noticed that the hashing of the objects happens independent of each other. Therefore they can be computed in parallel using a multi-core system.

For the implementation of the minhash algorithm, we use Rabin fingerprints as described by Broder [11] instead of computing a real permutation of the universe. An improvement over earlier work [10] where Rabin hashing was also used is due to the fact that we invert the bits of the input to the hashing function. We noticed that small inputs gave a fairly high number of collisions using the functions normally, while the inverted versions do hardly cause any.

For the random hyperplane hashing we use a hash function to imitate an infinite random vector. The way this works is that we interpret each word as a number, which we then take to be the index (in the vector) representing the frequency of the word. Then, to find the value of the random vector for that

---

[4] http://www.cs.ox.ac.uk/isg/projects/SEALS/oaei/2013/.

[5] http://sig.biostr.washington.edu/projects/fm/.

[6] http://www.obofoundry.org/cgi-bin/detail.cgi?id=ncithesaurus.

[7] http://www.ihtsdo.org/index.php?id=545.

[8] http://www.cs.ox.ac.uk/isg/projects/SEALS/oaei/2013/oaei2013_umls_reference. html.

[9] http://www.oxforddictionaries.com/words/the-oec-facts-about-the-language.

index, we hash the index with the hash function. This has the practical implication that there is no need to store a random vector in its entirety, nor is there a need to know all words of the corpus beforehand. As a hash function we use murmur3[10]. This choice is made because the hash function is fast, it provides reasonable mixing of the input bits, and has a close to uniform output range.

The outcome of RHH is binary and the trie used will be a binary tree as well (as opposed to the n-ary trie used for minhash). Because of this difference we can easily afford checking newly added data for exact duplicates. So, when we insert a knowledge token using RHH (or f-RHH) we check in the leaf nodes whether the already existing token has the same source concept and the same representation we ignore it immediately. This is as opposed to double insertions which happen in the case of minhash (see also the results in Sect. 5.1).

The experiments are performed on hardware with two Intel Xeon E5-2670 processors (totaling 16 hyper-threaded cores) and limited to use a maximum of 16 GB RAM.

4.1   Single Data Source—Single Tree

In this series of experiments, we use only one LSH tree and knowledge tokens from a single dataset. First, the ontology is parsed and all its concepts are tokenized as described above. The resulting knowledge tokens are hashed (with the different hash functions—minhash, RHH, and f-RHH) and then fed into an LSH tree. We then analyze the distribution of the knowledge tokens in the tree obtained for each hashing option. Concrete, we observe how deep the knowledge tokens are located in the tree and how many siblings the leaves in the tree have. Further, for the case of minhash, we investigate chains of nodes which are only there because of a low number of tokens at the bottom of the tree.

4.2   Connecting Knowledge Tokens Using LSH Forest, i.e. Matching

The objective of our the first experiment in this second series is to show how the ontology matching using LSH Forest compares to standard LSH. Besides the change in data structure we use the experimental set-up similar to what was used for testing standard LSH in our earlier research work [10]. In that work only Jaccard distance and minhashing were used and the best result for matching the SNOMED and NCI ontologies was obtained using 1 band of 480 rows which corresponds to 1 tree of maximum height $k_m = 480$. To keep the results comparable, we also do not use the reduced collision effect from inverting before hashing (see **Implementation** above). It needs to be noted, however, that we use a slightly different approach for selecting near neighbors compared to the standard LSH Forest approximate nearest neighbor querying. Since we are not interested in neighbors if they are to far away, we only take the siblings of each leaf into account when searching for related concepts. Further, we ignore concepts if they their similarity is less than 0.8. Next to the traditional ontology

---

[10] https://code.google.com/p/smhasher/wiki/MurmurHash3.

matching measures of precision, recall, and F-measure, the potential memory and processing power savings are evaluated.

In the second part of this series we use the properties of the tree and also experiment with RHH and f-RRH. For minhashing we use our improved version, applying the inversion before hashing. We also incorporate the knowledge from the previous experiments to test how LSH Forest can perform when connecting knowledge tokens using a shorter tree. We measure both runtime performance and quality metrics for a different number of trees.

In the last part we use the fact that there is no reason to limit ourselves to only using two data sources. Hence, we demonstrate scalability of the system by feeding all knowledge tokens created for all three datasets. We also analyze the time saving compared to performing three separate alignment tasks when pairs of datasets are used.

4.3 Adding Dynamics

In the final series of experiments we observe how the tree reacts to dynamic insertion of concepts. In the basic case, we select 10^6 knowledge tokens (from the three sets) using a uniform distribution. These are then one by one inserted into the tree. After every 10^4 insertions we measure number of hash operations used to measure the time complexity. The cumulative memory consumption is measured as the number of edges used in the trees. We also measure the real elapsed time after the insertion of every 10^5 knowledge tokens.

On an average system some knowledge tokens will be added much more frequently than others. This is due to the fact that the information or queries which the system processes are somehow focused on a certain domain. This also means that the tokens would not arrive according to a uniform distribution. A more plausible scenario is that certain concepts are very likely to occur, while others do hardly occur at all. We model this phenomena by using a so-called Zipf distribution with exponent 1 which causes few concepts to be inserted frequently while most are inserted seldom. Using this set-up we perform the same measurements as made for the uniform distribution.

It has to be noted that we need to make a minor change to the way our trees process the tokens. When a token already exists at a node, the standard implementation would build a chain which can only end at k_m. This is related to our above remark about the minimal distance between any two points. To solve this problem, the lowest internal nodes check whether the newly added representation is already existing and if so, it will ignore the representation. We shortly analyzed the effect of this change using the same set-up as in the second experiment series and noticed that this check does hardly affect runtime performance. The main effect is visible in the number of edges and hash operations which both drop by about 30%. Further, a marginal decrease of the precision and a marginal increase of the recall is observable.

5   Results

5.1   Single Data Source—Single Tree

For the first series of experiments, we look at the characteristics of the LSH tree for the distance metrics and hash functions. We start with the cosine distance, RHH and f-RHH (the variant described above) because the outcome of the hashing is binary. This binary tree makes it somewhat easier to analyze.

Cosine Distance—RHH, F-RHH. When measuring the frequencies of the depths of the leafs in the tree we obtain the results shown in Fig. 2. To obtain this figure we placed all knowledge tokens from a given dataset into a tree with $k_m = 80$ after hashing them using RHH and f-RHH, respectively. Then we measure the number of leaves at a given height. From the figure it can be seen that there are only slight differences between the way the different datasets are spread over the tree. From the exect numbers we observed that the fRHH histograms are slightly skewed to the right when compared to their RHH counterparts. This is as expected since fRHH will insert extra elements into the tree whenever the outcome of the hashing has both values at the same time. The tail of the histogram decays pretty fast for all data sets indicating that the tree is able to differentiate between the majority of the tokens after about 40 hashings.

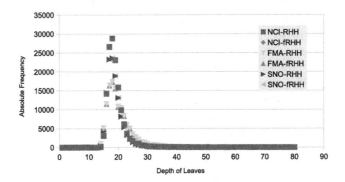

Fig. 2. The frequency of a leaf occurring at a given height for the knowledge tokens derived from the different data sets.

Jaccard Distance—Minhash. After feeding the minhashed knowledge tokens of each data set into their own single LSH Tree with $k_m = 80$, we find clusters of leaves as shown in Fig. 3. The figure shows how often a group of n siblings occurs as a function of the depth in the tree. Note that this figure is more complex than the figure we obtained for the (f-)RHH case. The reason for this complexity is that we are not dealing with a binary, but an n-ary tree.

What we notice in the figures is that most of the concepts are fairly high up in the tree. After roughly 30 levels all the concepts, except these residing at the bottom of the tree, are placed. It is also visible that most knowledge tokens

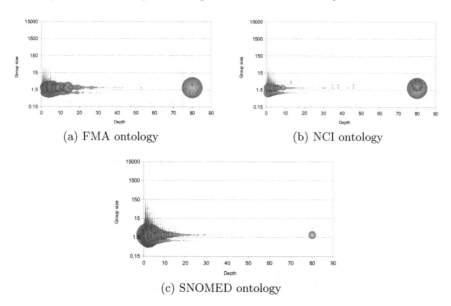

(a) FMA ontology   (b) NCI ontology

(c) SNOMED ontology

Fig. 3. Frequency of sibling groups of a given size at a given level in one LSH Tree. Note the logarithmic scale.

are located in the leaves which either have very few siblings or are located high up in the tree. This indicates that the tree is able to distinguish between the representations fairly fast. In both the FMA and NCI ontologies, we notice a high amount of knowledge tokens at the bottom of the tree, i.e., at level $k_m = 80$. We noticed that the same amount of concepts end up at the bottom of the tree even if k_m is chosen to be 1000, which indicates that hashing might be incapable to distinguish between the representations, i.e., they are so close that their hashes virtually always look the same. After further investigation, we found that the Jaccard similarities between the sibling concepts at the bottom of the tree are all equal to 1. This means that there are concepts in the ontology which have very similar labels, i.e., labels which (often because of our preprocessing steps) get reduced to exactly the same set of tokens. One problem with this phenomenon is that the tree contains long chains of nodes, which are created exclusively for these few siblings. We define an *exclusive chain* as the chain of nodes between an internal node at one level above the bottom of the tree, and another (higher) node which has more than one child. The lengths of these exclusive chains are illustrated in Fig. 4a.

We notice that mainly the NCI ontology causes long exclusive chains. The most plausible cause for this is that NCI has a higher average number of representations per concept (2.6) than the other two ontologies (1.7—FMA and 1.0—SNOMED). To investigate this further, we plot the number of classes which the siblings at the lowest level represent. The result of analyzing the number of classes represented by the leaves in each sibling cluster can be found in Fig. 4b.

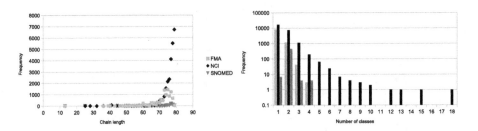

(a) Frequency of a given exclusive chain length for nodes at k_m

(b) Frequency of a given number of classes represented in a leaf at level k_m for each ontology. Note the log scale.

Fig. 4. Analysis for the leaf nodes

From the figure we notice that, indeed, very often there is a low number of classes represented by the siblings of the final nodes. We also notice that the NCI ontology has the most severe representation clashes.

5.2 Connecting Knowledge Tokens Using LSH Forest, i.e. Matching

Part 1. When matching the SNOMED and NCI ontologies using a single tree of height 480, we obtain the precision of 0.838, recall of 0.547, and hence F-measure of 0.662. These results are similar to the results of the standard LSH algorithm which attained the precision of 0.842, recall of 0.535, and F-measure of 0.654.

The LSH Forest algorithm, however, uses only 30% of the amount of hash function evaluations compared to the standard LSH algorithm. Furthermore, the Forest saves around 90% of the memory used for storing the result of the hash evaluations. This is because the tree saves a lot of resources by only computing and storing the part of the label which is needed. Further, a result is stored only once if the same outcome is obtained from the evaluation of a given hash function for different representations. It should, however, be noted that using LSH Forest also implies a memory overhead for representing the tree structure, while the standard algorithm can place all hash function evaluations in an efficient two dimensional table.

The speed of the two algorithms with the same set-up is very similar. Using the Forest, the alignment is done in 20.6 s, while the standard algorithm completes in 21.5 s.

Part 2. As can be seen in the distribution of the ontologies over the tree in our previous experiment series (Fig. 3) non-similar concepts remain fairly high up in the tree. Hence, when using the improved Rabin hashing technique described above, we can reduce the maximum height of the tree. Based on this information, we now choose the maximum height of the tree to be 30. We also use 10 as the highest level of interest and ignore all representations which are unable to get a lower positions in the tree. We vary the number of trees used between 1 and

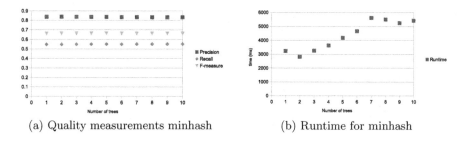

(a) Quality measurements minhash   (b) Runtime for minhash

Fig. 5. Quality measurements and runtime behavior for an ontology matching task using different number of trees for minhash.

10 and show the impact on the precision, recall and F-measure in Fig. 5a and timing in Fig. 5b.

From the quality measurements, we see that the number of trees has little effect. It is hard to see from the figure, but the precision lowers ever so slightly when more trees are used. Concretely, it goes from 0.836947 when using one tree to 0.831957 with 10 trees. The recall has the opposite behavior growing from 0.546824 to 0.550616. The net effect of these two on the F-measure is a slight increase when more trees are used, namely from 0.661472 to 0.662662. It needs to be noted that also these results are in the same range as the measures in the previous experiment. Hence, we can conclude that constraining the height of a tree does not affect the quality much, if at all. However, as can be seen in the timing chart, the tree works much faster when its height is reduced. When only one tree is used, roughly 3 s are needed to obtain results. Increasing the number of trees to 10 only doubles the time, most likely because the system is better able to use multiple threads or the virtual machine might do a better just-in-time compilation. In any case, we note that using the forest and better hashing, we can create a system which is roughly 7 times faster and produces results of similar quality.

Next, we experimented using the RHH and f-RHH hash functions. The quality measurements for these for trees with depth 80 are shown in Figs. 6a and b. Surprisingly and seemingly contradicting to the findings of [12] the performance of RHH and f-RHH are pretty low when compared to minhash. The reason for this low performance seems to be that in the case of the earlier work [12] the comparison was performed between a large set of complete web pages. The documents which we are working with in these experiments are much smaller, namely tens of words, instead of hundreds or thousands in the case of web pages. Further, we are looking for a high similarity in order to classify something similar, while the earlier work is focused on finding near-duplicate web pages. Finally, when comparing web pages there will often be a large impact from the frequencies of words. In the current work, however, the frequencies are usually very small numbers. Since these results are not satisfying for the setting we are developing, we will not continue using RHH and f-RHH for further experiments. However, we would still like to highlight the performance difference between RHH and

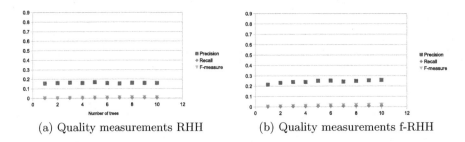

(a) Quality measurements RHH   (b) Quality measurements f-RHH

Fig. 6. Quality measurements of an ontology matching task using different number of trees using RHH and f-RHH.

f-RHH. As can be seen from the graphs, f-RHH achieves a much better precision compared to RHH Also the recall and hence F-measure are always higher than what we obtained using RHH. Hence, it would be worth investigating further whether f-RHH works better compared to normal RHH in other use cases.

Part 3. To try whether we can also use the tree for bigger datasets, we now feed all knowledge tokens created from all three ontologies into the system and present similar measurements in Fig. 7.

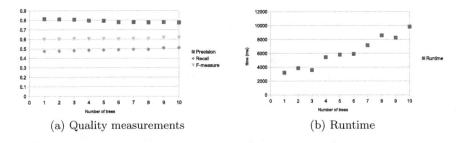

(a) Quality measurements   (b) Runtime

Fig. 7. Quality measurements and runtime behavior for a three way ontology matching task using different number of trees.

Now, we notice the effect on the precision and recall more profoundly. Also the runtime increases faster when the input is larger. We do however see only a three-fold increase when the number of trees is ten-folded. When comparing these results to our earlier work [10] we can see the speed-up of using LSH Forest and performing multiple alignments at once. In our previous work we used 45.5 s for doing three 2-way alignment tasks. Using the LSH Forest we can perform the 3-way alignment in less than 10 s. When using a single tree, we measured a time of 3.2 s yielding roughly a ten-fold speed-up.

5.3   Adding Dynamics

The results of adding knowledge tokens according to a uniform distribution are in Fig. 8. From the figures we note that the number of edges needed grows sublinear. This is as expected since both the fact that certain knowledge tokens will be selected more than once and the reuse of edges decreases the number of new edges needed. The number of hashes shows an initial ramp-up and then starts growing linear. We also note that the time used for adding is growing, but the growth slows down when more concepts are added. Moreover, if we try to fit a linear curve trough the cumulative runtime measurements, we notice that we can obtain a Pearson product-moment correlation coefficient of 0.9976, indicating that the increase is actually very close to linear.

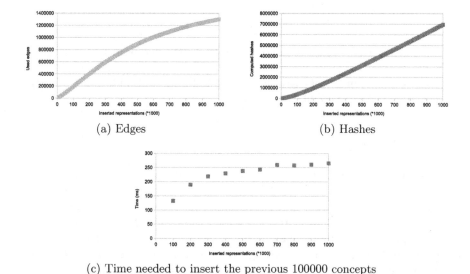

(a) Edges   (b) Hashes

(c) Time needed to insert the previous 100000 concepts

Fig. 8. Cumulative number of edges and hashes; and time needed for uniform adding of knowledge tokens

When choosing the representations using a Zipf distribution instead, we obtain the results as depicted in Fig. 9. When comparing the charts for insertion using the normal and Zipf distribution, we notice that the later puts much less of a burden upon the system. This is a desirable effect since it means that the system is likely to work well with more organic loads. Also here, we can fit a linear curve trough the cumulative runtime measurements with a high correlation coefficient of 0.9968.

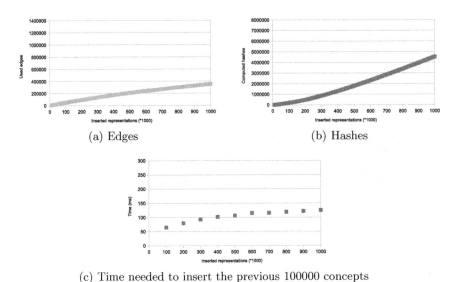

(a) Edges   (b) Hashes

(c) Time needed to insert the previous 100000 concepts

Fig. 9. Cumulative number of edges and hashes; and time needed for adding of knowledge tokens according to a Zipf distribution

6   Conclusions and Outlook

When trying to understand and follow what is happening around us, we have to be able to connect different pieces of information together. Moreover, the amount of information which we perceive does not allow us to look at each detail, instead we need to focus on specific parts and ignore the rest. When we want to built a system capable of embodying evolution in knowledge, similar challenges have to be tackled. In this paper we investigated one of the first steps needed for this type of system, namely bringing related pieces of knowledge together.

The system we envision is an Evolving Knowledge Ecosystem in which Knowledge Organisms are able to consume Knowledge Tokens, i.e., pieces of knowledge, which have been sown in the environment. In this paper we looked at the application of LSH Forest to dynamically sow knowledge tokens in the environmental contexts.

We found out that LSH Forest is a suitable approach because it is able to balance well between efficiency and effectiveness. This can be observed from the fact that the method scales well, both from a space and runtime perspective; and from the fact that the quality measures are sufficiently high when using minhash. Further, the Forest makes it possible to focus on these parts which need further investigation and it allows for connecting between the knowledge tokens. We also investigated the use of cosine distance using random hyperplane hashing. From our observations we noticed that this approach performs poorly in comparison to minhash. This seems contradictory to earlier findings [12], but is likely because of the fact that the documents which are being compared are very different in nature (short labels vs. complete web pages).

There are still several aspects of using LSH Forest which could be further investigated. First, the problem caused by exclusive chains could be mitigated by measuring the distance between knowledge tokens when they reach a certain depth in the tree. Only when the concepts are different enough, there is a need to continue; this however requires to parametrize the inequality. Another option to reduce at least the amount of used memory and pointer traversals is using PATRICIA trees as proposed by Bawa et al. [3].

Secondly, we noted that the LSH tree allows for removal of concepts and that this operation is efficient. Future research is needed to see how this would work in an evolving knowledge ecosystem. Besides, as described in [1], the knowledge tokens do not disappear at once from an environmental context. Instead, they might dissolve slowly, which could be thought of as a decreasing fuzzy membership in the context. One straightforward method for achieving this would be to use a sliding window which has an exponential decay. Also more complex ideas could be investigated, perhaps even providing a bonus for concepts which are queried often or using hierarchical clustering techniques to remove tokens from areas which are densely populated [13]. This would mean that some tokens remain in the system even when other (less popular or more common) concepts with similar insertion characteristics get removed.

Thirdly, we observed that f-RHH performed better than the traditional RHH. The improvement was still not enough to warrant its use in the context of this paper, however. As a further direction it would definitely be beneficial to see a large scale comparison between standard RHH, f-RHH, and perhaps multi-probe LSH [14].

Lastly, it would be interesting to see how the Forest would react when the input data becomes that big that it is impossible to keep the tree in the physical memory available. Then, using a distributed setting, ways should be found to minimize the overhead when concepts are added and removed from the tree. One promising idea is the use of consistent hashing for the distribution of knowledge tokens as proposed in [15].

Acknowledgments. The authors would like to thank the faculty of Information Technology of the University of Jyväskylä for financially supporting this research. Further, it has to be mentioned that the implementation of the software was greatly simplified by the Guava library by Google, the Apache Commons Math^{TM} library, and the Rabin hash library by Bill Dwyer and Ian Brandt.

References

1. Ermolayev, V., Akerkar, R., Terziyan, V., Cochez, M.: Towards evolving knowledge ecosystems for big data understanding. In: Big Data Computing, pp. 3–55. Taylor & Francis Group, Chapman and Hall/CRC (2014)

2. Cochez, M., Terziyan, V., Ermolayev, V.: Balanced large scale knowledge matching using LSH forest. In: Cardoso, J., Guerra, F., Houben, G.J., Pinto, A., Velegrakis, Y. (eds.) Semanitic Keyword-based Search on Structured Data Sources. LNCS, vol. 9398, pp. 36–50. Springer, Cham (2015). doi:10.1007/978-3-319-27932-9_4

3. Bawa, M., Condie, T., Ganesan, P.: LSH forest: self-tuning indexes for similarity search. In: Proceedings of the 14th International Conference on World Wide Web, pp. 651–660. ACM (2005)

4. Indyk, P., Motwani, R.: Approximate nearest neighbors: towards removing the curse of dimensionality. In: Proceedings of the Thirtieth Annual ACM Symposium on Theory of Computing, pp. 604–613. ACM (1998)

5. Andoni, A., Indyk, P.: Near-optimal hashing algorithms for approximate nearest neighbor in high dimensions. Commun. ACM 51(1), 117–122 (2008)

6. Rajaraman, A., Ullman, J.D.: Finding similar items. In: Mining of Massive Datasets, chap. 3, pp. 71–128. Cambridge University Press (2012)

7. Broder, A.Z.: On the resemblance and containment of documents. In: Proceedings of the Compression and Complexity of Sequences, pp. 21–29. IEEE (1997)

8. Charikar, M.S.: Similarity estimation techniques from rounding algorithms. In: Proceedings of the Thiry-Fourth Annual ACM Symposium on Theory of Computing, STOC 2002, pp. 380–388. ACM, New York (2002)

9. Ermolayev, V., Davidovsky, M.: Agent-based ontology alignment: basics, applications, theoretical foundations, and demonstration. In: Proceedings of the 2nd International Conference on Web Intelligence, Mining and Semantics, WIMS 2012, pp. 3:1–3:12. ACM, New York (2012)

10. Cochez, M.: Locality-sensitive hashing for massive string-based ontology matching. In: 2014 IEEE/WIC/ACM International Joint Conferences on Web Intelligence (WI) and Intelligent Agent Technologies (IAT), vol. 1, pp. 134–140. IEEE (2014)

11. Broder, A.: Some applications of Rabins fingerprinting method. In: Capocelli, R., De Santis, A., Vaccaro, U. (eds.) Sequences II, pp. 143–152. Springer, New York (1993). doi:10.1007/978-1-4613-9323-8_11

12. Henzinger, M.: Finding near-duplicate web pages: a large-scale evaluation of algorithms. In: Proceedings of the 29th Annual International ACM SIGIR Conference on Research and Development in Information Retrieval, pp. 284–291. ACM (2006)

13. Cochez, M., Mou, H.: Twister tries: approximate hierarchical agglomerative clustering for average distance in linear time. In: Proceedings of the 2015 ACM SIGMOD International Conference on Management of Data, pp. 505–517. ACM (2015)

14. Lv, Q., Josephson, W., Wang, Z., Charikar, M., Li, K.: Multi-probe LSH: efficient indexing for high-dimensional similarity search. In: Proceedings of the 33rd International Conference on Very Large Data Bases, pp. 950–961. VLDB Endowment (2007)

15. Karger, D., Lehman, E., Leighton, T., Panigrahy, R., Levine, M., Lewin, D.: Consistent hashing and random trees: distributed caching protocols for relieving hot spots on the world wide web. In: Proceedings of the Twenty-Ninth Annual ACM Symposium on Theory of Computing, STOC 1997, pp. 654–663. ACM, New York (1997)

Keyword-Based Search of Workflow Fragments and Their Composition

Khalid Belhajjame[1](✉), Daniela Grigori[1], Mariem Harmassi[1,2],
and Manel Ben Yahia[1]

[1] Université Paris-Dauphine, PSL Research University, CNRS, UMR [7243],
LAMSADE, 75016 Paris, France
{khalid.belhajjame,daniela.grigori,mariem.harmassi,
manel.benyahia}@dauphine.fr
[2] L3i Lab, Université de La Rochelle, La Rochelle, France
mariem.harmassi@univ-lr.fr

Abstract. Workflow specification, in science as in business, can be a difficult task, since it requires a deep knowledge of the domain to be able to model the chaining of the steps that compose the process of interest, as well as awareness of the computational tools, e.g., services, that can be utilized to enact such steps. To assist designers in this task, we investigate in this paper a methodology that consists in exploiting existing workflow specifications that are stored and shared in repositories, to identify workflow fragments that can be re-utilized and re-purposed by designers when specifying new workflows. Specifically, we present a method for identifying fragments that are frequently used across workflows in existing repositories, and therefore are likely to incarnate patterns that can be reused in new workflows. We present a keyword-based search method for identifying the fragments that are relevant for the needs of a given workflow designer. We go on to present an algorithm for composing the retrieved fragments with the initial (incomplete) workflow that the user designed, based on compatibility rules that we identified, and showcase how the algorithm operates using an example from eScience.

1 Introduction

Workflows are popular means for specifying and enacting processes in business as in science. For example, they are used in modern sciences to specify and enact in-silico experiments, thereby allowing scientists to gain better understanding of the phenomenon or hypothesis they are investigating. The design of scientific workflows can however be a difficult task as it requires a deep knowledge of the domain as well as awareness of the programs and services available for implementing the workflow steps. To overcome this obstacle and facilitate the design of workflows, many workflows repositories have emerged, e.g., myExperiment [1],

The research reported on this paper was supported by the french research agency (ANR-14-CE23-0006). M. Harmassi and M. Ben Yahia contributed to this work during their masters internship at the Lamsade Laboratory.

© Springer International Publishing AG 2017
N.T. Nguyen et al. (Eds.): TCCI XXVI, LNCS 10190, pp. 67–90, 2017.
DOI: 10.1007/978-3-319-59268-8_4

Crowdlabs [2] and Galaxy [3] to share, publish and enable reuse of workflows. For example, De Roure *et al.* [1] pointed out the advantages of sharing and reusing workflows as a solution to face the difficulty and cost of design.

Sharing and publishing workflows is however not sufficient to enable their reuse. Over the past years, an important number of workflows has been shared by scientists in several domains on the myExperiment workflow repository. However, their users face difficulties when it comes to exploring and querying workflows. Indeed, users still have to go through published workflows to identify those that are relevant for their needs. The situation is exacerbated by the fact that the number of workflows hosted by workflow repositories is rapidly increasing. To overcome this problem, mining techniques can be utilized to automatically analyze the workflows in the repository with the objective to provide templates that assist users in the design of their own workflows, thereby allowing them to take advantage of a knowledge-asset gained and verified by their peers.

Several works have been proposed in the literature for mining workflows (see, e.g. [4–6]). Unlike these proposals, our objective is not to propose yet another mining algorithm. Instead, we investigate the graph representations that can be used to encode workflow specifications into graphs before they are examined by existing graph mining algorithms. We are particularly interested in sub-graph mining techniques that find commonalities among fragments of workflows. Indeed, fragments that are common to multiple workflows are likely to be patterns that can be useful for designers when specifying new workflows. In elaborating possible representations, we take into consideration the cost in terms of time that the graph mining algorithm spends given a workflow representation, and the impact of the representation on the quality of the mining algorithm results.

As well as mining frequent workflows fragments, we investigate the problem of exploring them by designers using keyword search. In doing so, we augment traditional TF-IDF with semantic capabilities that take into consideration synonym relation between the keywords used by users in their query and the terms used to label the activities that compose workflow fragments. Furthermore, we elaborate an algorithm for assisting designers in the composition of the retrieved fragments with the initial (incomplete) workflows that they specified.

Accordingly, the contributions of this paper are as follows.

- We elaborate representation models for encoding workflows in the form of graphs that can be used as input to sub-graph mining algorithms, and systematically evaluate the effectiveness of such representations through an empirical evaluation (in Sect. 4).
- We present a keyword-based search method for identifying relevant frequent graphs (in Sect. 5).
- We present an algorithm for assisting designers in the composition of the workflow fragments with their (incomplete) workflow specification (in Sect. 6), and showcase how it operates using an example from eScience (in Sect. 7).

Furthermore, we present the overall approach (in Sect. 2), review and compare existing proposals to ours (in Sect. 3). Finally, we conclude the paper underlining the main contributions and discussing future research directions (in Sect. 8).

The work reported in this paper is an extended version of the work presented in [7]. In [7], we have investigated the representation models suitable for mining workflow fragments (Sect. 4). In the extended version reported on in this paper, we make the following new contributions. We (i) investigate keyword search of workflow fragments (Sect. 5), (ii) study the problem of workflow fragment composition (Sect. 6), (iii) show how the composition operates using an example (Sect. 7). Furthermore, we weave the three pieces of mining, keyword search, and composition of workflow fragments within a global method (Sect. 2), and extend related work analysis (Sect. 3).

2 Approach Overview

Designing a workflow is a time consuming and sometimes expensive task. The designer needs to be knowledgeable of the tools (services) that are available to implement the steps in the process she desires. Furthermore, she needs to know how such services can (or should) be connected together taking into consideration, amongst other criteria, the types and semantic domains of their input and output parameters. There has been a good body of work in the literature on workflow discovery, see e.g., [8–10]. The typical approach requires the user to specify a query in the form of a workflow that is compared with a collection of workflows. The workflows that are retrieved are then ranked taking into consideration, amongst other things, the structural similarity between the workflow issued by the user and the workflows retrieved. In our work, we focus on a problem that is different and that received little attention in the literature. Specifically, we position ourselves in a context where a designer is specifying her workflow and needs assistance to design parts of her workflow, e.g., because she does not know the services that are available and that can be used to enact the steps within the part in question. In certain situations, the designer may know the services that can be used for such purpose, but would still like to acquire knowledge about the best way/practice for connecting such services together. The solution we describe in this paper has been elaborated with the needs of such designers in mind. It can be used to assist them finding an existing fragment that can be used to complete the workflow being designed. Furthermore, we provide the user with suggestions on the way such fragments can be composed with the initial workflow.

Figure 1 illustrates our approach using two processes. Figure 1(a) illustrates the process that is enacted offline to build a repository of workflow fragments. Specifically, given a workflow repository, e.g., the myExperiment repository [1], the labels used to name the activities in the workflow are homogenized. Indeed, different designers are likely to use different labels to name activities that perform the same task. For this purpose, we use existing state of the art techniques, which consist in using shared vocabularies (dictionaries) to rename the activities of the workflow. Once the labeling of the workflows in the repository is homogenized,

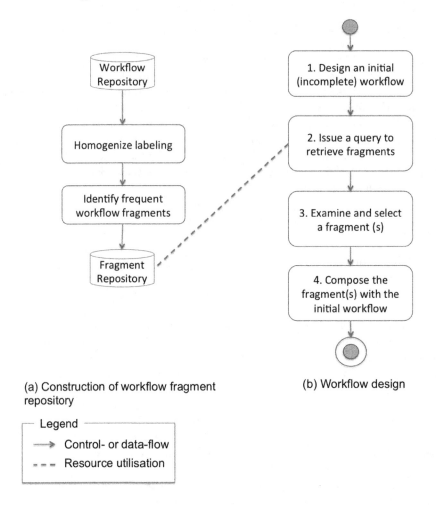

(a) Construction of workflow fragment repository

(b) Workflow design

Legend

⟶ Control- or data-flow

--- Resource utilisation

Fig. 1. An overview of the approach

we use sub-graph mining techniques, in particular the SUBDUE algorithm [11] to identify frequent fragments, which are stored in a dedicated repository. It is worth underlining that we only seek to mine frequent fragments since they are likely to represent patterns (and therefore best practices) that can be useful for the designer. Note also that our choice of Subdue is motivated by the popularity of this algorithm.

Figure 1(b) illustrates the process used to mine workflow fragments and exploit them when designing new workflows. In the first phase, the user starts by designing an initial workflow based on her objectives. There are some parts of the workflow that the designer may need assistance with. For a given part, which we name *fragment*, the designer issues a query against a repository of workflow fragments (phase 2). Such a query is composed of two elements: a set of keywords and a set of activities in the workflow being designed, which we name *joint activities*. The set of keywords are used to identify the fragments in the repository that are relevant. The joint activities specify the activities in the workflow being designed to which the relevant fragment(s) are to be connected to, to complete that workflow. This step returns a list of ranked candidates workflow fragments. The fragments are ranked based on the extent they match the keywords specified by the designer, but also based on their amenability to be connected to the joint activities in the workflow being designed. The user examines the top-k fragments and identifies the one or the ones she wishes to compose with the initial workflow (phase 3). Our system makes suggestions to the user on the way the composition can be performed (phase 4). The user accepts the suggestions she deems appropriate and complete the composition when necessary to obtain the desired workflow. We will present in more details the mining of frequent workflow fragments, their retrieval and their composition in Sects. 4, 5 and 6, respectively.

Workflow Model

For the work we present in this paper, we view a workflow as a graph $wf = (N, E)$, where N is a set of nodes composed of the activities A that constitute the workflow and control flow operators OP, i.e., $N = A \cup OP$. E represents the set of edges connecting activities and operators, i.e., $E \subseteq (N \times N)$. We consider the control flow operators supported by BPMN[1], namely sequence, and-split, and-join, or-split, or-join, xor-split and xor-split, the semantics of which is defined below.

- **Sequence:** The sequence flow connector (represented as an edge) is used to model the cases where the completion of the execution of an activity causes (or initializes) the execution of another activity.
- **And-split** and **And-join:** This operator is used when the completion of the execution of a given activity causes the execution of two or more activities, which are executed concurrently. The activities that are triggered by an and-split, or more precisely the workflow branches that are initialized by such activities, are usually synchronized by an and-join operator. Such an operator triggers the execution of the succeeding activity when the execution of given activities comes to completion.
- **Or-split** and **Or-join:** This operator is used when the completion of the execution of a given activity causes some or all of its subsequent activities within the workflow, which, as for and-split, are executed concurrently. The Or-join operator is usually used to synchronize the execution of workflow branches that were triggered by an or-split. It initializes the execution of the succeeding activity when the execution of some of the preceding activities terminates.

---

[1] http://www.bpmn.org.

– **Xor-split** and **Xor-join:** Unlike or-split, the xor-split is used when the activities (branches) that succeed a given activity are mutually exclusive. Therefore, during the execution one and only one of those activities are triggered. The xor-join is usually used to synchronize the branches that succeed an xor-split. It triggers the execution of the following activity once the execution of one of its preceding activities comes to completion.

Figure 2 illustrates a simple workflow composed of five activities. The workflow contains three control flow operators. The and-split connects the activity *att*1 to the activities *att*2 and *att*4, specifying that the execution of *att*2 and *att*4 is triggered once the execution of *att*1 terminates. The sequence connector is used to specify that the execution of *att*2 is followed by that of *att*3. Finally, the and-join operators connects the activities *att*3 and *att*4 to the activity *att*5, specifying that the execution of the latter is triggered once the execution of the formers terminates.

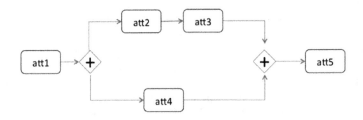

Fig. 2. A simple workflow

3   Related Work

There are three lines of work that are similar to our proposal which we analyze in this section and compare to our work: workflow similarity and mining, semantic enrichment as a means for improving workflow discovery and intelligent support for process modelling.

Workflow Similarity and Workflow Mining. The literature of business and scientific workflows is rich with proposals that seek to mine existing workflows and/or identify similarities between workflows. Existing work on workflow mining, focused mainly on deriving a workflow specification (usually as a petri-net) from logs of executions of the workflows. There are however some proposals that focused on examining workflow specifications using clustering [12] and case-based reasoning [13], among other techniques. For example, in the case of clustering-based techniques, several similarity measures were employed to estimate the distance between workflows. For example, Bae *et al.* [4] proposed a metric that uses tree structures to take into account control flow operators such as parallel branching and conditional choice. Diamantini *et al.* estimate the similarity between workflows based on the representation of workflows as Event Condition Action rules (ECA) [14]. Other authors apply sub-graph isomorphism techniques, see e.g. [5,6].

The above methods assess the similarity between entire workflows. In our work, we are interested in identifying the similarity between fragments of workflows. In this respect, our work is more related to the proposal by Diamantini *et al.* [14] who applied hierarchical graph clustering method in order to extract common fragments of workflows. We focus on fragments as opposed to entire workflows since there are more (realistic) opportunities for reuse at the level of the fragment as opposed to the entire workflow. In other words, the chances that the user finds a workflow that match her needs are slim. On the other hand, the chances that she finds workflows that contains one of more fragments that may contribute to her workflow are more likely.

Improving Similarity Using Semantic Enrichment. A comparative study of different methods for scientific workflow matching confirms that inclusion of external knowledge improves both computational complexity and result quality [15]. While the application of semantic enrichment has received notable attention in the literature as a means to enhance the quality of workflow matching, enhancing the quality of fragments matching has received less attention and is by and large unexplored.

One of the main issue that benefits from semantic enrichment is that of heterogeneity in naming the parameters of the workflows and their constituent activities. To do so, taxonomies are used to infer relationships between activities and their parameters [16,17]. We use a different strategy by augmenting existing sub-graph mining techniques [16–19] with a preprocessing phase for homogenizing workflow labels and by enriching user keywords query for searching fragments with synonyms. Trying to make a naive clustering of workflows in a repository would lead us to inefficient and limited method. Moreover, a striking distinction is that the previous works [17,18,20] propose the most reused fragments among the dataset as templates. Due to the large collection of available data on-line, the number of templates increases, which leads the designer to a heavy activity of browsing and analyzing the pool of templates in order to understand what could be useful to him. Instead, our work consists on assisting designer by using a simple keyword search to suggest the most probable component that could help her. We also offer support for integrating this fragment in her current workflow.

With the exception of the work by Diamantini *et al.* [14], we are not aware of any proposal that investigated the impact of the representation model used to encode workflows on the effectiveness and efficiency of workflow fragment mining. We proposed new models with respect to the work by Diamantini *et al.* We also conducted an empirical evaluation to investigate the advantages and limitations of each model. This study revealed that the representation model that we proposed out-preforms the remaining models both in terms of effectiveness and efficiency.

Advanced Support and Recommendation for Process Modelling. A categorization of recommendation techniques for process modelling is presented in [21], including textual recommendation, structural recommendation and linking recommendation. Following this classification, our technique would fall into the category of structural recommendation, that can be used for forward or backward completion. The approach in [22] aims also at helping designers to reuse parts of workflow models. In contrast with our approach, the user is required to describe the missing fragment using a dedicated query language.

Recommendation of an operator to extend a data analysis process is proposed in [23], based on a prediction model that is learned in a pre-processing phase using a pool of several thousand real-world data analysis workflows.

The notion of configurable operator that we use in our work is inspired by the works on configurable workflows (e.g., [24]), where it has a different goal, that of defining a generic process model whose behavior encompasses those of its variants. The configurable process model, resulting from the union of several alternative processes keeps information allowing analysts to track back, for each element, the process model form which it originates. Thus, the approach in [24] proposes to use it to construct the intersection of the process models, i.e., to identify common process fragments. A configurable business process is used also in [25] to create a Bayesian network to allow probabilistic recommendation queries.

Among the approaches for intelligent support for modelling, the work the most similar to the one presented in this paper is [26], which offers a search interface for process model fragments based on semantic annotations (tags). In contrast with our work, where process fragments are automatically extracted by mining the repository, users manually declare logically coherent process parts as fragments and assign titles to them.

To conclude, while similar works exist for different steps of our approach, the contribution presented in this paper is a complete and realistic solution for reusing process fragments starting from mining an heterogeneous repository using an efficient workflow encoding format, for offering a semantically enhanced keyword search, and for including support for their integration (composition) in a new workflow during the design task.

4   Mining Frequent Workflow Fragments

Given a repository of workflows, we would like to mine frequent workflow fragments, i.e., fragments that are used across multiple workflows. Such fragments are likely to implement tasks that can be reused in newly specified workflows. Mining workflows raises the following questions.

- *How to deal with the heterogeneity of the labels used by different users to model the activities of their workflows within the repository?* Different designers use different labels to name the activities that compose their workflow. We need a mean to homogenize the labels before mining the workflows in order not to miss relevant fragments.

- *Which graph representation is best suited for formatting workflows for mining frequent fragments?* We argue that the effectiveness and efficiency of the mining algorithm used to retrieve frequent fragments depend on the representation used to encode workflow specifications.

4.1 Homogenizing Activity Labels

To be able to extract frequent workflow fragments, we first need to identify common activities. Thus, activities implementing the same functionality should have the same names. Some workflow modelling tools (see for example Signavio[2]) handle a dictionary and allow to reuse dictionary entries via a search or by the auto-completion function (when user starts typing an activity label, the system suggests similar activity labels from the dictionary). If models in the repository come from different tools and use different naming conventions, a preprocessing step is applied to homogenize activity labels using a dictionary [27]. For facilitating this step, we rely on existing techniques like [28]. These techniques are able to recognize the labelling styles and to automatically refactor labels with quality issues. These labels are transformed into a verb-object label by the derivation of actions and business objects from activity labels. The labels of verb-object style contain an action that is followed by a business object, like *Create invoice* and *Validate order*. The benefits of this style of labeling have been promoted by several practical studies and modeling guidelines. Synonyms are also handled in this step. They are recognized using the WordNet lexical database and they are replaced with a common term.

4.2 Workflow Encoding

In order to extract frequent patterns, we use an existing graph mining algorithm, SUBDUE [11]. SUBDUE is a heuristic approach that uses a measure-theoretic information, the minimum description length, to find important subgraphs. Thus, the workflow model must be translated to a graph format. To this end, we studied some of the state of the art representation models and proposed one that can enhance the running time, the memory space required, and also the significance of the patterns extracted. In fact, we show that the representation model is of major importance.

The pre-processing phase consists of transforming a workflow into a compact graph representation. Indeed, the level of compactness depends on the representation model selected. As demonstrated by Diamantini *et al.* [14] and supported by our experimentation which we will report later on, the choice of the encoding model affects not only the time required for mining fragments, but also the relevance of the fragments returned.

In the experiment conducted by Diamantini and coauthors, three representation models A, B and C have been proposed (see Fig. 4). In all these models,

---

[2] www.signavio.com.

the activities are mapped to the so called activity nodes, while the representation of operators differs from one model to another. Specifically, in model A, each operator is represented by two nodes, called control nodes (to distinguish them from activities nodes): the first one is labeled "operator" and the second one is used to specify the type of operator. The labels that can be assigned to the latter one are: sequence, AND or XOR. The model A does not explicitly mention the difference between JOIN and SPLIT which can be deduced from the number of ingoing and outgoing arcs. The second model, model B assigns a control node to each operator, i.e., AND-split, XOR-split, AND-join, XOR-join. The operator SEQ is not explicitly represented by a node, instead it is translated into an edge connecting the activity nodes in question. Finally, the third model, C model simplifies the graph by removing both join and split nodes. XOR nodes are removed by generating a graph for each alternative path. In this way, the only nodes having several ingoing/outgoing activity are the AND nodes. As there is no ambiguity about these nodes, they can be removed also. Edges are labeled to maintain information about the type of the operator and its operand nodes.

Fig. 3. An example of BPMN process (figure extracted from [14]).

According to the experiments conducted by Diamantini *et al.*, model A is the most costly in terms of execution time and also the less effective as it generates the least significant patterns. Indeed, when using representation model A the majority of nodes are control nodes. On the other hand, the model C contains no control node. The advantage of the model C is that the edges conveys information about the nodes attached to and the nature of the operator connecting them, which resulted in a gain in terms of storage space and execution time required. However, the disadvantage of model C lies in the mapping of the "XOR" operator; a graph is generated for each alternative which makes spatio-temporal complexity grow exponentially with the size of input data. Indeed, let us consider the case, where during the parsing of the original business process to convert into graph format the next node type is XOR-split with at least two incidents arcs. In this case, the number of graphs generated is doubled. In addition, if we consider an example repository where one of its most common substructures includes an operator XOR, this knowledge will not be discovered. Each path of the XOR operator will be extracted separately, but the fragment of business processes which contains all of these alternatives will not be considered as a whole. However, the model C is suitable for the discovery of typical pathways, which can be useful for some application domains.

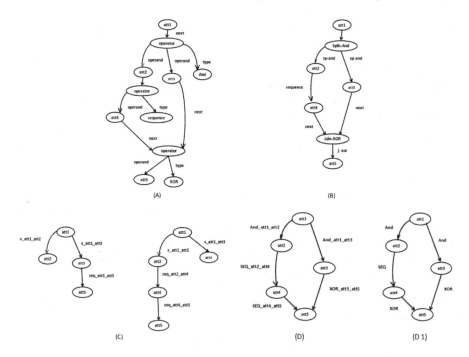

Fig. 4. Graphic of different representation models A, B, C and D.

Compared to model A and C, the model B has the higher level of compactness without a loss of information. In fact, representation model B reflects most closely the initial business process scheme. Therefore, patterns discovered based on this model are more interesting than those extracted by model A and C for searching and indexing cases.

We suggest a new representation model for workflows. We tried to take advantage of the previous models A, B and C and come up with a new model D that alleviates the disadvantages of such representation models. Specifically, we use the same strategy as the model C, in the sense that no control node is used. The edge connecting two activity nodes are labelled to indicate the kind of the control operator(s) connecting the nodes. We propose two variant representation models: D and D1. In the representation model D, the edges are labelled with the type of the operator and the labels of the activities that the operator connects. In the representation model D1, the edges are labeled only with the type of the control operator. That is, it does not consider the labels of the activities.

4.3   Empirical Evaluation

The methodology we have just described raises the following question: *Is the representation model that we propose suitable for mining frequent workflow fragments?* In this section we report on an empirical evaluation that we conducted to answer such a question.

Experimental Setting

We ran our experiment on a DELL machine with an Intel Core i7-2670QM processor with a 2.20 GHz frequency. We used the SUBDUE 5.5.2 tool in the fragment mining algorithm phase. We configured SUBDUE by choosing the MDL as a selection criterion with beam width equal to 4 and the number of top substructures returned set to 10.

We compared the representation models, namely A, B, C, D and D1. Our goal is to show, amongst other things, the drawbacks of the representation model C when it comes to dealing with datasets containing workflows with XOR operators. To do so, we generated three datasets composed of 30, 42 and 71 workflows. The datasets are composed of a mixture of some synthetic workflows that are obtained by mutating the workflow illustrated in Fig. 3 and some real ones selected from the Taverna 1 repository [1]. We manually examined the workflows generated to identify useful frequent fragments. Therefore, to measure the effectiveness of the representation models presented in this paper, we computed the precision and recall of the results obtained using each model.

Evaluation Results

Figure 5 illustrates the size of the graphs created using the different representation models. It shows that model A is the most expensive in term of space disk required to represent the dataset in graph format. Figure 6 compares the performances of the different representation models in terms of space disk, execution time and quality of results for different number of processes in the data set. Our results confirm those reported by Diamantnini *et al.* The A model requires the longest execution time (at least 7 times more than all other models); note this is not depicted in Fig. 6 for visibility reasons. Regarding the qualitative performance of the A model, we notice that when the number of workflows increases to 71, the recall decreases to 0%. This is due to the fact that control operators in the A model are represented by two nodes connected by an edge. For example the And-Split operator gives rise to two nodes connected by an edge: one is labelled "Operator" and the second "And-Split". Therefore, when mining the workflow repository using such a representation, the SUBDUE algorithm finds that the fragments representing control flow operators are the most frequent and returns them. However, they are useless for the designer as they do not implement any useful pattern that can be reused.

Concerning the C model, as expected, Fig. 5 shows that it may require more than twice the number of edges and nodes required by the models that we propose, namely D and D1. In addition, the model C is associated with a recall rate that varies between 32% and 34% for all tested databases which confirms that the C model can, at best, discover only one alternative at a time (in our case there are 2 alternatives attached to the XOR node).

Qualitatively, the B model performs much better than the A and C models. It retrieves successfully twice the number of significant elements retrieved using the C model and between 66% to 135% more than the A model. The B model was also able to discover more relevant workflow fragments than model D (about 10% more). This is due to the fact that the D model uses activity labels when labeling the edges. This over-specification of the labeling of the edges yields missing some fragments, and has therefore a negative impact on the recall. Note, however, that the B model returned more irrelevant workflow fragments (around 7%), which impacted negatively on the precision. Concerning the disk space requirements, the B model required between 25% up to 40% more space compared with the D and D1 models.

Based on the results illustrated in Fig. 6, we can observe a common precision performance between models D and D1. This performance is due to the fact that these two models do not use control nodes thereby avoiding retrieving false positive fragments, which will have a negative impact on the precision. We note, on the other hand, that the D1 model performs better than the D model when it comes to recall. This is due, as mentioned earlier, to the fact that the D model over-specifies the labels of the edges by using as well as the name of the control-operator, the labels of the activities connected by such an operator.

As SUBDUE loads the input data and performs all calculations in main memory, reducing the search space and the input file size, would also reduce the amount of memory required and computation time. Moreover, the D1 model also requires the smallest space compared with the other models. We can therefore conclude from this experiment that the D1 model was not only able to extract the most significant fragments but also did so in a relatively short execution time and required the least memory space. The performance achieved by the D1 model through this experiment has proven its effectiveness and efficiency.

5   Keyword-Based Search of Frequent Workflow Fragments

Given an initial workflow, the user issues a query to characterize the desired missing workflow fragment. The query is composed of two elements. The first element is a set of keywords $\{kw_1, \ldots, kw_n\}$ characterizing the functionality that the fragment should implement. The user selects the terms of her own choice. In other words, we do not impose any vocabulary for keyword specification. The second element in the user query specifies the activities in the initial workflow that are to be connected to the fragment in question, $A_{common} = \{a_1, \ldots, a_m\}$. Generally speaking, the user will specify one or two activities in the initial work-flow. We call such activities using the terms common activities or joint activities, interchangeably.

The first step in processing the user query consists in identifying the fragments in the repository that are relevant given the specified keywords. In doing so, we adopt the widely used technique of TF/IDF (term frequency/inverse document frequency) measure. It is worth mentioning here that the workflow fragments in the repository are indexed by the labels of the activity obtained after the homogenization of the workflow (see Sect. 4.1). We refer to such an

Input	Mod	V	E
9	A	128	132
	B	79	80
	C	123	102
	D	56	57
	D1	**56**	**57**
30	A	610	604
	B	340	330
	C	335	295
	D	268	250
	D1	**268**	**250**
42	A	908	897
	B	511	496
	C	473	421
	D	406	376
	D 1	**406**	**376**
71	A	1560	1541
	B	886	863
	C	777	706
	D	710	661
	D 1	**710**	**661**

Fig. 5. Size of the graphs using the different representation models.

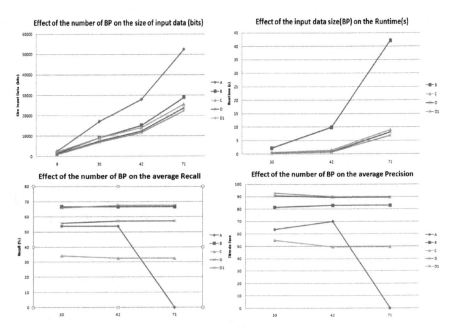

Fig. 6. Performances of the different representation models.

index by IDX. Applying directly TF/IDF based on the set of keywords provided by the user is likely to miss some fragments. This is because the designer provides keywords of her own choosing; a given keyword may not be present in the repository, while one of its synonyms could be present. To address this issue, we adopt the following method which augments traditional TF/IDF with a semantic enrichment phase. Specifically, given a set of keywords provided by the user $\{kw_1, \ldots, kw_n\}$, for each keyword kw_i we retrieve its synonyms, which we denote by $syn(kw_i)$ from an existing thesaurus, e.g., Wordnet [29] or a specialized domain specific thesaurus if we are dealing with workflows from a specific domain. The index IDX is trawled to identify if there is a term in $syn(kw_i) \cup \{kw_i\}$ that appears. If this is the case, then the term in the index is used to represent kw_i in the vector that will be used to compare the query with the vectors representing the workflow fragments in the repository.

Note also that multiple keywords, e.g., kw_i and kw_j, may be mapped to the same term kw_{IDX} in the index IDX, in this case we set the frequency of the kw_{IDX} to be the number of keywords it represents when computing the associated TF/IDF. In certain situations, we may need to use the hypernyms of kw_i. This is specifically the case when none of the terms in IDX appears in $syn(kw_i) \cup \{kw_i\}$. Using the hypernyms in such a case may allow us to identify a term in IDX that can be used to represent kw_i in the vector representing the user query.

Once the vector that represents the user query is constructed and the TF/IDF of its associated terms are calculated, it is compared against the vectors representing the workflow fragments in the repository using the cosine similarity [30].

The set of fragments retrieved in the previous step, which we call candidate fragments, are then examined. Specifically, their constituent activities are compared and matched against the activities in A_{common}, that are specified by the user. Given a candidate fragment wf_{frg}, each activity a_j in A_{common} is compared (matched) against the activities that constitute the fragment wf_{frg}. The objective of this step is to identify the activities that will be in common between the fragment and the initial workflow. Note that for a given activity a_j in A_{common} there may be more than one matching activity in the fragment wf_{frg}. In this case, we associate a_j with the activity in wf_{frg} with the highest matching score. Reciprocally, if two activities a_i, a_j in A_{common} are associated with the same activity in wf_{frg}, the one with the highest score is kept and other matcher is searched for the second one (such that the sum of the similarities of the global mapping is maximised). Note also that it is possible that a_j may not have any matching activities among those of the fragment wf_{frg}. The matching is performed using existing techniques for matching activity labels [31]. These techniques tokenize the activity labels, remove stop words and then apply syntactic string comparisons (string edit distance, number of common words) and take semantic relationships into account based on the lexical database WordNet.

The last step in the query processing consists in ranking the candidate fragments. The ranking takes into consideration the following factors.

1. The relevance score of the candidate fragment calculated based on TF/IDF given a user query uq. (We view a fragment as a document, or more specifically, we consider the terms labeling the activities in the fragment when computing the TF/IDF.) We use $Relevance(wf_{frg}, uq)$ to denote the relevance score associated with a candidate fragment wf_{frg} given the user query.
2. The frequency of use of the fragment in the repository. The fragment that are used across multiple workflows are likely to implement best practices that are useful for the workflow designer compared with workflow fragment that are used in, say, only 2 workflows. We use $Frequency(wf_{frg})$ to denote the frequency, i.e., the number of times a candidate fragment wf_{frg} appears in the mined workflow repository.
3. The compatibility of the candidate fragment with the inital workflow. To estimate the compatibility, we consider the number of activities in A_{common} that have a matching activity in the workflow fragment and their associated matching score. Specifically, we define the compatibility of a workflow fragment given the activities $uq.A_{common}$ specified in the user query uq as follows:

$$Compatibility(wf_{frg}, uq.A_{common}) = \frac{\sum_{a_j \in A_{common}} matchingScore(a_j, wf_{frg})}{|A_{common}|}$$

where $matchingScore(a_j, wf_{frg})$ is the matching score between a_j and the best matching activity in wf_{frg}, and $|A_{common}|$ the number of activities in A_{common}. $Compatibility(wf_{frg}, A_{common})$ takes a value between 0 and 1. The larger is the number of activities A_{common} that have a matching activity in wf_{frg} and the higher are the matching scores, the higher is the compatibility between the candidate workflow fragment and the initial workflow.

Based on the above factors, we define the score used for ranking candidate fragments given a user query uq as:

$$Score(wf_{frg}, uq) =$$

$$w_r.Relevance(wf_{frg}, uq) + w_f.\frac{Frequency(wf_{frg})}{MaxFrequency} + w_c.Compatibility(wf_{frg}, uq.A_{common})$$

where w_r, w_f and w_c are positive real numbers representing weights such that $w_r + w_f + w_c = 1$. $MaxFrequency$ is a positive number denoting the frequency of the fragment that appears the maximum number of times in the workflow repository harvested. Notice that the score takes a value between 0 and 1. Once the candidate fragments are scored, they are ranked in the descendant order of their associated scores. The top-k fragments, e.g., 5, are then presented to the designer who selects to the one to be composed with the initial workflow. Initially the weights w_r, w_f and w_c take equal values. Then, depending on the performance and the feedback provided by the user they can be adjusted.

6   Composing Workflow Fragments

Once the user has examined the fragments that are retrieved given the set of keywords she specified, she can choose a fragment to be composed with the initial workflow she was designing. We present in this section a method that can assist the designer in the composition task. Specifically, we consider that the user has designed an initial workflow $wf_{initial}$ and selected a fragment wf_{frg} to be composed with $wf_{initial}$. We turn our attention first to the case where $wf_{initial}$ and wf_{frg} has one activity in common a_{common}. We denote by $in(a_{common}, wf)$ the set of activities that precedes a_{common} in the workflow wf, and by $out(a_{common}, wf)$ the set of activities that succeed a_{common} in the workflow wf.

Algorithm Compose
Input: $wf_{initial}$ initial workflow
           wf_{frg}: workflow fragment
           a_{common}: activity in common between $wf_{initial}$ and wf_{frg}
Output: wf_{merge}: workflow obtained by composing $wf_{initial}$ and wf_{frg} based on a_{common}
Begin
1   **If** $(card(out(a_{common}, wf_{initial})) = 0)$ and $(card(in(a_{common}, wf_{frg})) = 0)$
2   **Then** connect in sequence $wf_{initial}$ followed by wf_{frg} using a_{common}
3   **If** $(card(in(a_{common}, wf_{initial})) = 0)and(card(out(a_{common}, wf_{frg})) = 0)$
4   **Then** connect in sequence wf_{frg} followed by $wf_{initial}$ using a_{common}
5   **If** $(card(in(a_{common}, wf_{initial})) \geq 1)and(card(in(a_{common}, wf_{frg})) \geq 1)$
6   **Then** create a configurable join operator and
7   connect it to the preceeding activities of $wf_{initial}$ and those of wf_{frg}
8   **If** $(card(out(a_{common}, wf_{initial})) \geq 1)and(card(out(a_{common}, wf_{frg})) \geq 1)$
9   **Then** create a configurable branching operator and
10   connect it to the succeeding activities of $wf_{initial}$ and those of wf_{frg}
11   wf_{merge} is the workflow obtained as a result of the above manipulation.
End

Fig. 7. Composition algorithm

Figure 7 sketches the algorithm used for composing $wf_{initial}$ and wf_{frg}. If there is no succeeding activity for a_{common} in wf_{intial} and there is no preceding activity for a_{common} in wf_{frg} then $wf_{initial}$ is composed in sequence with wf_{frg} based on a_{common} (*lines 1 and 2*). Inversely, if there is no preceding activity for a_{common} in $wf_{initial}$ and there is no succeeding activity for a_{common} in wf_{frg} then wf_{frg} is composed in sequence with $wf_{initial}$ based on a_{common} (*lines 3 and 4*). The above cases are illustrated using Fig. 8.

If a_{common} has preceding activities in both $wf_{initial}$ and wf_{frg} (*line 5*), then we connect the two workflows using a configurable join operator as illustrated in Fig. 8 (*lines 6 and 7*). We call such an operator configurable because it is up to the user to choose if such an operator is of a type $and - join$, $or - join$ or $xor - join$. The preceding activities of such an operator are the preceding activities of $wf_{initial}$ and wf_{frg}, and its succeeding activity is a_{common} (Fig. 9).

If a_{common} has succeeding activities in both $wf_{initial}$ and wf_{frg} (*line 8*), then we use a configurable split operator to connect the two workflows as illustrated in Fig. 10 (*lines 9 and 10*). We call such an operator configurable because it is up to the user to choose if such an operator is of a type *and-split, or-split* or *xor-split*. The preceding activity of such an operator is a_{common} and its succeeding activities are the succeeding activities of $wf_{initial}$ and wf_{frg}.

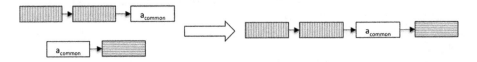

Fig. 8. Merging the initial workflow and a fragment in sequence based on the common activity a_{common}.

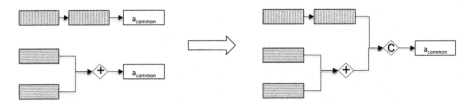

Fig. 9. Merging the preceding activities of the initial workflow and a fragment using a configurable join control operator.

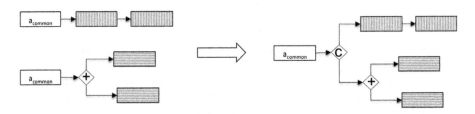

Fig. 10. Merging the succeeding activities of the initial workflow and a fragment using a configurable split control operator.

If the initial workflow and the fragment has more than one activity in common then we perform the processing we have just described above iteratively using one activity at a time. Note, however, that one would expect in the general case that there is one activity in common between the initial workflow and the fragment selected by the user. Having multiple activities in common between the initial workflow and the fragment is likely to lead to complex workflows that are difficult to understand thereby out-weighting the benefits that can be derived from fragment reuse. Once the initial workflow and the fragment selected are merged, the user examines the obtained workflow, makes changes in terms of activities and control flow connectors if necessary. In particular, the user will need to substitute configurable join and split operators with concrete operators, e.g., and-split or or-split, that meet the semantics of the process she has in mind. As mentioned earlier, the user may want to merge another fragment once the initial workflow and the current fragment has been merged. The same processing described above will be applied to the newly selected fragment.

7   Example from eScience

In this section, we illustrate the use of the method we have proposed in this paper to assist a designer of a workflow from the eScience field. Specifically, we show how the method described can help the designer specify a workflow that is used for analyzing Huntington's disease (HD) data. Huntington's disease is the most common inherited neurodegenerative disorder in Europe, affecting 1 out of 10000 people. Although the genetic mutation that causes HD was identified 20 years ago [32], the downstream molecular mechanisms leading to the HD phenotype are still poorly understood. Relating alterations in gene expression to epigenetic information might shed light on the disease aetiology. With this in mind, the scientist wanted to specify a workflow that annotate HD gene expression data with publicly available epigenetic data [33].

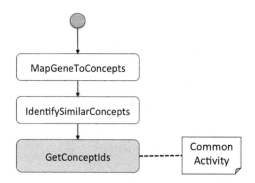

Fig. 11. Initial Huntington disease profiling workflow.

The initial workflow specified by the designer is illustrated in Fig. 11. The workflow contains three activities that are ordered in sequence. The first activity *MapGeneToConcept* is used to extract the concepts that are used in domain ontologies to characterize a given gene that is known or suspected to be involved in an infection or disease, in this case the Huntigton Disease. The second activity *IndentifySimilarConcepts* is then used to identify for each of those concepts, the concepts that are similar. The rational behind doing so is that genes that are associated with concepts that are similar to concepts that are involved in the disease have chances of being also involved in the disease. This activity involves running ontological similarity tests to identify similar concepts. The third activity *GetConceptIds* is then used to extract the identifiers of the similar concepts.

The workflow depicted in Fig. 11 does not completely implement the analysis that the designer would like. In particular, the designer would like to profile and rank the similar concepts that have been identified by the third activity but is unaware of the service implementations that can be used to do so. To assist the designer in this task, we asked him to identify the common activity to which the missing fragment is to be attached to. She identified the activity *GetConceptIDs* as the common activity. We then asked him to provide a set of keywords characterizing the desired fragment. She provided as a result the following set: $\{concept, score, rank, profile\}$. Using the method presented in Sect. 5, we retrieved candidate fragments. Figure 12 illustrates the fragment that was first ranked in the results and was selected by the user. The common activity is named *GetTermIdentifiers* in the fragment, which is different from the label of the common activity in the initial workflow, *GetConceptIds*. Still, our method was able detect it as a common activity thanks to the string similarity utilized.

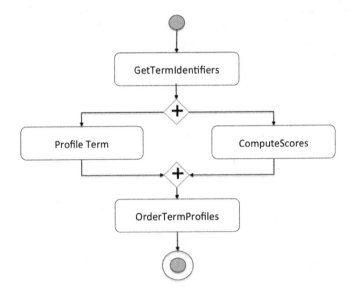

Fig. 12. Candidate fragment selected by the workflow designer.

By applying the composition algorithm presented in Sect. 6 to merge the initial workflow and the fragment selected by the user, we obtained the workflow depicted in Fig. 13. Indeed, the common activity has no succeeding activity in the initial workflow and has no preceding activity in the workflow fragment (*lines 1, 2* in Fig. 7). Therefore, the two workflows are connected ins sequence using the common activity.

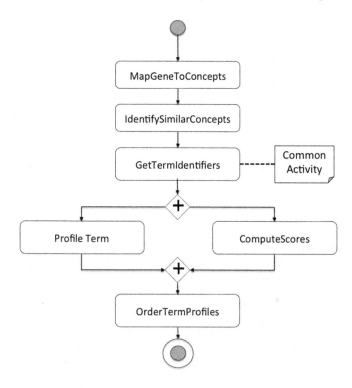

Fig. 13. Workflow obtained by merging the initial workflow and selected fragment.

8   Conclusion

We presented in this paper a methodology for improving the reusability of fragments within workflow repositories, with the objective of allowing workflow
designers to benefit from existing workflows (and the knowledge they encompass) when designing new workflows. Specifically, we examined the representation model that can be used for formatting workflows before they are mined.
In order to propose a realistic and complete solution, we showed also how to
deal with the heterogeneity of activity labels as a preprocessing step before mining. The experimentation shows the effectiveness of the representation model
in improving the performance of the mining task. The mined fragments can be
searched by designers using a simple free keyword search and automatically integrated in the initial workflow model. Our ongoing work aims to examine how
several fragments from different workflow specifications can be combined to meet
user needs. We also intend to perform a larger scale evaluation to assess the performance of the solution proposed and a user study to evaluate the efficiency
gain of a designer using our approach.

References

1. De Roure, D., Goble, C.A., Stevens, R.: The design and realisation of the my$_{experiment}$ virtual research environment for social sharing of workflows. Future Gener. Comput. Syst. **25**(5), 561–567 (2009)

2. Mates, P., Santos, E., Freire, J., Silva, C.T.: CrowdLabs: social analysis and visualization for the sciences. In: Cushing, J.B., French, J., Bowers, S. (eds.) SSDBM 2011. LNCS, vol. 6809, pp. 555–564. Springer, Heidelberg (2011). doi:10.1007/978-3-642-22351-8_38

3. Giardine, B., Riemer, C., Hardison, R.C., Burhans, R., Shah, P., Zhang, Y., Blankenberg, D., Albert, I., Miller, W., Kent, W.J., Nekrutenko, A.: Galaxy: a platform for interactive large-scale genome analysis. Genome Res. **15**, 1451–1455 (2005)

4. Bae, J., Caverlee, J., Liu, L., Yan, H.: Process mining by measuring process block similarity. In: Eder, J., Dustdar, S. (eds.) BPM 2006. LNCS, vol. 4103, pp. 141–152. Springer, Heidelberg (2006). doi:10.1007/11837862_15

5. Goderis, A., Li, P., Goble, C.: Workflow discovery: the problem, a case study from e-science and a graph-based solution. In: International Conference on Web Services, ICWS 2006, Chicago, IL, pp. 312–319. IEEE (2006)

6. Bergmann, R., Gil, Y.: Similarity assessment and efficient retrieval of semantic workflows. Inf. Syst. **40**, 115–127 (2014)

7. Harmassi, M., Grigori, D., Belhajjame, K.: Mining workflow repositories for improving fragments reuse. In: Cardoso, J., Guerra, F., Houben, G.-J., Pinto, A.M., Velegrakis, Y. (eds.) KEYSTONE 2015. LNCS, vol. 9398, pp. 76–87. Springer, Cham (2015). doi:10.1007/978-3-319-27932-9_7

8. Deutch, D., Milo, T.: Evaluating TOP-K queries over business processes. In: Proceedings of the 25th International Conference on Data Engineering, ICDE 2009, Shanghai, China, 29 March 2009–2 April 2009, pp. 1195–1198 (2009). http://dx.doi.org/10.1109/ICDE.2009.199

9. Goderis, A., Li, P., Goble, C.A.: Workflow discovery: requirements from e-science and a graph-based solution. Int. J. Web Serv. Res. **5**(4), 32–58 (2008). http://dx.doi.org/10.4018/jwsr.2008100102

10. Starlinger, J., Brancotte, B., Boulakia, S.C., Leser, U.: Similarity search for scientific workflows. PVLDB **7**(12), 1143–1154 (2014). http://www.vldb.org/pvldb/vol7/p.1143-starlinger.pdf

11. Jonyer, I., Cook, D.J., Holder, L.B.: Graph-based hierarchical conceptual clustering. J. Mach. Learn. Res. **2**, 19–43 (2001)

12. Yaman, M.B.F., Oates, T.: A context driven approach for workflow mining. In: Proceedings of the 21st International Joint Conference on Artificial Intelligence, Pasadena, California, USA, pp. 1798–1803. Morgan Kaufmann Publishers Inc. (2009)

13. Leake, D., Kendall-Morwick, J.: Towards case-based support for e-science workflow generation by mining provenance. In: Althoff, K.-D., Bergmann, R., Minor, M., Hanft, A. (eds.) ECCBR 2008. LNCS, vol. 5239, pp. 269–283. Springer, Heidelberg (2008). doi:10.1007/978-3-540-85502-6_18

14. Diamantini, C., Potena, D., Storti, E.: Mining usage patterns from a repository of scientific workflows. In: Proceedings of the ACM Symposium on Applied Computing, SAC 2012, Riva, Trento, Italy, 26–30 March 2012, pp. 152–157. ACM (2012). http://doi.acm.org/10.1145/2245276.2245307

15. Starlinger, J., Brancotte, B., Cohen-Boulakia, S., Leser, U.: Similarity search for scientific workflows. In: 40th International Conference on Very Large Data Bases, VLDB Endowment, Hangzhou, China, pp. 2150–8097 (2014)
16. Cuzzocrea, A., Diamantini, C., Genga, L., Potena, D., Storti, E.: A composite methodology for supporting collaboration pattern discovery via semantic enrichment and multidimensional analysis. In: 6th International Conference of Soft Computing and Pattern Recognition (SoCPaR), Tunis, Tunisa, pp. 459–464. IEEE (2014)
17. Garijo, D., Corcho, Ó., Gil, Y.: Detecting common scientific workflow fragments using templates and execution provenance. In: Proceedings of the Seventh International Conference on Knowledge Capture, pp. 33–40. ACM, New York (2013)
18. Diamantini, C., Genga, L., Potena, D., Storti, E.: Innovation pattern analysis. In: 2013 International Conference on Collaboration Technologies and Systems (CTS), San Diego, CA, pp. 628–629. IEEE (2013)
19. Garijo, D., Corcho, Ó., Gil, Y., Gutman, B.A., Dinov, I.D., Thompson, P.M., Toga, A.W.: Fragflow automated fragment detection in scientific workflows. In: 10th IEEE International Conference on e-Science, Sao Paulo, Brazil, pp. 281–289. IEEE (2014)
20. Diamantini, C., Genga, L., Potena, D., Storti, E.: Discovering behavioural patterns in knowledge-intensive collaborative processes. In: Appice, A., Ceci, M., Loglisci, C., Manco, G., Masciari, E., Ras, Z.W. (eds.) NFMCP 2014. LNCS, vol. 8983, pp. 149–163. Springer, Cham (2015). doi:10.1007/978-3-319-17876-9_10
21. Kluza, K., Baran, M., Bobek, S., Nalepa, G.J.: Overview of recommendation techniques in business process modeling. In: Proceedings of 9th Workshop on Knowledge Engineering and Software Engineering (KESE9) Co-located with the 36th German Conference on Artificial Intelligence (KI 2013), Koblenz, Germany, 17 September 2013
22. Awad, A., Sakr, S., Kunze, M., Weske, M.: Design by selection: a reuse-based approach for business process modeling. In: Jeusfeld, M., Delcambre, L., Ling, T.-W. (eds.) ER 2011. LNCS, vol. 6998, pp. 332–345. Springer, Heidelberg (2011). doi:10.1007/978-3-642-24606-7_25
23. Jannach, D., Jugovac, M., Lerche, L.: Adaptive recommendation-based modeling support for data analysis workflows, pp. 252–262 (2015)
24. Rosa, M.L., Dumas, M., Uba, R., Dijkman, R.M.: Business process model merging: an approach to business process consolidation. ACM Trans. Softw. Eng. Methodol. **22**(2), 11 (2013)
25. Bobek, S., Nalepa, G.J., Grodzki, O.: Integration of activity modeller with Bayesian network based recommender for business processes. In: Proceedings of 10th Workshop on Knowledge Engineering and Software Engineering (KESE10) Co-located with 21st European Conference on Artificial Intelligence (ECAI 2014), Prague, Czech Republic, 19 August 2014
26. Koschmider, A., Hornung, T., Oberweis, A.: Recommendation-based editor for business process modeling. Data Knowl. Eng. **70**(6), 483–503 (2011)
27. Peters, N., Weidlich, M.: Automatic generation of glossaries for process modelling support. Enterp. Model. Inf. Syst. Archit. **6**(1), 30–46 (2011)
28. Leopold, H., Smirnov, S., Mendling, J.: On the refactoring of activity labels in business process models. Inf. Syst. **37**(5), 443–459 (2012)
29. Princeton University (2010) About WordNet. http://wordnet.princeton.edu/wordnet/

90 K. Belhajjame et al.

30. Baeza-Yates, R.A., Ribeiro-Neto, B.A.: Modern information retrieval - the concepts and technology behind search, 2nd edn. Pearson Education Ltd., Harlow (2011). http://www.mir2ed.org/
31. Cayoglu, U., et al.: Report: the process model matching contest 2013. In: Lohmann, N., Song, M., Wohed, P. (eds.) BPM 2013. LNBIP, vol. 171, pp. 442–463. Springer, Cham (2014). doi:10.1007/978-3-319-06257-0_35
32. The Huntington's Disease Collaborative Research Group: A novel gene containing a trinucleotide repeat that is expanded and unstable on Huntington's disease chromosomes. Cell **72**(6), 971–983 (1993)
33. Mina, E., van Roon-Mom, W., 't Hoen, P.A., Thompson, M., van Schouwen, R., Kaliyaperumal, R., Hettne, K., Schultes, E., Mons, B., Roos, M.: Prioritizing hypotheses for epigenetic mechanisms in Huntington's disease using an e-science approach. J. BioData Min. (2014, submitted)

Scientific Footprints in Digital Libraries

Claudia Ifrim[1], Xenia Koulouri[2], Manolis Wallace[2], Florin Pop[1(✉)], Mariana Mocanu[1], and Valentin Cristea[1]

[1] Faculty of Automatic Control and Computers, Computer Science Department, University Politehnica of Bucharest, 060042 Bucharest, Romania
claudia.ifrim@hpc.pub.ro, florin.pop@cs.pub.ro

[2] Knowledge and Uncertainty Research Laboratory, Department of Informatics and Telecommunications, University of the Peloponnese, 22 131 Tripolis, Greece
gav@uop.gr
http://acs.pub.ro/, http://gav.uop.gr

Abstract. In recent years, members of the academic community have increasingly turned to digital libraries to follow the latest work within their own field and to estimate papers', journals' and researchers' impact. Yet, despite the powerful indexing and searching tools available, identifying the most important works and authors in a field remains a challenging task, for which a wealth of prior information is needed; existing systems fail to identify and incorporate in their results information regarding connections between publications of different disciplines. In this paper we analyze citation lists in order to not only quantify but also understand impact, by tracing the "footprints" that authors have left, i.e. the specific areas in which they have made an impact. We use the publication medium (specific journal or conference) to identify the thematic scope of each paper and feed from existing digital libraries that index scientific activity, namely Google Scholar and DBLP. This allows us to design and develop a system, the Footprint Analyzer, that can be used to successfully identify the most prominent works and authors for each scientific field, regardless of whether their own research is limited to or even focused on the specific field. Various real life examples demonstrate the proposed concepts and actual results from the developed system's operation prove the applicability and validity.

Keywords: Research impact · Citations · Publication medium · Digital library · Google Scholar · DBLP

1 Introduction

Electronic and online publishing has brought about a revolution in science [32]. Access to other people's work is now faster, easier and more universal than ever [33]. But new economic models originating from this trend have helped scientific publishing evolve into a lucrative business, and now a huge volume of scientific texts is added to existing literature daily [10]. As a result, although

© Springer International Publishing AG 2017
N.T. Nguyen et al. (Eds.): TCCI XXVI, LNCS 10190, pp. 91–118, 2017.
DOI: 10.1007/978-3-319-59268-8_5

each individual text is more accessible than before, studying the literature and getting or maintaining a clear view of the state of the art of a specific field remains a challenging task; only the challenge has now shifted from the acquisition of access to the papers to the selection of the right papers to focus on amongst the numerous published articles.

To put this in a more specific context, it is safe to assume that almost every reader going through the pages of this journal has had to at some point in the past, or is currently trying to, identify and study the most important researchers or papers in their field; this could, for example, be the fundamental first step towards a PhD [40]. And although powerful indexing and searching tools exist, such as DBLP [21], Google Scholar [59] or ScienceDirect [60], the way to efficiently search in such a large information space is not a straightforward one.

The difficulty stems from the type of indexing that such systems apply, which is quite different from what is required for the task at hand. Papers are indexed by their titles and journals they are published in; authors are indexed by the papers they have published and the keywords they use to characterize their own research interests. But all of these (titles, journals to submit to, description of interests) are determined by the authors based on a priori preferences and are not necessarily closely related to the a posteriori information regarding the actual areas that their work has an actual impact on. For example, authors may be more inclined to choose a shorter, rather than a lengthier and more accurate title for their work in order to maximize its impact [46], or in order to maximize their perceived activity in a specific field.

An example that is close to heart for some of this paper's authors is that of Human Computer Interaction. There exist of course important conferences and journals that focus on this field, and important researchers who list it as their primary focus. Still, some of the most prominent scientist working on HCI are psychologists (who list psychology as their only expertise) and the field's seminal papers have not been published in HCI related journals. Thus, current indexing and searching systems would fail to support a user in the identification of the key papers and researchers of the field.

To overcome this, we propose herein an alternative indexing approach that focuses on papers' and researchers' impact, not as defined by themselves but rather as assessed by their "footprints" in digital libraries, i.e. the specific areas of impact as indicated from citations. Our analysis is based on the detailed examination of citation records and combines information from multiple sources; DBLP and Google Scholar are the sources considered in this work, but extension to include more sources is straight forward.

More specifically, in order to overcome the subjective nature of a paper's metadata, such as the title and keywords that are selected by the authors themselves, we base our analysis on the publication medium (specific journal or conference) which provides a more objective estimation of the broader thematic scope [71]. Then, by examining which works cite each paper we can estimate the specific areas in which it has had an impact. This allows us to develop paper and author impact indices, that can be thematically searched, thus supporting queries that existing systems are no able to handle.

The main contributions of this paper are: the definition of a researcher's scientific footprint, a methodology to detect footprints in an objective and automated manner based on the analysis of citations, an extensible architecture that employs the notion of the footprint and is able to consider multiple information sources and the Footprint Analyzer, a preliminary implementation of the above. This paper is based on, and constitutes a combination and major extension of, paper "Agile DBLP: A Search-based Mobile Application for Structured Digital Libraries" presented at the 1st International KEYSTONE Conference (IKC 2015) [35] and paper "Extracting and visualizing research impact semantics" presented at the 9th International Workshop on Semantic and Social Media Adaptation and Personalization [71].

The remainder of this paper is organized as follows. In Sect. 2 we discuss existing approaches to the assessment and quantification of scientific impact and in Sect. 3 we review digital scientific libraries. In Sect. 4 we examine the types of contextual information related with citations, a notion upon which we base our definition of "footprints" in Sect. 5. In Sect. 6 we extend the notion into an algorithm, listing the steps required to generate semantic footprint indices, and in Sects. 7 and 8 we present the integrated system incorporating these notions and discuss some preliminary yet indicative results. Finally, in Sect. 9 we list our concluding remarks.

2   Scientific Impact

Scientific value and scientific recognition are subjective in their very nature, and often even random. There is no objective way by which to measure the degree of novelty or importance of a scientific proposition, and even the way it is perceived by the scientific community is not always to be trusted. A characteristic example is that of Dr. Zadeh's seminal paper on fuzzy sets [34], which was rejected and refused publication by three different journals, but has now defined not just a new subfield in applied mathematics but more importantly a whole new paradigm in scientific computing and computer engineering.

Still, a need exists to quantify the importance of scientific work; for example when wishing to comparatively assess candidates for academic positions. In order to overcome the highly subjective and unreliable nature of the related a priori information, the value of scientific work is evaluated based on the a posteriori information regarding its impact. For example, modern day Nobel prizes are decided primarily based on the actual impact candidate works have had on society and science, and the time period for the full impact of the work may be several decades; Chandrasekhar famously shared the 1983 Nobel prize in physics for work done in 1939 [15].

Although randomness and unfairness can still be claimed (potentially revolutionary works may go un-noticed and less deserving works may receive attention due to random shifts of the market's direction or simply because of an inspired title), at least objective (numerical) measures may can be defined. Despite known inherent weaknesses [27], citation counts are seen as the most trusted indications of scientific impact. An important driving factor for this is that they are quantitative and are easily and readily available in online systems such as Google Scholar.

2.1 Paper Impact

Thus, a paper's impact is quantified as the count of citations it has received from the day it was published and up to the day of examination. This, of course, favors papers that were published many years ago, as they have been accumulating citations for a longer period of time. This is not seen as a weakness of the measure; it is only natural that works that have been around for a long time have had the opportunity to have a greater impact on the works of others.

Besides, it has been observed that the yearly count of citations received by a paper diminishes after a few years; so, after some time, the advantage of earlier papers is diminished.

2.2 Journal Impact

Similar ideas are applied towards the evaluation of the scientific value of a publication medium, such as a journal, magazine or conference. There is, though, an important difference originating in the way to use the results of this evaluation.

Journals are not evaluated in order to assess which one has had the greatest overall impact on the scientific world. To the contrary, the goal is to assess the probability that an article published in a journal will make an impact in the future; readers consider this evaluation to select the journals to read and more importantly authors consider it in order to select the journals to submit to, thus maximizing the potential of their work. Therefore, the number of years that a journal has been publishing, or even the number of volumes per year or the number of articles per volume cannot be allowed to affect the evaluation.

The impact factor (IF) is the most trusted quantification of a journal's scientific potential. It is computed as the average count of citations articles published in the journal receive in the first two years after their publication; some limitations apply regarding the sources of these citations. It is clear to see that the IF is configured in a way that favors journals that publish carefully selected high quality articles, which is in accordance with the goals of journal evaluation.

2.3 Author Impact

Researchers' impact (and sometimes future potential too) is also assessed based on citations. The first, most common and straightforward approach is the consideration of the cumulative number of citations for the complete list of their published work.

But given the highly competitive nature of the scientific community, it is rather expected that the prime tool to assess and compare researchers has received a lot of attention, both in the form of criticism of its objectivity and in the form of attempts to affect its outcomes. Numerous weaknesses have been identified, related to the number of years of activity, the effect of cooperation networks, self-citations, outlier works, frequency of publication etc.

In order to deal with the aforementioned weaknesses of using citation count as a metric, numerous more elaborate metrics have been designed, such as the following.

Average Number of Citations per Paper. Using the average number of citations aims to compensate for the fact that some authors publish more papers and this leads them to have higher total number of citations, where in fact each of their individual works may be cited rarely. It also compensates for differences in the duration of the career, i.e. in the number of years researchers have been publishing.

Average Number of Citations per Author. Single author papers and cooperative works do not indicate the same level of personal involvement in the work. Thus, it makes sense to distribute the count of citations for each paper equally to the contributing authors. This is not the only approach in this direction; sometimes a greater part of the contribution is assigned to the leading author, or the amount of contribution is gradually reduced based on the author's position in the author list.

Average Number of Citations per Year. Researchers that have had a longer publishing career, have inevitably produced more work. This does not necessarily indicate that their research is more important than that of younger researchers. A workaround is to average citations over the count of years, which allows for a more fair comparison of veteran and new researchers.

h-Index and Similar Indices. Hirsch's h-index is the most well known and widely used metric after the citation count. An index of h indicates that h distinct papers of a given researcher have at least h citations each. Variations of the h-index emphasize different features, such as the number of authors in each paper [22] or the average value of the h-index over the years [69]. In [11] we see a partitioning of the h-index into $h1$, $h2$ and $h3$, which help discriminate between different types of researchers such as the perfectionists and the mass producers.

The g-index and the e-index are extensions of the h-index. In the g-index the citation count is averaged [25] and in the e-index the square root of citations in the h-set beyond h^2, is considered, i.e. square root of citations beyond the minimum number of citations required to achieve an h-index of h. The e-index is particularly useful when comparing researchers who have the same h-index [66].

s-Index. The s-index is based on the notion of entropy and provides a better basis for comparisons between researchers than h-index in the case of researchers who many citations [41].

i-**10 Index.** Google Scholar's *i*-10 is the count of articles that have ten or more citations [29].

3   Digital Libraries

There are various digital libraries of scientific content, that interested readers may turn to in order to search for and gain access to a specific paper; IEEEX-plore, ScienceDirect, SpringerOnline to mention just a few. But these are not the focus on this work. In this work we focus on digital libraries that can be used to assess scientific importance or equivalently, as explained in the previous section, scientific impact. Therefore, libraries such as the above (that only index content of partner publishers) are not a suitable source of information.

Others exist, on the other hand, that aim to generate an author's complete list of published works, regardless of where they have been published. The following are stand out examples of this category; DBLP due its highly accurate and well curated content regarding lists of published works by each author and Google Scholar due to the extensive and all inclusive citation lists it provides. We review then both below, as they form the basis for the system presented herein.

3.1   Google Scholar

Google Scholar is a web service engine provided by Google which indexes the full text of scholarly literature across various disciplines and publishing formats. Since its release in November 2004, Google Scholar has become one of the most popular academic search engines.

Although most academic databases and search engines allow the ranking of the results by certain factors, the Google Scholar ranking algorithm is still unknown to this date. According to various studies that have tried to reverse-engineering the algorithm, Google Scholar arranges results by putting weight especially on citation counts [9] and the occurrence of search terms in the article's title [8].

Since it was first introduced in November 2004, there has been abundant literature regarding the weak and strong points of Google Scholar. So far, the studies have varied in their approaches, differing from the analysis of the user interface functionality to the content covered by the search engine. In 2010, Xiaotian Chen did an empirical study of Google Scholar's coverage of scholarly journals five years after a similar study was performed. His findings showed a dramatic improvement: using the same database, Google Scholar's coverage has gone from an average of 60 to a range from 98 to 100% [16] (Fig. 1).

On the other hand, another interesting study conducted in the same year [7] showed that Google Scholar is far easier to spam than the Google Search for Web Pages. For example, it was demonstrated that Google Scholar counts references that were added to modified versions of already published articles, meaning that researchers could increase citation counts and rankings of the cited articles in order to increase their visibility on Google Scholar. Moreover, several studies have pointed out that the Google Scholar enforces the Matthew effect (sociology:"the rich get richer and the poor get poorer") by placing the high cited papers on top of the search results [9].

Google Scholar has a familiar search interface, similar to the classic Google Search. The search results are based on the terms/keywords typed in the search box. Within a Google Scholar search results, the following features are available:

- Abstract
- Cited by: Returns the list of articles that have cited the current article.
- Related articles: Returns a list of articles similar to the current article, ranked primarily by similarity but also by taking into account the relevance of each paper.
- All versions: Returns the list of all alternative sources for the current paper.
- Import citations: BibTex, EndNote, RefMan, RefWorks

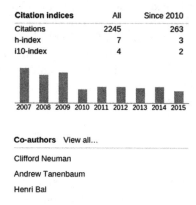

Fig. 1. Citation indices and co-authors.

Also, the following bibliometrics are available on each author profile:

- Co-authors
- Citations
- h-index
- i-10 index: The number of publications that have received at least 10 citations.

Metadata. Metadata cannot be easily obtained through Google Scholar: scraping is not allowed and the data is not exposed through an API.

Information Retrieval. P. Jacso, in his paper "Metadata mega mess in Google Scholar" [38], discusses some of the problems that exist with Google Scholar, particularly the incorrect field detection mechanism. The author found that Google

Scholar is especially "bad for metadata based searching when, beyond keywords in the title, abstract, descriptor and/or full text, the user also has to use the author's name, journal title and/or publication year in specifying the query".

Although many may argue that the "mess" can actually come from publishers and vendors, the author also pointed out that the Google Scholar developers decided not to use the metadata readily available from most of the scholarly publishers [48].

3.2 DBLP

DBLP is a digital library for computer science bibliography supported by University Trier from Germany. This project started in 1993 as a experimental server meant to test web technology, but evolved continuously, based on ad hoc solutions. The project policy is to keep the application as stable as possible. For example, URLs are only changed if they prevent an important functionality, and not because the people simply perceive them as unaesthetic.

In June 2015, DBLP indexes more the 3 million publications from major information sources: VLDB[1], IEEE transactions[2] and ACM transactions[3].

In comparison with Google Scholar or CiteSeer[4], that crawl the web to extract metadata from publications in order to operate their journal collections, the DBLP collections are maintained with great human effort by having the data inserted manually. One of the consequences of this is that authors are disambiguated more accurately.

The complete DBLP dataset is available at http://dblp.uni-trier.de/xml/dblp.xml. This project has evolved from an experimental Web Server to a popular digital library service for the computer science community, but it's documentation is limited.

In the paper "DBLP - Some Lessons Learned", Michael Ley described the evolution of DBLP from the data modeling point of view. Apart from being available online, the DBLP database can be also downloaded as a large XML file (http://dblp.uni-trier.de/xml/dblp.xml.gz) and a schema is available as a DTD file, making it easy for researchers to integrate the data in their work (over 400 publications mention the use of DBLP for a variety of purposes [47]) (Fig. 2).

Above, you have a graphical representation of sample-information extracted from [19] in March 2012. It allows access to relatively static and limited information, showing only the publications (nodes with green color - 10 co-authored or more), and authors (orange nodes - 200 publications or more), and their interconnectivity. This interconnections show only static information, because it is only one moment in time; it is also a limited information, because it doesn't show the entire population of the database, but only the higher values. Furthermore, it doesn't have a statistical value, as it is a sample which not relevantly chosen from the entire population (Fig. 3).

---

[1] http://www.vldb.org/.

[2] http://www.ieee.org/publications_standards/publications/services/journals.html.

[3] http://dl.acm.org/pubs.cfm.

[4] http://citeseerx.ist.psu.edu/.

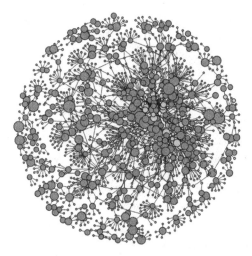

Fig. 2. DBLP graph.

Metadata. The complet DBLP dataset is exposed in JSON and XML formats.

DBLP contains the following types of entries: article, book, in proceedings, in collection, master's/ph.d thesis, proceedings, www and provides medata like: title, author, pages, volume, journal, publisher, year. Metadata for publications are available in BibTex format and articles are identified by URIs like this: http://dblp.unitrier.de/rec/bibtex/journals/computer/TanenbaumHB06 Access to the bibliographic metadata is available to everyone as of 2011 (relased under ODC-By).

```
▼<dblp>
  ▼<article key="journals/computer/TanenbaumHB06" mdate="2006-11-10">
      <author>Andrew S. Tanenbaum</author>
      <author>Jorrit N. Herder</author>
      <author>Herbert Bos</author>
      <title>Can We Make Operating Systems Reliable and Secure?</title>
      <pages>44-51</pages>
      <year>2006</year>
      <volume>39</volume>
      <journal>IEEE Computer</journal>
      <number>5</number>
    ▼<ee>
        http://doi.ieeecomputersociety.org/10.1109/MC.2006.156
      </ee>
      <url>db/journals/computer/computer39.html#TanenbaumHB06</url>
    </article>
  </dblp>
```

Fig. 3. Example of DBLP XML record.

Although the data retrieved from the DBLP database is well-formatted and the author names are disambiguated, it lacks citation references, having no indicators in assessing the relevance of the papers. Also, DBLP is limited to computer science and, as pointed out by another study in [58], it does not cover all sub-fields of computer science to the same degree.

Information Retrieval. CompleteSearch DBLP is a tool that provides extended search capabilities for DBLP. The following features are available: phrase search, prefix search, exact word match, only first-authored papers, specify number of authors etc.

4   Citation Context

In Sect. 2 we saw how metrics based on citations are used to evaluate and quantify scientific impact. But these metrics do not make any distinction between citations, thus failing to consider contextual information. In this section we take a closer look at two different aspects of context in citations and discuss how they can be used in order to define new, more information rich citation metrics.

4.1   Role of Referenced Work

In each paper there are various citations, but they do not all have the same role. Whilst some citations may provide the theoretical and technical foundation of the presented work, indicating a true connection between the papers, others are used to compare results or just in the discussion of previous related, or broadly related, work. To further emphasize this, in the current paper we have split the references in two sections. The first part lists works that relevant to the work presented, whilst the second part lists works that are mentioned in the discussion but whose content is never discussed. In a conventional citation count both parts of our references would be counted as equally important, which is clearly unfair to the authors of the papers listed in the first part.

To deal with this, we should be able to first determine and then consider the role that each entry in the references has in a paper. We meet a similar concept in CiteSeer^X, the "citation context", but that is only presented as additional information; it does not affect the calculation of the number of citations [17].

This would be a tenuous task that cannot be performed automatically considering the current state of the art in text analysis and understanding. It requires the work of human experts in the area of the considered papers who will study the papers and evaluate what the exact role of each reference is. This is not only expensive, it also introduces subjectivity, as it is up to the expert to decide the degree to which a citation reflects actual contribution. Therefore, this type of context cannot be practically considered, at least with the current state of the art.

An alternative consideration of context could focus on the part of the text where the citation is referenced. Citations, for example, in the introduction and the section on related work typically have had little or no impact on the considered work, citations in the results are typically used as benchmarks whilst citations in the description of the proposed methodology have most probably been used as a methodological basis and are the ones with the highest true impact. This is also not possible to apply in an automated manner, and in some cases not even in a manual manner, as on the one hand not all sections in a paper can be clearly identified as related work, methodology or results, and, on the other hand, sometimes some references are not at all listed in the text which makes it impossible to determine their citation context.

The unfortunate conclusion is that, although this type of contextual information could provide very rich information regarding the nature and value of citations, it is quite improbable that is will be used in citation analysis, for the reasons explained above.

4.2   Scientific Scope

In the previous subsection we discussed how we could evaluate the importance of a cited work in a paper. In this section we examine not the importance but the topic of the citation.

Many papers are monothematic. But theare are also those works that are interdisciplinary and/or rely on ideas from different scientific fields. When examining a paper's references we can understand if it interdisciplinary by examining the topic of each cited work, but it is debadable whether that would give some important insight regarding the importance of the paper. But the reverse is a lot more interesting: by examining the topics of the papers that reference a work we can see which scientific areas have been affected by that work.

Of course there is a practical question here: how could one determine in an automated and reliable manner the scientific scope of any given paper. The listed Keywords could be useful when existing, but they are not always standardized - some authors write in their owns without choosing from a predetermined list - and in many publications keywords are not used at all. Paper titles could also be used, but they are often misleading. Abstract texts are less misleading, but the current state of the art in text analysis and understanding is not mature enough to provide reliable results when applied to short texts without any additional contextual information.

The publication medium (the journal, conference, edited book etc. in which a paper is included) can provide reliable evidence regarding the scientific scope of the work. When a submission is considered for publication, either by a journal or by a conference, one of the first and most important checks is whether it falls within the thematic scope; scientific quality is examined secondly. Therefore, the editorial process guarantees that, for example, papers published in LNCS Transactions on Computational Collective Intelligence are related to CCI and papers included in this special issue are additionally related to keyword searching in Big Data.

Almost all conferences, journals etc., in short publications that follow and editorial process, have clearly defined scopes and often also provide potential authors with lists of relevant topics. And for those that do not have such information readily available it is quite easy to produce them manually. Especially since this would be done only one time for each publication medium. Therefore, this can provide the basis for an automated and objective (i.e. without a human experts examining the article and providing a subjective evaluation) consideration of the scientific scope of a published paper.

Moreover, this is also interesting in the scope of citation analysis, as it provides richer insight into the impact that a paper has had.

5   Scientific Footprints

In this work we look more closely at citation records, examining scientific scope, in order to acquire deeper insight on researchers' impact. In order to better explain what type of insight we are looking at, we start by listing below details from the citation records of two higly cited authors, namely Dr. Cynthia Whissel and Dr. Theodore Simos.

5.1   Two Indicative Examples

Cynthia Whissell. Cynthia Whissell is a professor in the Psychology Department at Laurentian University and she is a psychologist. In her own description of her research interests she lists language and the way language conveys emotion [50]. Therefore, based on studies, professional affiliation and title, as well as on her own description of herself, professor Whissell works in psychology and lingustics. It would only be natural for one to expect the impact of the work of professor Whissell to be in those fields as well.

Looking at her citation list we quickly identify paper *The dictionary of affect in language* [51] as her seminal work, as it has received by far the most citations and considerably more than her next most cited work. Looking at the title, the abstract or even the content of the paper we can determine that this specific work is also in the field of psychology and linguistics. As far as the publication medium is concerned, it is included in a book titled *Emotion: Theory, Research, and Experience*, again clearly in the field of psychology. If we examine more of her works we will reach similar conclusions; overall there is nothing to imply that the work and expertise of professor Whissell might be of interest to scientific fields other than psychology and linguistics.

But when we examine her citation list, there are some interesting surprises. For example, there is this paper:

S. Soroka, M.A. Bodet, L. Young, B. Andrew, *Campaign news and vote intentions*, Journal of Elections, Public Opinion and Parties, no. 19(4), pp. 359–376, 2009.

The title of the paper and the name of the journal point towards politics. When reading the paper we find that the content of the paper is also focused on politics. Linguistics and psychology are briefly considered in the analysis, but they are the tools, not the core subject of the work. If we study this paper more carefully we find that the role of Whissell's paper is fundamental in the design and application of the work. In other words, Soroka et al's paper shows that professor Whissell has made through her work an impact not only in psychology and linguistics but also in political analysis.

This paper is neither an outlier nor an exception. In the citations of the aforementioned paper of professor Whissell we find evidence that it has made an impact in psychology [4,5,49], biology [57], affective computing [24,63–65], artificial intelligence [28,36,44,56,62,72,73,75], multimedia and image processing [37,55,67], speech and liguistics [18,20,31,68], management [1,12,23,26,42, 70], music [6,14], gender [45], politics [52,53,74], bilingualism [2,3] and more.

Theodore Simos. Theodore Simos is a professor in the Department of Informatics and Telecommunications of the University of Peloponnese. He studies include a bachelor degree in engineering and a PhD in mathematics. His teaching and research is in mathematics and on his homepage he describes himself as a researcher of mathematics [61].

At [61] we can find a list of citations for professor Simos. Almost all of the papers listed in it are published in journals and conferences in the fields of mathematics, computational chemistry and computational physics, in other words solely in theoretical and applied mathematics.

5.2 Following the Footprints

What the above examples indicate is that there are different types of scientific impact. Professor Simos's work has a very deep impact in mathematics (he has more than 2000 citations in the field) but little or no impact outside that field. Professor Whissell's work on the other hand has a very broad impact in science which is not limited to psychology and linguistics. The question is, what consequences could this observation have on the design and development of digital libraries and the indexing/searching mechanisms that support them.

The answer lies with Dr. Whissell's example. We have already seen that her work is relevant to fields outside psychology. What we have not seen, because it could not be seen in the independent analysis of her citation records, is that her work is actually important in other fields. For example, researchers from the field of affective computing will be quick to identify Dr. Whissell as not only relevant but also central in the literature related to facial expression recognition.

Dr. Whissell's great impact in the field of affective computing has left its trace, or "footprint", in digital libraries. Specifically, if we were to analyze all citations found in papers of the field of affective computing, we would find a disproportionably high number of references to the work of Dr. Whissell.

The work presented herein is based on this very notion of footprint in digital libraries. Specifically, by examining citation records we aim to detect and index the footprints of all works and authors. Thus, our system will be able to handle queries not only of the form "Who are the most cited researchers *of* HCI" which limit results to those working in the field but also of the form "Who are the most cited researchers *in* HCI". This will allow for the automatic detection of the most important people (or articles) for a field and will also facilitate people, such as first year PhD students, who wish to get acquainted with a new field by reading the most important works in it.

6   Semantic Citation Analysis

In order for the aforementioned notions to be put into application, footprint indices are required, linking each article and each author to their respective areas of impact.

As we have already explained, most metadata linked to an article are inherently subjective and unreliable, as they are defined by the authors and most commonly are not independently reviewed and verified; the most reliable source of semantic information regarding the articles is the publication medium itself, as the editorial process involves a rigorous control of the thematic scope. For this reason our analysis is based on the examination of the publication medium.

Of course, this is not a trivial task. The way to describe the thematic scope of journals, magazines and conferences is not standardized, in many cases there is only a textual description without keywords, there may be huge differences in the breadth of the thematic scope, etc. Even the compilation of a comprehensive and universally accepted list of scientific scopes is hard to achieve. Overall, our approach for the population of the footprint indices includes a preparatory step and processing steps for articles and authors, which are further analyzed in the following sections.

6.1   Preparatory Steps

The preparatory steps involve the establishment of the knowledge base that is required for the execution of the processing steps, as follows:

1. Develop a list of thematic areas
2. Compile a list of publication media (journals, magazines, conferences)
3. Assign thematic areas to each publication medium

Thematic Areas. The list of scientific fields does not change; or at least it does not change often and drastically. Therefore a reasonable first step is to develop this hierarchy. Existing hierarchies exist that may be considered as a basis, as for example the one found in [30] or [13].

Wikipedia classifies sciences in 4 main fields. Natural sciences (sciences that study the laws that condition the nature), formal sciences (sciences that have a specific methodology, instead of what actually happens in reality), social sciences (which study the human and the society behavior), and applied sciences (which implement scientific knowledge for practical purposes) [76] (Fig. 4).

Another hierarchy of sciences which we can find at Physics Portal at South Carolina State University categorizes them in three main classes: formal, natural and humanistic science. The 3 classes can be divided to 6 more subclasses: mathematics, logic, physical, biological, behavioral and social [54].

We are going to choose as our basis the classification we found in paper has been visually "mapped" according to various branches of sciences [43]. According this paper sciences are divided in more main classes which is comfier and more useful in our paper, in order to categorize the list of means of publication, according to this hierarchy. The hierarchy that we are going to use contains 16 main divisions each of one's has its own smaller classes (subdivisions). The 16 main classes are: mathematics, physics, chemistry, physical chemistry, biochemistry, computer sciences, engineering, earth science (geoscience), infectious disease, medical specialties, brain research, health services, psychology, social sciences and humanities.

We can observe that these 16 fields are dependant. There are areas where they can be overlapped in the map of sciences or there can be sciences that they are linked by different ways. Fields that can be enlisted in more than one classes are name interdisciplinary fields. In the map of sciences, the edges between the scientific fields demonstrate the links of sciences.

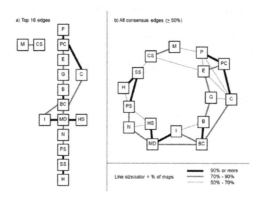

Fig. 4. Links of scientific fields.

Publication Media. We have used DBLP metadata in order to acquire a first list of previous and running journals and conferences, knowing that although this list is long it is far from complete. A comprehensive list of publication media is not easy to establish. Moreover, the list is not static as some conferences disappear whilst new ones appear every year; there are similar changes to the list of journals, but they are less frequent and thus easier to tackle.

Therefore the pre-processing step regarding the acquisition of publication media is not meant to produce a complete and finalized list. As we will explain in the following, the list of media can be updated during the processing steps; the role of this pre-processing step is to facilitate the initiation processing steps by dealing with the problem of cold start.

Medium to Area Assignments. Although the DBLP metadata are carefully curated, they do not contain semantic information regarding the thematic scope of the included publication media, other than their title. This title is often, but not always, enough to have a rough idea of the thematic coverage.

In order to overcome this, we follow a semi-automatic approach to the identification of the links between publication media and the thematic areas: we start by applying and automated string matching approach to identify probably links (differences between UK and US spellings, synonyms etc. limit the success of this step) and continue with a manual step during which the journal's of conference's site is examined and the description of the scope is used to determine which thematic areas are most and truly associated with it.

The initial step is to collect all the publication media that are shown up in the record of the list or references. Afterwards, we checked each of their names and we studied the subjects which they were dealing and that they are published each year. In that way, we choose which sciences and which scientific field each publication deals with. So we took into consideration the hierarchy of sciences that we created and we exhibited in Sect. 6, in order to match the correspondences of sciences that we found in our previous step, in our hierarchy.

6.2 Processing Steps, for Each Work

For each considered article, we examine the list of citations as follows:

1. Acquire the list of citations
2. Identify the thematic area of each citing work
3. Aggregate findings and populate the article footprint index

List of Citations. We use Google Scholar to acquire comprehensive lists of citation for the articles that we examine. Of course, since the database is not curated, there are numerous errors (false positives, incorrectly assigned fields, damaged titles, repetitions etc.).

In a parallel work (which is not yet completed and is expected to be sent for publication in 2016) we are examining the validity of Google Scholar by comparing its automated results with manually established lists of citations. Our early findings indicate that, although error rates are high (often exceeding 20%), the deviation is small. Thus citations retrieved by Google Scholar are a relatively reliable source given that the error rate is similar for different articles and authors (Fig. 5).

The acquisition of the list is non-trivial, as the system does not provide an open version of the data or a freely accessible API. Quite the contrary, there are provisions to block repeated access in order to prohibit robotic crawling. Our approach includes an automated tool that queries the website and processes the HTML results in order to extract citation data (Fig. 6).

Different fields are identified, allowing for the establishment of a structured XML document as seen in Fig. 7. The acquired list is them trimmed, to remove self citations and repetitions, to the extend that they can be identified in an automated manner.

Limitations set by Google results in an upper threshold to the frequency of access and therefore to the speed of crawling. What is permitted is enough for the system presented herein to work as a proof of concept, but a more open access to the data will be required for a full scale application.

Fig. 5. Google Scholar.

Fig. 6. HTML source.

Thematic Area of Each Citation. In earlier sections we have explained that we will use the publication medium to identify the thematic scope, we have developed the lists of publication media and scopes and established the associations between publication media and thematic areas. In the previous paragraph we also saw how the publication medium is acquired as a separate field in an XML document.

Unfortunately, this does not imply that this is a simple task. The publication medium included in the XML document comes from the uncurated Google Scholar system, whilst the entries in the publication media to thematic scope association table come from the DBLP sytem. The titles between the two do not match an a manual matching step is required. This is a highly time consuming step for the first runs, but as more links (between Scholar titles and DBLP titles) are established the need for manual intervention diminishes.

In the end, each citing article is associated to a publication medium, and by extension to its thematic areas.

Aggregated Impact for Each Work. Conventionally all citations associated with a published work are considered equally and uniformly, and overall impact is given as the count of citations. Given the additional thematic information that now becomes available, a rising question is the validity of considering uniformly

```
- <paper>
    <title>Context-aware recommender systems</title>
    <author>G Adomavicius</author>
    <author>A Tuzhilin</author>
    <author> </author>
    <journal> - Recommender systems handbook, 2011 - Springer</journal>
  </paper>
```

Fig. 7. XML document.

references that have been published in a publication medium with an impact on a single science and references whose publication medium influences more than a single science. Our approach is a variable weighting factor for the two cases. In case that the papers influence a single scientific field weight will be equal to 1, whereas the weight will be distributed uniformly when multiple fields are impacted.

The reasoning behind this is not so much that impact is distributed between the different fields, but rather that it is not possible to safely detect the field of impact without firsts performing a deeper semantic analysis, for example by reading the full text of the paper. Thus the reduced weight denotes the reduced confidence regarding the association between the considered citation and the actual field of impact. Distributing the weight differently allows for the overall counts to be unaffected; this is fair, as otherwise works published in interdisciplinary journals and conferences would have a greater (or smaller) weight in the assessment of impact and there is no evidence to support this.

The aggregated impact for each work is given as the sum of weights, for each scientific field; as expected the impact is not calculated as a single number but rather as an array of numbers, one per field.

6.3   Processing Steps, for Each Author

For each considered article, we examine the list of public works as follows:

1. Acquire the list of published works
2. Identify the impact of each work
3. Aggregate results and populate the author footprint index

List of Published Works. The list of published works is extracted from DBLP, using the provided APIs. We do this knowingly that DBLP is limited to computer science, and thus this first implementation of our approach will serve as a proof of concept. A latter implementation will extend to other fields.

Impact for Each Work. For each work attributed to the author by DBLP, the impact is readily available in the article footprint index, through the process of Sect. 6.2. In most cases there are no differences between article titles as they are reported in DBLP and Google Scholar, so querying the index is straightforward.

Aggregated Impact for Each Author of Results. In the conventional approach, an author's citation count is calculated as the sum of citations for all of the author's published works. By extension, in our work we calculate an author's impact in each field as the sum of the impact values for that field for all of the author's works. Thus, the aggregated impact for the author is a vector calculated as the sum of the impact vectors of all of the author's published works, as calculated above.

7   Integrated System

In order to automate the steps described in Sect. 6 and to have a consistent and accurate dataset to analyze we developed a prototype, named Footprint Analyzer, that aggregates information from DBLP and Google Scholar. Other digital libraries could (and will in the future) also be considered as sources, but the integration with more sources is outside the scope of this paper and this feature is not included in the current version of the Footprint Analyzer.

Footprint Analyzer is a web application implemented in NodeJS. For a given author name, we extract all the important elements that define a person's scientific interests that we can collect from Google Scholar and DBLP: frequent keywords, conferences attended, collaborative colleagues (co-authors), top 5 most important co-authors and published work.

For citation tracking we use data from Google Scholar. Google's algorithms allow it to retrieve a large number of citations results, which we then clean as they often include duplicates and citations that simply aren't real.

Footprint Analyzer exposes an interface that allows the user to enter an author's name or the title of an article. To control the results, a user can also specify years of publishing activity or restrict to one thematic area.

We populate our database with the list of conferences and their assigned articles, using the list that we retrieve from DBLP.

For each conference we have assigned thematic areas form our nomenclator defined in Sect. 6.

Results are loaded as soon as a user runs a query. They can be sorted by clicking on each label heading of the table of results (footprint index, author, title, year of publication, publication media). The user can uncheck any entry in the results that is irrelevant, a case in which the footprint index is automatically updated.

In order to calculate the footprint index of each author we followed the steps described in Sect. 6.

The main focus of our work isthe analysis of an author's impact, but is also possible to use Footprint Analyzer to analyze the impact of a specific article.

The power of any data-mining project lies in the amount of data that can be processed to provide meaningful and statistically relevant information. Merging information form two digital libraries is necessary in order to obtain an accurate scientific footprint of each publication or author; the consideration of more sources in the future can further enhance the accuracy and reliability of the results.

Once extracted, the metadata is stored in a MySQL database. In the current status of the Footprint Analyzer the data inserted in the database is based on XML responses from DBLP and BibTex format for Google Scholar.

7.1   Architecture

The main tasks performed by the implemented Footprint Analyzer prototype are the following:

1. Acquire published author's records
2. Analyze author's domains of interest based on keywords from their publications
3. Establish links between publication media and our nomenclator of thematic areas
4. Analyze citations of each article
5. Remove self-citations and repetitions
6. Retrieve the distributed knowledge from different digital libraries by using exposed APIs and lightweight web-crawling methods
7. Calculate footprint index of an author or journal

For digital libraries that don't expose an API, the following principles of web-crawling are employed by the system:

1. Starts with a set of seeds (i.e., author names, titles) which represent the list of URLs to visit (used in constructing URL requests)
2. Crawler starts fetching pages
2. Result pages are parsed to find link tags that might contain other useful URLs to fetch (e.g., publications, profile pages, etc.)
4. New URLs are constructed (child URLs from the initial parent URLs)
5. Continue until all necessary info has been retrieved

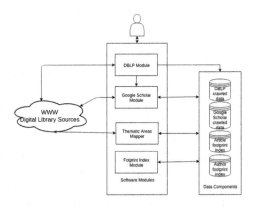

Fig. 8. Footprint analyzer prototype architecture.

Figure 8 describes the main components of the Footprint Analyzer and the way they interact.

DBLP Module - sends the query to DBLP based on parameters received from the user (e.g. author name, years, etc.), parses the response received from DBLP, saves the information in the MySQL database and sends to **Google Scholar Module** the list of published works for citation tracking.

Google Scholar Module - retrieves and saves in our database information regarding citations of articles returned by **DBLP Module**.

Thematic Areas Mapper - retrieves the list of conferences and published articles and assigns them to thematic areas.

Footprint Index Module - calculates the footprint index for an author or an article as described in Sect. 6 based on results from our database.

7.2   Problems Encountered

As part of our project to automatically retrieve and analyse scholarly literature, Google Scholar and DBLP were considered as data sources.

Google Scholar. "Google Scholar is a freely available service with a familiar interface similar to Google Web Search" [58]. Google indexes articles from most major academic repositories and publishers. The results retrieved from a Google Scholar search are an important aspect of the research tool we are considering.

Many scholarly publishers, databases, and products offer APIs (application programming interface) to allow users with programming skills to more power-fully extract data to use for a variety of purposes. Some APIs allow programmatic bibliographic searching of a citation database, others allow extraction of statistical data, while others allow dynamic querying and posting of blog content.

Although being probably one of the most useful tools on the web today for academics, Google Scholar does not provide any API or other automated data extraction means. There is a lot of complaining on the web about Google's failure to provide an API for web search, which leaves people writing custom scrapers in Python, Perl, R, etc. As first part of our work, we scrap Google Scholar pages for the extraction and processing of information about author's articles, citations, years of publishing, etc.

Technical Details and Limitations.

First of all, Google's Terms of Service do not allow "the sending of automated queries of any sort without express permission in advance from Google" [48]. In agreement with Google Scholar terms of service which prohibits the automatic querying, only the displayed result page can pe processed.

In February 2013 Google Scholar reduced the maximum number of results per page from 100 to 20 results and if an excessive number of queries is detected, Google Scholar will refuse to accept further queries from the requester's IP address.

Since there are no APIs for Google Scholar, we have to parse directly the HTML of Google Scholar's response page about the requested author/requested article. Starting from the data retrieved we will make some computations and statistic analysis.

We started by trying to retrieve information from Google Scholar using a custom parser. The plan is to make a query to Google Scholar using a cookie and to be able to retrieve the HTML file with the results.

Generating a cookie is mandatory if we want access to the BibTeX files provided in the search results - the BibTeX entries are not displayed by default and are only showed if they are manually enabled in the Google Scholar search settings. We will need to parse the BibTex entries as well in order to retrieve the list of author names of a certain publication.

After analyzing the structure of the webpage, we consider the following:

- Number of results retrieved - gs_ab_md CSS class
- Titles - gs_rt CSS class
- Number of citations - gs_fl CSS class
- BibTeX entry

All this information has been extracted by means of mechanisms for regular expressions.

DBLP. A record from DBLP data set can be:

- article
- book
- incollection
- inproceedings
- proceedings
- mastersthesis, phdthesis, www

For each record we have one or more of the following metadata fields: title, booktitle, author, editor, pages, year, publisher, address, journal, volume, number, month, cdrom, url, ee, cite, note, crossref, series, isbn, school, chapter.

We can identify the following links:

- a publication is linked to the authors and editors
- a paper is linked to the journal, proceedings or book in which it was published
- citation links are created for each non-empty "cite" element in a publication's record.

On http://dblp.uni-trier.de/, DBLP provides a primitive form to search for persons inside the bibliography. The Footprint Analyzer accesses DBLP data records by retrieving author information, parsing it and then requesting additional data records based on the processed data.

7.3   Software Licensing

As part of our future work, once the Footprint Analyzer has reached the desired level of maturity and stability, we plan to release the full integrated code under a GPLv3 license. Early versions of parts of the code (the module extracting citation information from Google Scholar and the module processing citation lists to extract footprint information) are already released under a GPLv3 license at GitHub [39].

8   Experimental Results

As an experimental result we will analyze the author **Cynthia Whissell**, author mentioned also in the example described in Sect. 5.

When we query DBLP on author **Cynthia Whissell** published work we receive two records:

– The Times and the Man as Predictors of Emotion and Style in the Inaugural Addresses of U.S. Presidents. Computers and the Humanities 35(3): 255–272 (2001)
– Traditional and emotional stylometric analysis of the songs of Beatles Paul McCartney and John Lennon. Computers and the Humanities 30(3): 257–265 (1996)

The first article has 16 citations and the second one 43. After retrieving the lists of citations for each record and removing irrelevant records, the footprint index module has all de data in order to calculate the footprint index for our author.

Our thematic areas mapper identified three thematic areas for our author: psychology, social science and computer science.

For the first article we have 3 citations mapped on social science thematic area, 13 citations in psychology and none in computer science.

For the second article of our author we marked as irrelevant 7 records out of 43 citations (we preprocess the list of citations received from Google Schoolar). For this article, the citations were categorized as follow: 8 citations in social science, 21 in psychology and 7 in computer science.

9   Conclusions

In this paper we have presented the notion of a footprints in the academic world, defined as the traces of impact that an article, or an author, has had in different scientific fields. In order to avoid subjectivity in the estimation and quantification of the footprint we have opted to avoid author defined parameters and have instead focused our analysis on the journal or conference where a citing article has been published. This provides an objective and reliable indication of thematic scope, which allows us to see, in a semi-automated manner, which scientific areas have been affected by an author's work.

These steps allow us to develop semantic footprint indices, associating articles and authors with the fields where they have made an impact. Querying such indices we can provide semantic services that were unimaginable before, such as the automated identification of the most prominent works and authors for each field, regardless of their originally intended scope.

In our paper we have presented various real life examples to support the validity of our approach, and have also presented a preliminary integrated implementation, the Footprint Analyzer, based on information acquired from DBLP and Google Scholar. Constraints set by Google Scholar and DBLP limit the extent of our experimentation, but the presented results suffice for a proof of concept. Besides, the architecture makes it straightforward to link more academic sources, particularly those that provide structured exposed APIs.

Of course our work is not complete. As part of our future work we would like to develop a more complete hierarchy of scientific fields which includes the whole spectrum of scientific fields in a greater depth and making an automatic match of journals with the multiple scientific fields. As we intend to use Apacge Solr[5] in order to index our database and to create a section for manual mach the papers that have inconsistancies in titles or author names and to mark them as duplicates.

Acknowledgments. This work has been supported by COST Action IC1302: Semantic keyword-based search on structured data sources (KEYSTONE).

This work has been partially funded by the Sectoral Operational Programme Human Resources Development 2007–2013 of the Ministry of European Funds through the Financial Agreement POSDRU/187/1.5/S/155536 and partially supported by "DataWay - Real-time Data Processing Platform for Smart Cities: Making sense of Big Data" grant of the Romanian National Authority for Scientific Research and Innovation, CNCS – UEFISCDI, project number PN-II-RU-TE-2014-4-2731.

References

1. Armenakis, A.A., Harris, S.G.: Reflections: our journey in organizational change research and practice. J. Change Manag. **9**(2), 127–142 (2009)
2. Altarriba, J.: Cognitive approaches to the study of emotion-laden and emotion words in monolingual and bilingual memory. Bilingual Educ. Bilingualism **56**, 232–256 (2006)
3. Altarriba, J.: Emotion, memory, and Bilingualism. In: Heredia, R.R., Altarriba, J. (eds.) Foundations of Bilingual Memory, pp. 185–203. Springer, New York (2014). doi:10.1007/978-1-4614-9218-4_9
4. Altarriba, J., Bauer, L.M., Benvenuto, C.: Concreteness, context availability, and imageability ratings and word associations for abstract, concrete, and emotion words. Behav. Res. Methods **31**, 578–602 (1999)
5. Altarriba, J., Bauer, L.M.: The distinctiveness of emotion concepts: a comparison between emotion, abstract, and concrete words. Am. J. Psychol. **117**, 389–410 (2004)
6. Barthet, M., Fazekas, G., Sandler, M.B., Recognition, M.E.: From content- to context-based models. In: International Symposium on Computer Music Modeling and Retrieval (CMMR), pp. 228–252 (2012)
7. Beel, J., Gipp, B.: Academic search engine spam and Google Scholar's resilience against it. J. Electr. Publishing **13**(3) (2010)
8. Beel, J., Gipp, B.: Google Scholar's ranking algorithm: the impact of citation counts (an empirical study). In: Third International Conference on Research Challenges in Information Science (RCIS), pp. 439–446. IEEE (2009)
9. Beel, J., Gipp, B.: Google Scholar's ranking algorithm: an introductory overview. In: Proceedings of the 12th International Conference on Scientometrics and Informetrics (ISSI 2009), vol. 1, pp. 230–241 (2009)

---

[5] http://lucene.apache.org/solr/.

10. Bornmann, L., Mutz, R.: Growth rates of modern science: a bibliometric analysis based on the number of publications and cited references. J. Assoc. Inf. Sci. Technol. **66**(11), 2215–2222 (2015)
11. Bornmann, L., Mutz, R., Daniel, H.D.: The h index research output measurement: two approaches to enhance its accuracy. J. Informetrics **4**(3), 407–414 (2010)
12. Byron, K.: Carrying too heavy a load? The communication and miscommunication of emotion by email. Acad. Manag. Rev. **33**, 309–327 (2008)
13. ScienceDirect, Classification of topics. http://www.sciencedirect.com/. Accessed Dec 2016
14. Canazza, S., De Poli, G., Roda, A., Vidolin, A.: An abstract control space for communication of sensory expressive intentions in music performance. J. New Music Res. **32**(3), 281–294 (2003)
15. Chandrasekhar, S.: An Introduction to the Study of Stellar Structure. University of Chicago Press, Chicago (1939)
16. Chen, X.: Google Scholar's dramatic coverage improvement five years after debut. Serials Rev. **36**(4), 221–226 (2010)
17. CiteSeeer^X. http://citeseerx.ist.psu.edu/. Accessed Dec 2016
18. Clavel, C., Vasilescu, I., Devillers, L., Richard, G., Ehrette, T.: Fear-type emotion recognition for future audio-based surveillance systems. Speech Commun. **50**(6), 487–503 (2008)
19. Visualisation of DBLP's Bibliography Samples. http://suksant.com/tag/dblp/. Accessed Dec 2015
20. Cowie, R., Cornelius, R.R.: Describing the emotional states that are expressed in speech. Speech Commun. **40**(12), 5–32 (2003)
21. DBLP. http://dblp.uni-trier.de. Accessed Dec 2016
22. Batista, P.D., Campiteli, M.G., Konouchi, O., Martinez, A.S.: Is it possible to compare researchers with different scientific interests? Scientometrics **68**(1), 179–189 (2006)
23. Djamasbi, S., Strong, D.M.: The effect of positive mood on intention to use computerized decision aids. Inf. Manag. **45**(1), 43–51 (2008)
24. Douglas-Cowie, E., Cowie, R., Sneddon, I., Cox, C., Lowry, O., McRorie, M., Martin, J.-C., Devillers, L., Abrilian, S., Batliner, A., Amir, N., Karpouzis, K.: The HUMAINE database: addressing the collection and annotation of naturalistic and induced emotional data. In: Proceedings of 2nd International Conference on Affective Computing and Intelligent Interaction, Lisbon, Portugal (2007)
25. Egghe, L.: Theory and practise of the g-index. Scientometrics **69**(1), 131–152 (2013)
26. Elsbach, K., Barr, P.S.: The effects of mood on individuals' use of structured decision protocols
27. Figa-Talamanca, A.: Strengths and weaknesses of citation indices and impact factors. Qual. Assess. High. Educ., 83–88 (2007)
28. Fragopanagos, N., Taylor, J.G.: Emotion recognition in human-computer interaction. Neural Netw. **18**(4), 389–405 (2005)
29. Google Scholar Blog, Google Scholar Citations Open To All, Google, 16 November 2011. http://googlescholar.blogspot.gr/2011/11/google-scholar-citations-open-to-all.html. Accessed Dec 2016
30. Glanzel, W., Schubert, A.: A new classification scheme of science fields and subfields designed for scientometric evaluation purposes. Scientometrics **56**(3), 357–367 (2003)

31. Graciarena, M., Shriberg, E., Stolcke, A., Enos, F., Hirschberg, J., Kajarekar, S.: Combining prosodic, lexical and Cepstral systems for deceptive speech detection. In: Proceedings of IEEE International Conference on Acoustics, Speech, and Signal Processing (ICASSP), Toulouse (2006)

32. Harnad, S.: Post-Gutenberg Galaxy: the fourth revolution in the means of production of knowledge. Publ.-Access Comput. Syst. Rev. **2**(1), 39–53 (1991)

33. Harnad, S.: The Optimal and Inevitable Outcome for Research in the Online Age, pp. 46–48. CILIP, Update (2012)

34. Zadeh, L.A.: Fuzzy sets. Inf. Control **8**(3), 338–353 (1965)

35. Ifrim, C., Pop, F., Mocanu, M., Cristea, V.: AgileDBLP: a search-based mobile application for structured digital libraries. In: Cardoso, J., Guerra, F., Houben, G.-J., Pinto, A.M., Velegrakis, Y. (eds.) KEYSTONE 2015. LNCS, vol. 9398, pp. 88–93. Springer, Cham (2015). doi:10.1007/978-3-319-27932-9_8

36. Ioannou, S., Caridakis, G., Karpouzis, K., Kollias, S.: Robust feature detection for facial expression recognition. EURASIP J. Image Video Process. **2**, 2007 (2007)

37. Kierkels, J.J.M., Soleymani, M., Pun, T.: Queries and tags in affect-based multimedia retrieval. In: Proceedings of the IEEE International Conference on Multimedia and Expo, pp. 1436–1439. IEEE Press, Piscataway (2009)

38. Jacsó, P.: Metadata mega mess in Google Scholar. Online Inf. Rev. **34**(1), 175–191 (2010)

39. Knowledge and Uncertainty Research Laboratory GitHub. https://github.com/gavlab-gr/. Accessed Dec 2016

40. Foss, S.K.: Destination Dissertation: A Traveler's Guide to a Done Dissertation. Rowman and Littlefield Publishers, Maryland (2007)

41. Silagadze, Z.K.: Citation entropy and research impact estimation. Acta Physica Pol. B **41**, 2325–2333 (2009)

42. Keyton, J., Smith, F.L.: Distrust in leaders: dimensions, patterns, and emotional intensity. J. Leadersh. Organ. Stud. **16**(1), 6–18 (2009)

43. Klavans, R., Boyack, K.W.: Toward a consensus map of science. J. Am. Soc. Inf. Sci. Technol. **60**(3), 455–476 (2009)

44. Kostoulas, T., Mporas, I., Kocsis, O., Ganchev, T., Katsaounos, N., Santamaria, J.J., Jimenez-Murcia, S., Fernandez-Aranda, F., Fakotakis, N.: Affective speech interface in serious games for supporting therapy of mental disorders. Expert Syst. Appl. **39**(12), 11072–11079 (2012)

45. Dubois, S.L.: Gender differences in the emotional tone of written sexual fantasies. Can. J. Sex. **6**(4), 307–315 (1997)

46. Letchford, A., Moat, H.S., Preis, T.: The Advantage of Short Paper Titles, Royal Society Open Science. The Royal Society (2015). 10.1098/rsos.150266

47. Ley, M., et al.: DBLP-some lessons learned. Proc. VLDB Endowment **2**(2), 1493–1500 (2009)

48. Google Scholar's Ghost Authors. http://lj.libraryjournal.com/2009/11/industry-news/google-scholars-ghost-authors/. Accessed Dec 2015

49. Bartunek, J.M., Rousseau, D.M., Rudolph, J.W., DePalma, J.A.: On the receiving end sensemaking, emotion, and assessments of an organizational change initiated by others. J. Appl. Behav. Sci. **42**(2), 182–206 (2006)

50. C.M. Whissell, Homepage. http://laurentian.ca/faculty/cwhissell. Accessed Dec 2016

51. Whissell, C.M.: The dictionary of affect in language. In: Plutchik, R., Kellerman, H. (eds.) Emotion: Theory, Research, and Experience, pp. 113–131. New York, Academic Press (1989)

52. Soroka, S.N., Bodet, M.A., Young, L., Andrew, B.: Campaign news and vote intentions. J. Elections Publ. Opin. Parties **19**(4), 359–376 (2009)
53. Soroka, S.N.: Negativity in Democratic Politics: Causes and Consequences. Cambridge University Press, Cambridge (2014)
54. Physics Portal at South Carolina State University, The Branches of Science. http://www.cnrt.scsu.edu/~psc152/A/branches.htm. Accessed Dec 2016
55. Raouzaiou, A., Tsapatsoulis, N., Karpouzis, K., Kollias, S
56. Reyes, A., Rosso, P.: Making objective decisions from subjective data: detecting irony in customer reviews. Decis. Support Syst. **53**(4), 754–760 (2012)
57. Richards, P., Persinger, M.A., Koren, S.A.: Modification of semantic memory in normal subjects by application across the temporal lobes of a weak (1 microT) magnetic field structure that promotes long-term potentiation in hippocampal slices. Electro Magnetobiol. **15**(2), 141–148 (1996)
58. Mayr, P., Walter, A.-K.: Studying journal coverage in Google Scholar. J. Libr. Adm. **47**(1–2), 81–99 (2008)
59. Google, Scholar. https://scholar.google.com/. Accessed Dec 2016
60. ScienceDirect. http://sciencedirect.com/. Accessed Dec 2016
61. Simos, T.: Homepage. https://users.uop.gr/~simos/CV_Simos_EV.pdf. Accessed Dec 2016
62. Scherer, S., Schwenker, F., Palm, G.: Classifier fusion for emotion recognition from speech, invited book chapter contribution. Adv. Intell. Environ. **5**, 95–117 (2009)
63. Schroder, M.: Dimensional emotion representation as a basis for speech synthesis with non-extreme emotions. In: André, E., Dybkjær, L., Minker, W., Heisterkamp, P. (eds.) Affective dialogue systems. LNCS, vol. 3068, pp. 209–220. Springer, Heidelberg (2004). doi:10.1007/978-3-540-24842-2_21
64. Schuller, B., Vlasenko, B., Eyben, F., Wollmer, M., Stuhlsatz, A., Wendemuth, A., Rigoll, G.: Cross-corpus acoustic emotion recognition: variances and strategies. IEEE Trans. Affect. Comput. (TAC) **1**(2), 119–131 (2010)
65. Send, Z., Pantic, M., Huang, T.S.: Emotion recognition based on multimodal information. In: Tao, J., Tan, T. (eds.) Affective Information Processing, pp. 241–266. Springer, London (2009)
66. Zhang, C.T.: The e-index, complementing the h-index for excess citations. PLoS ONE **5**(5), e5429 (2009)
67. Tsapatsoulis, N., Karpouzis, K., Stamou, G., Piat, F., Kollias, S
68. Vlasenko, B., Prylipko, D., Bock, R., Wendemuth, A.: Modeling phonetic pattern variability in favor of the creation of robust emotion classifiers for real-life applications. Comput. Speech Lang. **28**(2), 483–500 (2014)
69. von Bohlen und Halbach, O.: How to judge a book by its cover? How useful are bibliometric indices for the evaluation of "scientific quality" or "scientific productivity"? Ann. Anat. **193**(3), 191–196 (2011)
70. Mossholder, K.W., Settoon, R.P., Harris, S.G., Armenakis, A.A.: Measuring emotion in open-ended survey responses: an application of textual data analysis. J. Manag. **21**(2), 335–355 (1995)
71. Wallace, M.: Extracting and visualizing research impact semantics. In: Proceedings of the 9th International Workshop on Semantic and Social Media Adaptation and Personalization, Corfu, Greece (2014)
72. Yi, J., Niblack, W.: Sentiment Mining in WebFountain. In: Proceedings of 21st International Conference on Data Engineering, pp. 1073–1083 (2005)
73. Yi, J., Nasukawa, T., Bunescu, R., Niblack, W.: Sentiment analyzer: extracting sentiments about a given topic using natural language processing techniques. In: Proceedings of the IEEE International Conference on Data Mining (ICDM) (2003)

74. Young, L., Soroka, S.N.: Affective news: the automated coding of sentiment in political texts. Polit. Commun. **29**, 205–231 (2012)
75. Zeng, Z., Pantic, M., Roisman, G.I., Huang, T.S.: A survey of affect recognition methods: audio, visual, and spontaneous expressions. IEEE Trans. Pattern Anal. Mach. Intell. **31**(1), 39–58 (2009)
76. WikiPedia, Branches of science. https://en.wikipedia.org/wiki/Branches_of_science. Accessed Dec 2016

Mining and Using Key-Words and Key-Phrases to Identify the Era of an Anonymous Text

Dror Mughaz[1,2(✉)], Yaakov HaCohen-Kerner[2], and Dov Gabbay[1,3]

[1] Department of Computer Science,
Bar-Ilan University, 5290002 Ramat-Gan, Israel
myghaz@gmail.com, dov.gabbay@kcl.ac.uk
[2] Department of Computer Science,
Lev Academic Center, 9116001 Jerusalem, Israel
kerner@jct.ac.il
[3] Department of Informatics,
Kings College London, Strand, London WC2R 2LS, UK

Abstract. This study is trying to determine the time-frame in which the author of a given document lived. The documents are rabbinic documents written in Hebrew-Aramaic languages. The documents are undated and do not contain a bibliographic section, which leaves us with an interesting challenge. To do this, we define a set of key-phrases and formulate various types of rules: "Iron-clad", Heuristic and Greedy, to define the time-frame. These rules are based on key-phrases and key-words in the documents of the authors. Identifying the time-frame of an author can help us determine the generation in which specific documents were written, can help in the examination of documents, i.e., to conclude if documents were edited, and can also help us identify an anonymous author. We tested these rules on two corpora containing responsa documents. The results are promising and are better for the larger corpus than for the smaller corpus.

Keywords: Hebrew-Aramaic documents · Key-phrases · Key-words · Knowledge discovery · Text mining · Time analysis · Undated documents · Undated references

1 Introduction

Determining the time frame of a book or a manuscript and identifying an author are important and challenging problems. Time-related key-words and key-phrases with references can be used to date and identify authors. Key-phrases and key-words have great potential to provide great information in many domains, such as academic, legal and commercial. Thus, the automatic extraction and analysis of key-phrases and key-words is growing rapidly and gaining momentum. Web search engines, machine learning, etc. are based on key-phrases and key-words. As a result, features are extracted and learned automatically; thus, the analysis of key-phrases and key-words has enormous importance. Key-phrases and key-words are essential features not only of the

© Springer International Publishing AG 2017
N.T. Nguyen et al. (Eds.): TCCI XXVI, LNCS 10190, pp. 119–143, 2017.
DOI: 10.1007/978-3-319-59268-8_6

needs of scientific papers or for industry and commerce but also of rabbinic responsa (answers written in response to Jewish legal questions authored by rabbinic scholars).

Key-phrases, key-words and citations/references included in rabbinic responsa text are more complex to define and to extract than key-phrases, key-words and citations/references in academic papers because:

(1) There is an interaction with the complex morphology of Hebrew, Aramaic and Yiddish (e.g. various citations can be presented with different types of prefixes included in the name of a citation, e.g., "and ...", "when ...", "and when ...", "in ...", "and in ...", "and when in ...");

(2) Natural language processing (NLP) in Hebrew, Aramaic and Yiddish has been relatively little studied;

(3) In contrast to academic papers, there is no reference list that appears at all, even not at the end of a responsa;

(4) Many references in Hebrew-Aramaic-Yiddish documents are ambiguous. For instance: (a) a book titled מגן-אבות (magen-avot) was composed by four different Jewish authors; and (b) The abbreviation מ"ב (m"b) relates to two different Jewish authors and has also other meanings, which are not authors' names; and

(5) At least 30 different syntactic styles (see next paragraph) are used to present references. This number is higher than the number of citation patterns used in academic papers written in English (e.g., see [1]).

Each specific document written by a specific author can be referred to in at least 30 general possible citation syntactic styles. For example, the pardes book written by the famous Jewish author Rabbi Shlomo Yitzhaki, known by the abbreviation Rashi, can be referenced using the following patterns: (1) "Shlomo son of Rabbi Yitzhaki", (2) "Shlomo son of Yitzhaki", (3) "Shlomo Yitzhaki", (4) "In the name of Rashi who wrote in the pardes book", (5) "In the complete pardes book of Rashi", (6) "Rashi of blessed memory in the pardes book", (7) "In Rashi in the pardes", (8) "Rashi the possessor of the pardes of blessed memory", (9) "In the name of of Rashi in the pardes", (10) "The pardes responsa of Rashi", (11) "Which wrote Rashi in the pardes", (12) "Rashi in the pardes book", (13) "The pardes book of Rashi", (14) "The pardes b' of Rashi", (15) "In the name of the pardes book", (16) "Rashi the possessor of the pardes", (17) "In the name of the pardes b'", (18) "Rashi in the pardes", (19) "The great pardes book of Rashi", (20) "The great pardes book", (21) "The great pardes", (22) "The pardes book", (23) "The pardes responsa", (24) "The possessor of the pardes", (25) "In the name of the pardes", (26) " The pardes b'" (27) "In the name of Rashi", (28) "There, chapter-number, sentence-number" (there refers to the book/paper mentioned on the latest reference), (29) "There, there, sentence-number" (the first there refers to the book/paper mentioned in the latest reference and the second there refers to the chapter-number mentioned in the latest reference), and (30) "There, there, there" (refers to the book/paper, chapter-number and sentence-number mentioned on the latest reference).

Furthermore, each citation pattern can be expanded to many other specific citations by replacing the name of the author and/or his book/responsa by each of their other names (e.g., different spellings, full names, short names, first names, surnames, and nicknames with/without title) and abbreviations of their names or their book titles.

Hebrew-Aramaic-Yiddish documents in general and Hebrew responsa in principle present various interesting text mining problems: (1) the morphology in Hebrew is richer than in English. Hebrew has 70,000,000 valid forms, while English has only 1,000,000 [2]. Declensions in Hebrew can be up to 7000 for one stem, while in English, there are only a few declensions; (2) responsa documents have a high rate of abbreviations (nearly 20%) while more than one third of them (about 8%) are ambiguous [3].

This research estimates the date of undated documents of authors using (1) the year (s) mentioned in the text, (2) "late" ("of blessed memory") key-phrases, (3) "rabbi" key-phrases, (4) "friend" key-phrases that are mentioned in the texts and (5) undated references of other dated authors that refer to the considered author or are mentioned by him. The assessments are with different degrees of certainty: "iron-clad", heuristic and greedy. The rules are based on key-phrases with and without references.

This paper is organized as follows: Sect. 2 gives background concerning the extraction and analysis of key-phrases and citation. Section 3 presents the boosting extraction key-phrases algorithm. Section 4 presents various rules of some degrees of certainty: "iron-clad", heuristic and greedy rules, which are used to assess writers' birth and death years. Section 5 presents the model description. Section 6 familiarizes the dataset, experiments, results and analysis. Section 7 includes the summary, conclusions and future works.

2   Related Research

Following the explosion of electronic information, there has been a growing need for extracting key-phrases and key-words automatically. Many studies have been made in this area for different purposes and from different perspectives. Key-words in documents allow for quick search on multiple large databases [4]. Key-words can also help to improve the NLP performance, as well as the information retrieval performance in issues such as text summarization [5], text categorization [6], topic change during conversational text [7], and opinion mining [8].

Although key-words are important in many computer applications, there is still much to be done in this area, and the state-of-the-art methods underperform compared to other NLP core tasks [9].

There are several difficulties in extracting key-phrases and key-words. One is the length of the documents. In scientific articles, although there can only be approximately 10 key-words or key-phrases and approximately another 30 candidates in the abstract section, the rest of the article may contain hundreds of candidate key-phrases or key-words [10]. Moreover, key-words can also appear at the end of an article. If key-phrase or key-word appears at the beginning and at the end of an article, it indicates the importance of that key-phrase or key-word [11].

When documents are structured, key-words extraction is easier. For example, in scientific papers, most of the key-words appear in the abstract, in the introduction and in the title [12]. In other cases, key-phrases can be automatically extracted from web page text and from its metadata [13] for the purpose of advertisement.

One possible way to date a document and determining who the writer of a document is to use visual image of the document. Analyzing image of a document generally consists, of: locating the place where the document was written (different climate types mean different erosion, discoloration and degradation), extracting features from letters, words and empty regions. Features can be extracted by the use of the contours of the alphabet shapes of the text, [14]; by extracting features that not related to a specific text [15, 16] or by geometric patterns.

Bar-Yosef et al. [17] developed a multi-phase binarization method using concavity (also of cavities), moments, among other features for identification, verification and classification of writers of historical Hebrew calligraphy texts. They performed an experiment on erosion letters of a 34 writers and the identification experiment yielded result of 100% correct classification.

The problem with those methods (e.g., signal or image processing) is that they can find the writer but not necessarily the author. We mean that an author, i.e., the original author, wrote a book or an article and after 200 or 400 years the paper disintegrated. The text was important so it copied, thus those methods may find the era of the copier/writer but not the epoch of the author.

Automatic extraction and analysis of references from academic papers was first proposed by Garfield [18]. Berkowitz and Elkhadiri [19] extracted writers' names and titles from articles. A knowledge-based system was used by Giuffrida et al. [20] to derive metadata, including writers' names, from computer science journal articles. Hidden Markov Models were used by Seymore et al. [21] to extract writer names from a limited collection of computer science articles. The use of terms leads to progress in the extraction of information. Selecting text before and after references to extract good index terms to improve retrieval effectiveness was done by Ritchie et al. [22]. Bradshaw [23] used terms from a fixed window around references.

In contrast with scientific articles, the documents we are working on are from the Responsa Project[1]; they are without any structural base, usually contain a mixture of at least two languages, and contain noise (e.g., editorial additions). Previous research on the Responsa Project dealt with text classification [24]. They checked whether classification could be done over the long axis of ethnic groups of authors with stylistic feature sets. HaCohen-Kerner and Mughaz [25] investigated in which era rabbis lived using undated Responsa, but they did not address the problem of how to extract time-related key-words or key-phrases. This article is a continuation research of this issue, i.e., determining when writers lived using key-phrases.

3 Semi-automatic Boosting Mining of Key-Phrases

We want to mine the time-related key-phrases automatically. We found that most of the sentences that contain time-related concepts (i.e., time-related words and phrases) to rabbinic literature (e.g., "late", "friend") are usually nearby rabbinic names/nicknames/acronyms/abbreviations/book-names. We developed a semi-automatic algorithm that boosts concepts mining in order to mine the time-related concepts. The main idea is to

---

[1] Contained in the Global Jewish Database (The Responsa Project at Bar-Ilan University). http://www.biu.ac.il/ICJI/Responsa.

extract sentences that contain names of rabbis so that the words and phrases that are nearby the rabbinic names are treated as the key-phrases (among others) that we look for. Now, we present a general description of our mining algorithm and after that Illustration of the run of the algorithm.

3.1   The Algorithm

Notations:

TP – temporal vector of Time-related Phrases.

RN – vector of Rabbinic Names.

n – number of iterations of the algorithm.

TRC – set of Time-Related Concepts starting with, e.g., year, life, fiend and era.

TP ← TRC // initiate TP with the value of TRC

For i = 1 to n do:

- Search for sentences that contain the last concepts that was added to TP
- Extract new rabbinic names from those sentences
- Add the new rabbinic names to RN
- Search for sentences that contain the last rabbinic names that was added to RN
- Mine time-related concepts from the new sentences:
  - Delete stop words.
  - Add the new time-related concepts to TP
  - Add the new time-related words and phrases to TRC (with their frequencies) and for the "old" time-related words and phrases only add their frequencies

Sort TRC by the frequency of time-related words and phrases in decreasing order (normally, concepts have larger number of appearances). Select from TRC the most frequent time-related concepts.

Bellow we present several examples of sentences, which contain rabbinic names, rabbinic acronym names and rabbinic books names (in Hebrew with translation to English)

(1) שו״ת יחל ישראל סימן מה
... וכבר ביאר זאת מורי ורבי הגרש״ז אויערבך זצ״ל בספרו מעדני ארץ

(1) Responsa Yahel Israel chapter 45

... and *my teacher and Rabbi* Hgrsh"z (acronym of the genius Rabbi Shlomo Zalman) Auerbach *za"l* (acronym of *righteous memory*) already explained it in his ma'adany eretz book ...

(2) שו״ת היכל יצחק אבן העזר ב סימן נג
תשובה בשאלה הקודמת, מאת הרב שלמה זלמן אויערבאך שליט״א ראש ישיבת קול תורה בירושלים. בענין שליח בי״ד של חיפה שנתמנה בחו״ל להיות שליח להולכת גט ומת פתאום ...

(2) **Responsa Hechal Yitzchak Even HaEzer part 2 chapter 53**

Answer to the previous question, from Rabbi Shlomo Zalman Auerbach *shlit"a* (acronym of *may he live a good long life, Amen*) head of Kol Torah yeshiva (talmudic college) in Jerusalem. In the matter of a courier of the Haifa court that appointed abroad, to be an emissary to conveyance get (divorce certificate) and died suddenly ...

(3) שו"ת הר צבי יורה דעה סימן יט

בספר ציץ אליעזר לידידי הגאון הגרא"י ולדינברג שליט"א אב"ד בה"ד ירושלם ...

(3) **Responsa Har-Zvi yore dea'a chapter 19**

In the book Tzitz-Eliezer written by *my friend* the genius Hgra"i (acronym of the genius Rabbi Eliezer Yehuda) Waldenberg *shlit"a* (acronym of *may he live a good long life, Amen*) ab"d (acronym of head of rabbinical court) of the city of Jerusalem ...

Illustration of the run of the algorithm

We searched for the time-related phrase *"righteous memory"* (from TRC).
   One of the results was sentence 1.
From sentence 1 we extracted the name "Rabbi Shlomo Zalman Auerbach".
   Then we searched for "Rabbi Shlomo Zalman Auerbach".
   One of the results was sentence 2.
From sentence 2 we extracted the time-related phrase *"Shlit"a"* (and insert it to the TRC).
   Then we search for *"Shlit"a"*.
   One of the results was sentence 3.
From sentence 3 we extracted the name "Rabbi Eliezer Waldenberg".

Then we continue until there were no more new time-related phrases (to insert to TRC).

3.2   Algorithm Results

After using the algorithm, we mine time-related key-words, key-phrases and acronyms (a partial list is shown in Table 1).
We divided the Hebrew and Aramaic key-words and key-phrases into three sets:
   Late – addressing a person who has already died.
   Friend – addressing another person as a friend, i.e., there is a large overlap between the lifetime of one author and the lifetime of another person who is referred to by the first author as a friend.
   Rabbi – addressing another person as a rabbi/master, i.e., there is overlap between the lifetime of one author and the lifetime of another person who is referred to by the first author as rabbi.
   Table 1 presents a partial list of Hebrew and Aramaic key-words and key-phrases and a few acronyms in Hebrew and their translation into English.

Table 1. Hebrew and Aramaic cue words partial list

Set	Key-phrase in Hebrew	Translation of the key-phrase
Late	זכור לטוב	Remembered for good
	זכרו לברכה קדוש צדיק וטהור	of blessed memory; holy, righteous and pure
	זכרו לברכה	of blessed memory
	זכר קדוש וצדיק לברכה	may the holy and righteous be of blessed memory
	זצוק"ל	acronym: may the righteous and holy be of blessed memory
	זקוצ"ל	acronym: may the holy and righteous be of blessed memory
	יז"ל	acronym: May his memory be forever
	זי"ע	acronym: May his virtue stand for us
	ז"ל	acronym: of blessed memory
Friend	ידידי הרב הגדול	My friend the Great Rabbi
	ידידי הרב הגאון	My friend the Gaon Rabbi
	ידידי הרב	My friend (the) Rabbi
	השם ישמרהו ויחיהו	may G-D preserve him and grant him life
	ידידו הקטן	his young friend
	ישמרהו השם ויחיהו	may G-D preserve him and grant him life
	ידידי הרה"ג	partially acronym: My friend HaRav HaGaon
	שליט"א	acronym: may he live a good long life, Amen
	יה"ו	acronym: may G-D preserve him and grant him life
Rabbi	יורנו רבנו	May the Rabbi guide us
	מרא דאתרא	the local rabbinic authority
	רבי ומורי	My Rabbi and teacher
	מרנא	Our teacher
	רבינו	Our Rabbi
	מו"ר	acronym: My Teacher and my Rabbi

4 Rules-Based Constraints

This section presents the rules, based on key-phrases and references, formulated for the estimation of the birth and death years of an author X (the extracted results point to specific years) based on his texts and the texts of other writers (Yi) who mention X or one of his texts. We assume that the birth years and death years of all writers are known, excluding those that are under interrogation. Now, we will give some notions and constants that are used: X – The writer under consideration, Yi – Other writers, B – Birth year, D – Death year, MIN – Minimal age (at present, 30 years) of a rabbinic writer when he starts to write his response, MAX – Maximal age (at present, 100 years) of a rabbinic author, and RABBI_DIS – The gap age between rabbi and his student (at present, 20 years). The estimations of MIN, MAX, and RABBI_DIS constants are heuristic, although they are realistic on the basis of typical responsa authors' lifestyles.

Different types of references exist: general references with and without key-phrases, such as "rabbi", "friend" and "late". There are two types of references: those referring to living authors and those referring to dead authors. In contrast to academic papers, responsa include many more references to dead authors than to living authors.

We will introduce rules based on key-phrases and references of different degrees of certainty: "iron-clad" (I), heuristic (H) and greedy (G). "Iron-clad" rules are always true, without any exception. Heuristic rules are almost always true. Exceptions can occur because the heuristic estimates for MIN, MAX and RABBI_DIS are incorrect. Greedy rules are rather reasonable rules for responsa authors. However, wrong estimates can sometimes be drawn while using these rules. Each rule will be numbered and its degree of certainty (i.e., I, H, G) will be presented in brackets.

4.1 "Iron-Clad" and Heuristic Rules with Key-Phrases

First, we present one general iron rule and two general heuristic rules, which are based on regular citations (i.e., without any key-phrase), based on authors that cite X.

General rule based on authors that were mentioned by X

$$D(X) >= MAX(B(Yi))   (0 \ (I))$$

$$D(X) >= MAX(B(Yi)) + MIN   (1 \ (H))$$

X must have been alive when he referred to Yi, so we can use the earliest possible age of publishing of the latest born author Yi as a lower estimate for X's death year. The heuristic rule includes the addition of MIN, which is the minimum age where Yi starts to write his response.

General rule based on authors that referred to X

$$B(X) <= MIN(D(Yi)) - MIN   (2 \ (H))$$

All Yi must have been alive when they referred to X, and X must have been old enough to publish. Hence, we can use the earliest death year amongst such authors Yi as an upper estimate of X's earliest possible publication age (and thus his birth year).

General rules based on year mentioning Y that appeared in X's documents

$$D(X) >= MAX(Y)   (3 \ (I))$$

X must have been alive when he mentioned the year Y. We can use the most recent year mentioned by X to evaluate the death year of X as an estimation of X's death year.

Posthumous Key-Phrase Rules

Posthumous rules estimate the birth and death years of an author X based on references of authors who refer to X with the key-phrase "late" ("of blessed memory") or on references of X that mention other authors with the key-phrase "late". Figure 1 describes possible situations where various types of authors Yi (i = 1, 2, 3) refer to X with the key-phrase "late". The lines depict writers' life spans; the left edges represent the birth years and the right edges represent death years. In this case (as all Yi refer to X with the key-phrase "late"), we know that all Yi passed away after X, but we do not

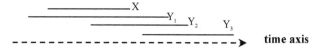

Fig. 1. References mentioning X with the key-phrase "late".

know when they were born in relation to X's birth. Y1 was born before X's birth; Y2 was born after X's birth but before X's death; and Y3 was born after X's death.

$$D(X) <= MIN(D(Yi)) \quad (4 \ (I))$$

However, we know that X must have been dead when Yi referred to him with the key-phrase "late"; thus, we can use the earliest born Y's death year as an upper estimate for X's death year. Like all writers, dead writers of course have to comply with rule (2) as well.

Now, we look at the cases where the author X that we are studying refers to other authors Yi with the key-phrase "late". Figure 2 describes possible situations where X refers to various types of authors Yi (i = 1, 2, 3) with the key-phrase "late". All Yi passed away before X's death (or X may still be alive). Y1 died before X's birth; Y2 was born before X's birth and died when X was still alive; Y3 was born after X's birth and passed away when X was still alive.

$$D(X) >= MAX(D(Yi)) \quad (5 \ (I))$$

X must have been alive after the death of all Yi who were referred by him with the key-phrase "late". Therefore, we can use the death year of the latest-born Y as a lower estimate for X's death year.

$$B(X) >= MAX(D(Yi)) - MAX \quad (6 \ (H))$$

X was probably born after the death year of the latest-dying person that X wrote about. Thus, we use the death year of the latest-born Y minus his max life-period as a lower estimate for X's birth year.

Fig. 2. References by X who mentions others with the key-phrase "late".

Contemporary Key-Phrases Rules

Contemporary key-phrases rules calculate the upper and lower bounds of the birth year of a writer X based only on the references of known writers who refer to X as their friend/rabbi. This means there must have been at least some period of time when both were alive together. Figure 3 shows possible situations where various types of writers

Yi refer to X as their friend/rabbi. Y1 was born before X's birth and died before X's death; Y2 was born before X's birth and died after X's death; Y3 was born after X's birth and passed away before X's death; Y4 was born after X's birth and passed away after X's death. Like all writers, contemporary authors of course have to comply with rules 1 and 2 as well.

$$B(X) >= MIN(B(Yi)) - (MAX - MIN) \quad (7 \ (H))$$

All Yi must have been alive when X was alive, and all of them must have been old enough to publish. Thus, X could not have been born MAX-MIN years before the earliest birth year amongst all authors Yi.

$$D(X) <= MAX(D(Yi)) + (MAX - MIN) \quad (8 \ (H))$$

Again, all Yi must have been alive when X was alive, and all of them must have been old enough to publish. Hence, X could not have been alive MAX-MIN years after the latest death year amongst all writers Yi.

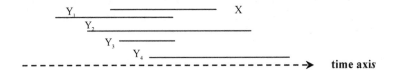

Fig. 3. References by authors who refer to X as their Friend/Rabbi.

4.2 Greedy Rules

Greedy rules bounds are sensible but can sometimes lead to wrong estimates.

Greedy rule based on authors who are mentioned by X

$$B(X) >= MAX(B(Yi)) - MIN \quad (9 \ (G))$$

Many of the references in our research domain relate to dead authors. Thus, most of the references within X's texts relate to dead authors. Namely, many Yi were born before X's birth and died before X's death. Thus, a greedy assumption would be that X was born no earlier than the birth of the latest author mentioned by X; however, because there may be at least one case where Y was born after X was born, we subtract MIN.

Greedy rule based on references to year Y made by X

$$B(X) >= MAX(Y) - MIN \quad (10 \ (G))$$

When X mentions years, he usually writes the current year in which he wrote the document or a few years ahead. Most of the time, the maximum year, Y, minus MIN is larger than X's birth year.

Greedy rule based on authors who refer to X

$$D(X) <= MIN(D(Yi)) - MIN \quad (11 \ (G))$$

As mentioned above, most of the references within Yi texts refer to X as being dead. Hence, most Yi died after X's death. Therefore, a greedy assumption would be that X died no later than the death of the earliest author who referred to X minus MIN.

Rules refinements 9–11 are presented by rules 12–17. Rules 12–14 are due to X referring to Yi and rules 15–17 are due to Yi referring to X.

Greedy rule for defining the birth year based only on authors who were referred to by X with the key-phrase "late"

$$B(X) >= MAX(D(Yi)) - MIN \quad (12 \ (G))$$

When taking into account only references that were written in X's texts, most of the references are related to dead authors. That is, most Yi died before X's birth. Moreover, an author does not write from his birth; rather, he usually begins near his death. Thus, a greedy assumption would be that X was born no earlier than the death of the latest author mentioned by X minus MIN.

Greedy rule for defining the birth year based only on authors who are mentioned by X with the key-phrase "friend"

$$B(X) <= MIN(B(Yi)) + RABBI\_DIS \quad (13 \ (G))$$

When taking into account only references that are mentioned by X, which are related to contemporary authors, a greedy rule could be that X was born no later than the birth of the earliest author mentioned by X with the key-phrase "friend". Because many times the older author refers to the younger author as "friend", we need to add RABBI_DIS.

Greedy rule for defining the birth year based only on authors who are mentioned by X with the key-phrase "rabbi"

$$B(X) <= MIN(B(Yi)) + RABBI\_DIS \quad (14 \ (G))$$

When taking into account only references written in X's texts, which are related to contemporary authors, a greedy rule could be that X was born no later than the birth of the earliest author mentioned by X as a "rabbi". Due to the age difference between a student and his rabbi being approximately 20 years, we need to add RABBI_DIS.

Greedy rule for defining the death year of X based only on authors who referred to X with the key-phrase "late"

$$D(X) <= MIN(B(Yi)) + MIN \quad (15 \ (G))$$

When taking into account only references written in Yi texts that refer to X with the key-phrase "late", a greedy assumption could be that X died no later than the birth of the earliest author who referred to X with the key-phrase "late"; because an author does not writes from birth, we need to add MIN.

Greedy rule for defining the death year of X based only on authors who referred to X with the key-phrase "friend"

$$D(X) >= MAX(D(Yi)) - RABBI\_DIS \quad (16\ (G))$$

When taking into account only references written in Yi texts that refer to X with the key-phrase "friend", all Yi must have been alive when X was alive, and all of them must have been old enough to publish; also, many times, the older author refers to the younger author with the key-phrase "friend", and the opposite never occurs. Therefore, a greedy assumption would be that X died no earlier than the death of the latest author who referred to X with the key-phrase "friend" minus RABBI_DIS.

Greedy rule for defining the death year of X based only on authors who referred to X with the key-phrase "rabbi"

$$D(X) >= MAX(D(Yi)) - RABBI\_DIS \quad (17\ (G))$$

This follows the same principle as the rule for defining the birth year, but because this time the student mentions the rabbi, we need to reduce RABBI_DIS.

4.3   Birth and Death Year Tuning

Application of the Heuristic and Greedy rules can lead to abnormalities, such as an author's death age being unreasonably old or young. Another possible anomaly is that the algorithm may result in a death year greater than the current year (i.e., 2015). Hence, we added some tuning rules: D – death year, B – birth year, age = D – B.

Current Year: if (D > 2015) {D = 2015}, i.e., if the current year is 2015, then the algorithm must not give a death year greater than 2015.

Age: if (age > 100), {z = age − 100; D = D − z/2; B = B + z/2}, and if (age < 30), {z = 30 − age; D = D + z/2; B = B − z/2}. Our postulate is that a writer lived at least 30 years and no more than 100 years. Thus, if the age according to the algorithm is greater than 100, we take the difference between that age and 100, and then we divide that difference by 2 and normalize D and B to result in an age of 100.

4.4   Example of the Use of a Certain Heuristic Rule and the Key-Phrase "Late"

Below we present texts written by Rabbi Herzog Yitzchak (1889–1959):

(1) שו"ת היכל יצחק אבן העזר ב סימן מג

... ויעויין ב"ח סי' קל"ד שהקדימני בחילוקי בין לפני הכתיבה וכו' (לב"ח זה העירני הרב הגר"י עדס,
חד מבי דינא רבא שליט"א) ...

(1) Responsa Hechal Yitzchak Even HaEzer part 2 chapter 43

... and inspecting (book) bayit chadash chapter 134 that was ahead of me to the
differences between before writing etc. (to this bayit chadash, turned my attention the
genius Rabbi **Yehuda Ades**, One of the religious court judges of the court shlit"a) ...

(2) שו"ת היכל יצחק אבן העזר ב סימן מז

... והנה אני מתבונן עכשיו בשו"ת מהרש"ם ז"ל בחלק ב' סימן ק"מ בענין החרשים אלמים מסוג זה
שגמרו ביה"ס שלהם ... שגט חרש הוא ככל הגטין, לא מתחוור לי כלל. ולדעתי אין ההשגות של
הגרבצ"ע ז"ל עומדות כנגדו.

(2) Responsa Hechal Yitzchak Even HaEzer part 2 chapter 47

... and here I am now looking at the responsa of **Maharsham** *of blessed memory* in
part 2 chapter 140 in the matter of deaf mute who finished their school ... that the
divorce certificate of a deaf is as like divorce certificates, It is not clear to me at all. And
in my opinion the objections of the genius Rabbi **Ben-Zion Uziel** *of blessed memory*
are not opposite to him.

(3) שו"ת היכל יצחק אבן העזר ב סימן עז

תשובת הגאון בעל חזון איש זצ"ל בשאלה הקודמת ...

(3) Responsa Hechal Yitzchak Even HaEzer part 2 chapter 77

The response of the genius the author of **Chazon Ish** book *of blessed memory* in the
previous question ...

Figure 4 shows the timeline of the authors that are relevant to the texts that appear
above (Table 2).

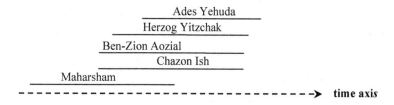

Fig. 4. Herzog Yitzchak refers to other fore Rabbis

Table 2. Birth and death years of authors that relate to the example

Name	Birth	Death	Mentioned as "late"
Maharsham	1835	1911	Yes
Chazon Ish	1879	1954	Yes
Ben-Zion Uziel	1880	1953	Yes
Herzog Yitzchak	1889	1959	— (the author)
Ades Yehuda	1898	1963	No

We use a heuristic rule to improve the assessment of the death year of Rabbi Herzog Yitzchak:

Activate the iron rule (formula (0(I))): $D(X) >= MAX(B(Yi)) \rightarrow D(X) >= 1898$ (Distance from the real death year (1959) is 61)

Activate the heuristic rule (formula (1(H))): $D(X) >= MAX(B(Yi)) + min \rightarrow D(X) >= 1898 + 30 = 1928$ (Distance from the real death year (1959) is 31)

We use the key-phrase "late" to improve the assessment of the death year of Rabbi Herzog Yitzchak:

Activate the iron rule (formula (0(I))): $D(X) >= MAX(B(Yi)) \rightarrow D(X) >= 1898$ (Distance from the real death year (1959) is 61)

Activate the iron key-phrase "late" rule (formula (5(I))): $D(X) >= MAX(D(Yi))$ $D(X) > = 1953$ (Distance from the real death year (1959) is 6)

We can see that the heuristic rule (1(H)) improves the result. However, with the use of the key-phrase "late", rule (5(I)), the result is much better.

5   The Model

The main steps of the model are presented below

1. **Cleaning the texts.** Because the responsa may have undergone some editing, we must make sure to ignore the possible effects of differences in the texts resulting from variant editing practices. Therefore, we eliminate all orthographic variations.
2. **Boosting mining key-phrases and key-words.**
3. **Normalizing the references in the texts.** For each author, we normalize all types of references that refer to him (e.g., various variants and spellings of his name, books, documents and their nicknames and abbreviations). For each author, we collect all references syntactic styles that refer to him and then replace them with a unique string.
4. **Building indexes,** e.g., authors, references to "late"/"friend"/"rabbi", and calculating the frequencies of each item.
5. **Performing various combinations of "iron-clad" and heuristic rules** on the one hand **and greedy rules** on the other hand to estimate the birth and death years of each tested author.
6. **Calculating averages** for the best "iron-clad", heuristic and greedy versions.

6 Examined Corpus, Experiments and Results

The documents of the examined corpus were downloaded from Bar-Ilan University's Responsa Project. The examined corpus contains 15,495 responsa written by 24 scholars, averaging 643 files for each scholar. The total number of characters in the whole corpus is 127,683,860 chars, and the average number of chars for each file is 8,240 chars. These authors lived over a period of 229 years (1786–2015). These files contain references; each reference pattern can be expanded into many other specific references [26].

Reference identification was performed by comparing each word to a list of 339 known authors and many of their books. This list of 25,801 specific references refers to the names, nicknames and abbreviations of these authors and their writings. Basic references were collected and all other references were produced from them.

We split the data into two corpora: (1) 10,561 responsa authored by 12 rabbis, with an average of 876 files for each scholar and each file containing an average of 1800 words spread over 135 years (1880–2015); (2) 15,495 responsa authored by 24 rabbis, with an average of 643 files for each rabbi and each file containing an average of 1609 words spread over 229 years (1786–2015) (the set of 24 rabbis contains the group of 12 rabbis). For more detailed information on the data set, refer to Table 5 in the appendix at the end of this article.

Because of the nature of the problem, it is difficult to appraise the results in the sense that although we can compare how close the system guess is to the actual birth or death years, we cannot assess how good the results are, i.e., there is no real notion of what a 'good' result is. For now, we use the notion Distance, which is defined as the estimated value minus the ground truth value.

The outcomes appear in the following histograms. Each histogram shows the results of one algorithm – Iron+Heuristic or Greedy. Each algorithm was performed on two groups of authors: a group of 12 writers and a group of 24 writers. For both algorithm executions, there are outcomes containing estimated birth years and death years. The results shown in the histograms are the best birth/death date deviation results. In every histogram, there are eight columns; there are two quartets of columns in each histogram: the right quartet indicates the deviation from the death year, while the left quartet indicates deviations from the birth year. Each column represents a deviation without a key-phrase or with the year that was mentioned in the text, a deviation with the "late" key-phrase, with the "rabbi" key-phrase, and with the "friend" key-phrase. Moreover, we used two manipulations – Age and Current year. The column with a gray background contains the best results. Each histogram contains 8 columns (results); there are 16 histograms, so there are, in total, 128 results.

The Age manipulation is very helpful; we used it in 94.5% of the experiments (i.e., $121/128 = 0.945$) for all of the refinements, in both algorithms, with or without constants.

Examination of the effect of mentioning a year, listed in Figs. 5, 6, 7 and 8, compared with Figs. 9, 10, 11 and 12 regarding death year deviation, indicates that the contribution of referencing a year leads to an improvement of 2.8 years on average.

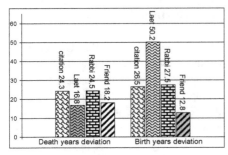

Fig. 5. 12 authors I+H no constant

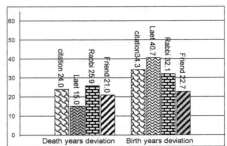

Fig. 6. 24 authors I+H no constant

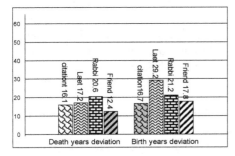

Fig. 7. 12 authors Greedy no constant

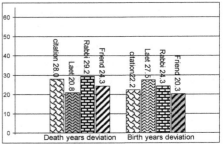

Fig. 8. 24 authors Greedy no constant

This phenomenon is more noticeable in Iron+Heuristic (average upswing of 4.2 years) than with Greedy (average deviation upswing of 1.4 years). The main reason for this is that a writer usually writes until close to his death. Additionally, when a year is mentioned in the text, it is often the year in which the writer wrote the document. Because an author writes, in many cases, until near his death year, the maximum year mentioned in his texts is close to the year of his death.

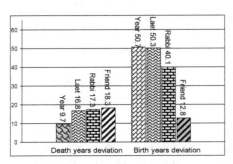

Fig. 9. 12 authors I+H no constant

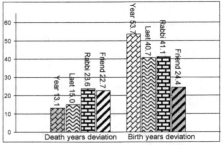

Fig. 10. 24 authors I+H no constant

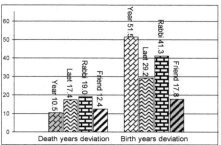

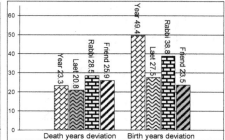

Fig. 11. 12 authors Greedy no constant

Fig. 12. 24 authors Greedy no constant

In contrast to the death year assessment, birth year assessment has a negative impact; the deviation increases by 10.4 years, on average. It is essential to note that we are now evaluating the impact of the year mentioned in the text. If the results without using the year mentioned are better than the results using the year mentioned, it means that we should not use it. For example: the result of the birth year using Greedy rules, without year mentioning and without any refinement, for the 12 authors has a deviation of 16.7 years. After using the year mentioned, the deviation is 51.5 years, decreasing the accuracy by 34.83 years. The result of the birth year using the Iron+Heuristic, without year mentioning and without key-phrases, for the 12 authors has a deviation of 26.5 years. After using a reference to years, the deviation is 50.7 years, decreasing the accuracy by 24.2 years, i.e., the deviation with the use of year mentioning is greater. An analysis of the formulas shows that the formula that determines the birth year in the Greedy (10(G)) uses the most recent year the writer writes in his texts. The most recent year that the rabbi mentions is usually near his death, as explained above; therefore, very poor birth results are obtained, with a decline of 12.5 years. The results of the Greedy are better than Iron+Heuristic (decline of 8.4 years), but the effect of year mentioning on the results of Iron+Heuristic is less harmful. Thus, to estimate the death year, we will use the Iron+Heuristic algorithm with the use of year mentioning without any key-phrases.

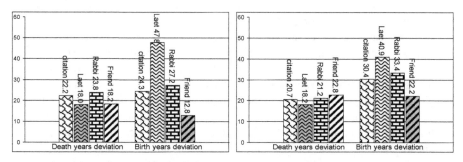

Fig. 13. 12 authors I+H with constant   **Fig. 14.** 24 authors I+H with constant

The use of the key-phrase "friend" for birth year assessment gives the best results compared with the other key-phrases – "late", "rabbi" or none. This is because friends are of the same generation and more or less the same age; thus, they are born in roughly the same year. Thus, for a writer addressing another author as his friend, the assessment of his birth year will give good results. For the death year, however, this is not assured because there may be a much greater period between the deaths of friends (one may die at the age of 50, while his friend at the age 75). Hence, the "friend" key-phrase usually gives better birth year assessment than death year assessment.

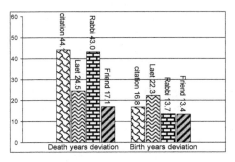

Fig. 15. 12 authors Greedy with constant

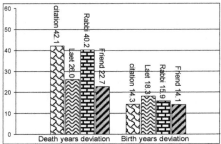

Fig. 16. 24 authors Greedy with constant

After we found that the best results for the birth year are always with the "friend" key-phrase (except for one case), we investigated at greater depth and found that this occurs specifically with the use of constants. Constants are important, resulting in an average improvement of 6.3 years in the case of Greedy (for the 12 and 24 authors). In general, a Posek is addressed in responsa after he has become important enough to be mentioned and regarded in the Halachic Responsa, which is usually at an advanced age.

We stated above that the use of Greedy rules with constants gives the greatest improvement. Even without the use of constants, Greedy produces the best results. The reason lies in the formulae; formula (13(G)) finds the lowest birth year from the group of authors that the arbiter mentioned. Unlike the Greedy, the Iron+Heuristic formula (7 (H)) reduces the constant (at present, 20); therefore, the results of the Greedy are better. In conclusion, to best assess the birth year, we apply the Greedy algorithm, using constants and also the key-phrase "friend".

The best results when evaluating birth year occurred when using the Greedy algorithm with constants and without mentioning years. The best results when evaluating death year occurred when using the Iron+Heuristic algorithm with constants and without mentioning years. When we compare these results with the results shown in Figs. 17, 18, 19 and 20 we find that in the case of Greedy, when we add more authors, there is an improvement only in one case, i.e., for the 12 authors using the "late" key-phrase; the remaining results show a decline in performance. The reason for this phenomenon may lie in the Greedy formula; when an author is more successful, in addition to being mentioned by others many times, he is mentioned at a younger age by authors that are older than him; therefore, the estimation is less accurate. For example:

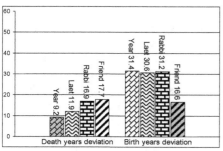

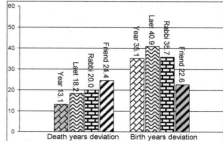

Fig. 17. 12 authors I+H with constant and year

Fig. 18. 24 authors I+H with constant and year

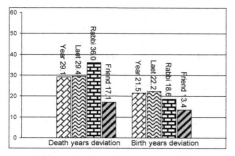

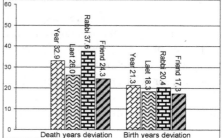

Fig. 19. 12 authors Greedy with constant and year

Fig. 20. 24 authors Greedy with constant and year

the estimation of the death year of the late Rabbi Ovadia Yosef has an error of 61 years (instead of 2014, the algorithm result is 1953), determining that he died at an age of 34; using the Iron+Heuristic algorithm, there was a decrease in two results and an improvement in 5 results. For Iron+Heuristic, there is an average improvement of 0.64 years and, in fact, the best death year result estimation. The quality of the Greedy algorithm birth year results estimation using year mentioning pretty severely impairs the results (explained above). A possible explanation for this is that the improvement that comes from using constants cannot overcome the deterioration that comes from year mentioning. In contrast, when assessing the death year, using year mentioning with Iron+Heuristic significantly improves the results, and using constants improves them a little more; therefore, a combination of constants + year mentioning brings better assessment of the death year. Therefore, when assessing birth year and death year, it is not enough to use references; we have to use key-words and key-phrases. To estimate death year, we will use the year(s) mentioned in the text and constants with the Iron+Heuristic algorithm; to estimate birth year, we will run the Greedy algorithm using constants and the "friend" key-phrase without year mentioning.

The Effect of the Relatively Larger Corpus

We compared between the results that achieved for the corpora containing responsa written by 12 and by 24 authors. We enlarged not only the number of authors but also the number of the responsa; from 10,561 files for 12 authors to 15,495 files for 24 authors and from 19,011,130 words for 12 authors to 24,930,082 words for 24 authors. The time-frame of the 12 authors spread over 135 years, while the time-frame of the 24 authors spread over 229 years. Because the span of the years of 24 authors is almost twice bigger than time-frame of the 12 authors, we must compare the results relative to the year's amplitude. When we analyze the results proportionally to the span of the years, we find that when we have a larger data-set we get better results (for 90.6% of the results as shown in Figs. 5, 6, 7, 8, 9, 10, 11, 12, 13, 14, 15, 16, 17, 18, 19 and 20). For instance, in Fig. 17, (12 authors) the smallest deviation predicting death year, i.e., the deviation of the best result, is 9.2, $9.2/135 \rightarrow 6.8\%$; in Fig. 18, (24 authors) the smallest deviation predicting death year is 13.1, $13.1/229 \rightarrow 5.7\%$ (improvement of 16%). In Fig. 17, (12 authors) the smallest deviation predicting birth year is 16.6, $16.6/135 \rightarrow 12.3\%$; in Fig. 18, (24 authors) the smallest deviation predicting birth year is 22.6, $22.6/229 \rightarrow 9.8\%$ (improvement of 20%).

The number of a general citation composed of a name/acronym/abbreviation/ \book-title of an author is very large (see Table 3). In many cases, the references to author appear with affixes of Rabbi, friend or "late" (see Sect. 3.1). A citation with time-related phrase is a citation of author's name and it is close to the time-related phrase. This fact leads us to the fact that the number of occurrences of general citations contains the number of occurrences of reference with time-related phrases. From Table 3 we can see that the number of general citations and "late" citations occurrences are the largest, also per author, so we would expect them to be the most influential. However, as we wrote above, the experiments indicate that the best results are using time-related phrases of a friend and references to years.

Table 3. Full details about the citations in the corpora

Citation	12 authors	24 authors	Average citation per author	12 authors	24 authors
General citation	314831	404116	General citation	26235.9	16838.2
"Late" citation	10492	12974	"Late" citation	874.3	540.6
"Rabbi" citation	14	39	"Rabbi" citation	1.2	1.6
"Friend" citation	707	813	"Friend" citation	58.9	33.9
Year citation	691	833	Year citation	57.6	34.7

From a glance at Table 3 the time-related phrase "Rabbi" is negligible certainly relative to other time-related phrases. We also can see that the number of occurrences of "Rabbi" time-related phrase is the lowest, and per author it is less than two. But when we look deeper, we see that despite the minimal number of occurrences to time-related phrase "Rabbi" it sometimes gives better results than general citations or references to the time-related phrase "late" (the two, general citation and "late" time-related phrase are with the largest number of occurrences). For example, Fig. 15, the greedy algorithm for the birth year assessment using references to time-related phrase "Rabbi" gives a deviation of 13.7 years from the truth birth years; in the same Fig. 15, references to "late" time-related phrase gives a result of 22.3 years deviation, which is worse by 62.8%. Also in Fig. 15, a general citation gives deviation of 16.8 years which is worse by 22.6% compared to the "Rabbi" time-related phrase. We can see a similar phenomenon in Figs. 6 and 9 using the Iron+Heuristic algorithm to estimate the birth years. The phenomenon that the key-phrase with a few occurrences can achieve a better result than a key-phrase with many occurrences is due to the structure of the rules (Sects. 4.1 and 4.2). The rules are using the minimum and the maximum functions. Because the nature of the minimum/maximum functions a few occurrences of citations can affect the results. As a result, occasionally the references to the time-related phrase "Rabbi" (which appears a few times) give better results than using the general citations or "late" time-related phrase that appear much more.

Current Research Versus First Research

In this research, various novelties are presented comparing to HaCohen-Kerner and Mughaz [25]:

1. There are two corpora of responsa composed by 12 authors and 24 authors, instead of one corpus (12 authors and with a far fewer files);
2. There is a use of years that are mentioned in the text documents (the text was not labeled with a date or year but sometimes years can appear in the text, e.g., quotation from a contract, which contains the year of the agreement);
3. Heuristics were added to the Greedy algorithm by adding a few greedy constraints;
4. New Rabbi's constrains were formulated;
5. Two new manipulations, "Current Year" and "Age" were added.

HaCohen-Kerner and Mughaz [25] examined a corpus, which includes 3,488 responsa authored by 12 Jewish rabbinic scholars, while in this research the current corpus for 24 authors contains 15,495 responsa and the current corpus for 12 authors contains 10,561 responsa. The 3,488 responsa used in HaCohen-Kerner and Mughaz [25] are included in these 10,561 responsa.

Table 4 presents a comparison between the results of our current work and the best results of HaCohen-Kerner and Mughaz [25]. This table shows that three results (out of four results) for 12 authors in the current research are much better (in their quality) than the corresponding results reported in HaCohen-Kerner and Mughaz [25]. Only one

Table 4. Current results vs. HaCohen-Kerner and Mughaz [25] results for the 12 authors corpus (the results are with years deviation)

Rule type	Birth/Death	HaCohen-Kerner and Mughaz [25]	Current results
Iron+Heuristic	Birth	22	12.8 (Fig. 5)
	Death	22.67	9.2 (Fig. 17)
Greedy	Birth	13.04	13.42 (Figs. 15 and 19)
	Death	15.54	10.5 (Fig. 11)

result (the birth years using the Greedy algorithm) was slightly worse. The results of 24 authors were not presented in HaCohen-Kerner and Mughaz [25].

Using the Iron+Heuristic algorithm, we reduced the years deviation, compared to HaCohen-Kerner and Mughaz [25], for death years by 60% (from 22.67 to 9.2 years) and for birth years by 42% (from 22 to 12.8 years). Using the Greedy algorithm, we reduce the deviation for death years by 32% (from 15.54 to 10.5 years); however for the birth years we got a slightly worse result of about 3% (from 13.04 to 13.4 years).

7   Summary, Conclusions and Future Work

We investigated the estimation of the birth and death years of authors using year mentioning, the "late" ("of blessed memory") key-phrase, the "rabbi" key-phrase, the "friend" key-phrase and undated references that are mentioned in documents of other dated authors that refer to author being considered or those mentioned by him. This research was performed on responsa documents, where special writing rules are applied. The estimation was based on the author's texts and texts of other authors who refer to the discussed author or are mentioned by him. To do so, we formulated various types of iron-clad, heuristic and greedy rules. The best birth year assessment was achieved by using the Greedy algorithm with constants and the "friend" key-phrase. The best death year assessment was achieved by using the Iron+Heuristic algorithm with year mentioning.

We plan to improve this research by (1) testing new combinations of iron-clad, heuristic and greedy rules, as well as a combination of key-phrases (e.g., "late" and "friend"); (2) improving existing rules and/or formulating new rules; (3) defining and applying heuristic rules that take into account various details included in the responsa, e.g., events, names of people, new concepts and collocations that can be dated; (4) conducting additional experiments using many more responsa written by more authors to improve the estimates; (5) checking why the iron-clad, heuristic and greedy rules tend to produce more positive differences; and (6) testing how much of an improvement we can obtain from a correction of the upper bound of D(x) and how much we will, at some point, use it for a corpus with long-dead authors.

Appendix

Data Set Information.

Table 5. Full details about the data set

# of authors		Death year	Birth year	Author's name	# of files	# of words	# of chars
24	12	2015	1914	Vozner Shmuel	1807	1,490,463	7,768,059
		2014	1920	Yosef Ovadya	1283	4,578,049	22,933,473
		2006	1917	Waldenberg Eliezer	1639	3,197,662	16,589,888
		1995	1910	Auerbach Shlomo Zalman	229	793,706	4,087,592
		1989	1902	Weiss Yitzchak	1468	2,311,927	11,695,021
		1989	1911	Stern Bezalel	663	1,080,452	5,390,661
		1986	1895	Feinstein Moshe	1831	2,306,526	11,959,224
		1969	1890	Hadaya Ovadia	210	713,341	3,683,787
		1963	1898	Ades Yaakov	131	310,585	1,604,218
		1959	1901	Havita Rahamim	736	898,543	4,655,681
		1959	1889	Herzog Yitzchak	190	430,259	2,210,586
		1953	1880	Ben-Zion Meir Hai Uziel	374	899,617	4,621,414
		1948	1880	Boimel Yehoshua	129	237,093	1,227,007
		1942	1873	Baer Weiss Yitzchak	497	243,789	1,257,633
		1935	1865	Kook Abraham Yitzchak	681	750,145	3,892,610
		1921	1854	Allouch Faraji	112	205,258	1,069,460
		1911	1835	Schwadron Sholom Mordechai	1574	1,657,860	8,560,084
		1889	1813	Somekh Abdallah	86	80,508	412,486
		1896	1817	Spektor Yitzchak Elchanan	301	1,159,019	5,843,696
		1893	1820	Trunk Israel Yehoshua	281	132,257	689,598
		1880	1790	Abuhatzeira Yaakov	146	177,411	917,682
		1874	1801	Edery Abraham	119	176,849	918,564
		1866	1794	Assad Yehuda	882	880,361	4,565,230
		1843	1786	Birdugo Yaakov	126	218,402	1,130,206

References

1. Powley, B., Dale, R.: Evidence-based information extraction for high accuracy citation and author name identification. In: RIAO 2007 (2007)
2. Wintner, S.: Hebrew computational linguistics: past and future. Artif. Intell. Rev. **21**(2), 113–138 (2004)
3. HaCohen-Kerner, Y., Kass, A., Peretz, A.: HAADS: A Hebrew Aramaic abbreviation disambiguation system. J. Am. Soc. Inf. Sci. Technol. JASIST **61**(9), 1923–1932 (2010)

4. Gutwin, C., Paynter, G., Witten, I., Nevill-Manning, C., Frank, E.: Improving browsing in digital libraries with key-phrase indexes. Decis. Support Syst. **27**(1), 81–104 (1999)
5. Zhang, Y., Zincir-Heywood, N., Milios, E.: World wide web site summarization. Web Intell. Agent Syst. **2**(1), 39–53 (2004)
6. Hulth, A., Megyesi, B.B.: A study on automatically extracted key-words in text categorization. In: Proceedings of the 21st International Conference on Computational Linguistics and the 44th Annual Meeting of the ACL, pp. 537–544 (2006)
7. Kim, S.N., Baldwin, T.: Extracting key-words from multi-party live chats. In: Proceedings of the 26th Pacific Asia Conference on Language, Information, and Computation, pp. 199–208 (2012)
8. Berend, G.: Opinion expression mining by exploiting key-phrase extraction. In: IJCNLP, pp. 1162–1170 (2011)
9. Liu, Z., Huang, W., Zheng, Y., Sun, M.: Automatic key-phrase extraction via topic decomposition. In: Proceedings of the 2010 Conference on Empirical Methods in Natural Language Processing, pp. 366–376. ACL (2010)
10. Hasan, K.S., Ng, V.: Conundrums in unsupervised key-phrase extraction: making sense of the state-of-the-art. In: Proceedings of the 23rd International Conference on Computational Linguistics: Posters, pp. 365–373. ACL (2010)
11. Medelyan, O., Frank, E., Witten, I.H.: Human-competitive tagging using automatic key-phrase extraction. In: Proceedings of the 2009 Conference on Empirical Methods in Natural Language Processing, vol. 3, pp. 1318–1327. ACL (2009)
12. Kim, S.N., Medelyan, O., Kan, M.Y., Baldwin, T.: Automatic key-phrase extraction from scientific articles. Lang. Resour. Eval. **47**(3), 723–742 (2013)
13. Yih, W.T., Goodman, J., Carvalho, V.R.: Finding advertising key-words on web pages. In: Proceedings of the 15th International Conference on World Wide Web, pp. 213–222. ACM (2006)
14. Schomaker, L., Bulacu, M.: Automatic writer identification using connected-component contours and edge-based features of uppercase western script. IEEE Trans. Pattern Anal. Mach. Intell. **26**(6), 787–798 (2004)
15. Said, H., Tan, T., Baker, K.: Personal identification based on handwriting. Pattern Recogn. **33**(1), 149–160 (2000)
16. Bulacu, M., Schomaker, L.: Text-independent writer identification and verification using textural and allographic features. IEEE Trans. Pattern Anal. Mach. Intell. **29**(4), 701–717 (2007)
17. Bar-Yosef, I., Beckman, I., Kedem, K., Dinstein, I.: Binarization, character extraction, and writer identification of historical Hebrew calligraphy documents. IJDAR **9**(2–4), 89–99 (2007)
18. Garfield, E.: Can citation indexing be automated? In: Stevens, M. (ed.) Statistical Association Methods for Mechanical Documentation, Symposium Proceedings, vol. 269, pp. 189–192. National Bureau of Standards Miscellaneous Publication, Washington, D.C. (1965)
19. Berkowitz, E., Elkhadiri, M.R.: Creation of a Style Independent Intelligent Autonomous Citation Indexer to Support Academic Research, pp. 68–73 (2004)
20. Giuffrida, G., Shek, E.C., Yang, J.: Knowledge-based metadata extraction from postscript files. In: Proceedings of the 5th ACM conference on Digital libraries, pp. 77–84. ACM (2000)
21. Seymore, K., McCallum, A., Rosenfeld, R.: Learning hidden Markov model structure for information extraction. In: AAAI-1999 Workshop on Machine Learning for Information Extraction, pp. 37–42 (1999)

22. Ritchie, A., Robertson, S., Teufel, S.: Comparing citation contexts for information retrieval. In: The 17th ACM Conference on Information and Knowledge Management (CIKM), pp. 213–222 (2008)
23. Bradshaw, S.: Reference directed indexing: redeeming relevance for subject search in citation indexes. In: Koch, T., Sølvberg, I.T. (eds.) ECDL 2003. LNCS, vol. 2769, pp. 499–510. Springer, Heidelberg (2003). doi:10.1007/978-3-540-45175-4_45
24. HaCohen-Kerner, Y., Beck, H., Yehudai, E., Rosenstein, M., Mughaz, D.: Cuisine: classification using stylistic feature sets and/or name-based feature sets. J. Am. Soc. Inf. Sci. Technol. (JASIST) 61(8), 1644–1657 (2010)
25. HaCohen-Kerner, Y., Mughaz, D.: Estimating the birth and death years of authors of undated documents using undated citations. In: Loftsson, H., Rögnvaldsson, E., Helgadóttir, S. (eds.) NLP 2010. LNCS, vol. 6233, pp. 138–149. Springer, Heidelberg (2010). doi:10.1007/978-3-642-14770-8_17
26. HaCohen-Kerner, Y., Schweitzer, N., Mughaz, D.: Automatically identifying citations in Hebrew-Aramaic documents. Cybern. Syst.: Int. J. 42(3), 180–197 (2011)

Toward Optimized Multimodal Concept Indexing

Navid Rekabsaz[1]([⊠]), Ralf Bierig[2], Mihai Lupu[1], and Allan Hanbury[1]

[1] Information and Software Engineering Group, Vienna University of Technology,
1040 Vienna, Austria
{rekabsaz,lupu,hanbury}@ifs.tuwien.ac.at
[2] School of Computing, National College of Ireland, Dublin 1, Ireland
ralf.bierig@ncirl.ie

Abstract. Information retrieval on the (social) web moves from a pure term-frequency-based approach to an enhanced method that includes conceptual multimodal features on a semantic level. In this paper, we present an approach for semantic-based keyword search and focus especially on its optimization to scale it to real-world sized collections in the social media domain. Furthermore, we present a faceted indexing framework and architecture that relates content to semantic concepts to be indexed and searched semantically. We study the use of textual concepts in a social media domain and observe a significant improvement from using a concept-based solution for keyword searching. We address the problem of time-complexity that is a critical issue for concept-based methods by focusing on optimization to enable larger and more real-world style applications.

Keywords: Semantic indexing · Concept · Social web · Word2Vec

1 Introduction

The past decade has witnessed the massive growth of the social web, the continued impact and expansion of the world wide web and the increasing importance and synergy of content modalities, such as text, images, videos, opinions, and other data. There are currently about 200 active social networks[1] that attract visitors in the range of the 100s of millions each month. Online visitors spend considerable amounts of time on social network platforms where they constantly contribute, consume, and implicitly evaluate content. The Facebook community alone, with over 1.2 billion members, shares the impressive amount of 30 billion pieces of content every month [17]. The knowledge contained in these massive data networks is unprecedented and, when harvested, can be made useful for many applications. Although research has started to automatically mine information from these rich sources, the problem of knowledge extraction from multimedia content remains difficult. The main challenges are the heterogeneity

---

[1] http://en.wikipedia.org/wiki/List_of_social_networking_websites.

© Springer International Publishing AG 2017
N.T. Nguyen et al. (Eds.): TCCI XXVI, LNCS 10190, pp. 144–161, 2017.
DOI: 10.1007/978-3-319-59268-8_7

of the data, the scalability of the processing methods and the reliability of their predictions.

In order to address these challenges in the social web domain, recent researches exploit the use of semantics in multimodal information retrieval and specially in image retrieval [12]. However, the focus resided on image processing and, so far, the methods used for text similarity for the purpose of multimodal retrieval are fairly mainstream [24]. In this work, we focus on semantic-based keyword search while specifically considering the optimization of the processing time, thus making our approach manageable in an information system.

This paper has four contributions. The *first* contribution presents a general investigation into semantic similarity matching for three types of information retrieval tasks: sentence paraphrasing, sentence-to-paragraph similarity matching and document matching. We applied a semantic similarity algorithm with a threshold filter to leverage its semantic preciseness. While discovering that the chosen threshold has a large effect on performance, we also found that only certain tasks benefit from such a parameterized approach. As the *second* contribution, we explored the effect of semantic similarity and optimization methods in text-based image retrieval in social media by applying Word2Vec [18] and Random Indexing (RI) [23]. This represents one possible form for a semantic concept index. As the *third* contribution we provide an optimization for these algorithms to allow them to scale to real-world collection sizes for more effective semantic-based keyword search on the (social) web. With an execution time that is about 40 times slower than standard TF-IDF in Solr, especially with longer documents, it is clear that optimization is paramount for allowing semantic search to become applicable and useful. We applied and evaluated two optimization techniques to contribute to this essential and important goal. The *fourth* contribution is a framework for integrating and evaluating algorithms and methods for semantic indexing and keyword search. It is designed as a combined faceted index for multimodal content collections, such as MediaEval Diverse Images [10,11]. The framework is based on a flexible document model and incorporates concepts as a semantic extension toward more generalized forms of information search that exceed the classic bag-of-words approach. The interlinked nature of these parts has the benefit of being flexible with respect to many kinds of multimodal and also multilingual documents. Each of these facets can be transformed into a semantic representation based on a dynamic and exchangable set of algorithms. The index itself is implemented effectively by using flexible facet indices that can be combined within a flexible document format based on the data at hand. The previous contributions additionally serve as an application use-case for this framework.

The following section describes the related work surrounding the domains of faceted, multi-modal and semantic indexing and search. In particular, we cover concept-based information retrieval. We describe our indexing architecture together with an application example of semantic index in Sects. 4 and 3. Focusing on questions of optimization, we explain two methods, followed by discussion and comparison in Sect. 5. We summarize our findings in Sect. 6, and subsequently elaborate on a range of future plans.

2   Related Work

While different modalities often occur together in the same document (scientific paper, website, blog, etc.), search through these modalities is usually done for each modality in isolation. It is well known that combining information from multiple modalities assists in retrieval tasks. For instance, the results of the ImageCLEF campaign's photographic retrieval task have shown that combining image and text information results in better retrieval performance than text alone [19]. There are two fundamental approaches to fusing information from multiple modalities: early fusion and late fusion [8].

Late fusion is widely used, as it avoids working in a single fused feature space but, instead, fusing results by reordering them based on the scores from the individual systems. Clinchant et al. [4] propose and test a number of late fusion approaches involving the sum or product combination of weighted scores from text and image retrieval systems. Difficulties arise from

- weights that must be fixed in advance or that need to be learned from difficult to obtain training data
- modality weights that might be query dependent and
- weights that are sensitive to the IR system performance for the various modalities [8]

Separate queries are needed for each modality, so that for example to find a picture of a cat in a database of annotated images, one would need to provide a picture of a cat and text about the cat. There are ways of getting around this limitation, such as choosing the images for the top returned text documents as seeds in an image search [8], but these are generally ad-hoc.

With early fusion, a query would not have to contain elements from all modalities in the dataset. To continue the previous example, pictures of a cat could be found only with text input. Early fusion suffers from the problem that text tends to sparsely inhabit a large feature space, while non-text features have denser distributions in a small feature space. It is however possible to represent images sparsely in higher-dimensional feature spaces through the use of bags of 'visual words' [5] that are obtained by clustering local image features. The simplest approach to early fusion is to simply concatenate the feature vectors from different modalities. However, concatenated feature vectors become less distinctive, due to the curse of dimensionality [8], making this approach rather ineffective. A solution proposed by Magalhaes and Rüeger [16] is to transform the feature vectors to reduce the dimension of the text feature vectors and increase the dimension of the image feature vectors using the minimum description length (MDL) principle.

Textual features has been used in many multimodal retrieval systems. For instance, recently, Eskevich et al. [9] considered a wide range of text retrieval methods in the context of multimodal search for medical data, while Sabetghadam et al. [22] used text features in a graph-based model to retrieve images from Wikipedia. However, these works do not particularly exploit text semantics.

In the text retrieval community, text semantics started with Latent Semantic Analysis/Indexing (LSA/LSI) [7], the pioneer approach that initiated a new trend in surface text analysis. LSA was also used for image retrieval [20], but the method's practicality is limited by efficiency and scalability issues caused by the high-dimensional matrices it operates on. Explicit Semantic Analysis (ESA) is one of the early alternatives, aimed at reducing the computational load [14]. However, unlike LSA, ESA relies on a pre-existing set of concepts, which may not always be available. Random Indexing (RI) [23] is another alternative to LSA/LSI that creates context vectors based on the occurrence of word contexts. It has the benefit of being incremental and operating with significantly less resources while producing similar inductive results as LSA/LSI and not relying on any pre-existing knowledge. Word2Vec [18] further expands this approach while being highly incremental and scalable. When trained on large datasets, it is also possible to capture many linguistic subtleties (e.g., similar relation between Italy and Rome in comparison to France and Paris) that allow basic arithmetic operations within the model. This, in principle, allows exploiting the implicit knowledge within corpora. All of these methods represent the words in vector spaces.

In order to compare the text semantic approaches, Baroni et al. [3] systematically evaluates a set of models with parameter settings across a wide range of lexical semantics tasks. They observe an overall better performance of state-of-the-art context-based models (e.g., Word2Vec) than the classic methods (e.g., LSA).

Approaching the text semantics, Liu et al. [15] introduced the Histogram for Textual Concepts (HTC) method to map tags to a concept dictionary. However, the method is reminiscent of ESA described above, and it was never evaluated for the purpose of text-based image retrieval.

3   Concept-Based Multimedia Retrieval

In this section, first we explain the architecture of our system for semantic indexing and keyword search.

We introduce a framework for multimodal concept and facet-based information retrieval and, in the scope of this paper, focus on the indexing component, particularly the semantic indexing features. The interaction between the components of the indexing framework is depicted in Fig. 1. These components represent the conceptual building blocks of the indexing architecture as part of the general framework. The figure presents the document model, the concept model and the indexing model with its individual document facets, such as text-, tag-, and image-typed content. We additionally depicts the information flow between these parts in a simplified form.

The *document model* defines a document that functions as the basic unit for content that is composed of facets. A facet is either a text, a tag or an

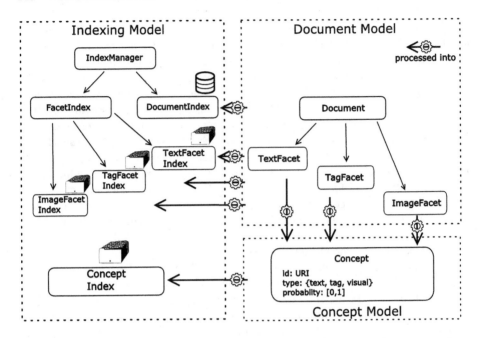

Fig. 1. Interaction between document model, concepts and (semantic) concept index

image. This allows many content structures to be created and organized, such as Wikipedia pages, scientific articles, websites, or blogs that often consist of such text, tag and image facets in various combinations. This structure also covers all unimodal variants, such as pure picture collections, since each document may contain any facet type in any order.

The *concept model* defines the structure of concepts. All concepts share a common identifier (usually a URI) that uniquely represents and differentiates them. A concept can describe either one of the three facet types, expressed as a type. That means, the concept can either be a text concept, a tag concept or a visual concept. Furthermore, a concept has a probability of being true, that allows a learning algorithm to store its confidence.

The *indexing model* is managed by the IndexManager, which controls the creation process of all indices, based on the configuration of the entire system. Facets are processed into respective indices that are all variations of a general FacetIndexer. TextFacets are indexed as a TextFacetIndex and TagFacets as a TagFacetIndex which are both based on Lucene[2] that stores it as separate, for their purpose optimized, inverted index file structures. ImageFacets are transformed into an ImageFacetIndex that is processed based on Lire, a Lucene derivative that is specialized on visual features. The indexing architecture therefore has three types of facet indexers, one per facet type, but maintains an arbitrary number of instances for each of them based on the structure of the

---

[2] http://lucene.apache.org/core.

content collection that is indexed. The DocumentIndex is a data structure that is implemented as a Database that connects all facets to make them accessible and usable for applications.

The *concept model* provides a definition of concepts for the framework. Concepts are processed into a ConceptIndex that is separate from the DocumentIndex and the FacetIndices. This concept model is used to translate facets into concepts. The ConceptIndex merges both text- and visual concepts into a common concept index space. In the next section, we demonstrate a first step into this direction by applying it solely on text concepts that are represented as an index of word vectors. Future work will expand on this by mapping concepts in an inverted index using Lucene covering both text, tag and visual concepts and representing it by a single index space.

In the following, we describe an application of semantic indexing in a social media domain. We specifically evaluate the effect of semantic-based retrieval on the textual features of multimodal documents.

4   Application of Concept-Based Retrieval

Based on the architecture discussed in the previous section, an application use-case is applied on the MediaEval Diverse Social Images task [10,11], using textual concepts. Our concept-based approach shows a significant improvement for keyword search on the test collection in the social media domain.

We explore the effect of semantic similarity and optimization methods on text-based image retrieval in social media as well as sentence paraphrasing and sentence-to-paragraph similarity. We introduce two semantic similarity methods, namely *Combinatorial* and *Greedy*, and evaluate them on the tasks using Word2Vec and Random Indexing word representations in different dimensions. This represents one possible scenario for a semantic concept index as shown in Fig. 1 and also examines the effectiveness of concept-based retrieval in this domain.

4.1   Experiment Setup

The evaluation on document retrieval was conducted using Flickr data, in particular in the framework of the MediaEval Retrieving Diverse Social Images Task 2013/2014 [10,11]. The task addresses result relevance and diversification in social image retrieval. We merged the datasets of 2013 (Div400) [11] and 2014 (Div150Cred) [10] and denoted it as MediaEval. It consists of about 60k photos of 300 world landmark locations (e.g., museums, monuments, churches, etc.). The provided data for each landmark location include a ranked list of photos together with their representative texts (title, description, and tags), Flickr's metadata, a Wikipedia article of the location and a user's credibility estimation (only for the 2014 edition). The name of each landmark location (e.g., Eiffel Tower) is used as the query for retrieving its related documents. For semantic text similarity, we focus on the relevance of the representative text of the photos containing title, description, and tags. We removed HTML tags and decompounded the terms using a dictionary obtained from the whole corpus.

We consider the evaluation metric as the precision at a cutoff of 20 documents (P@20) which was also used in the official runs. In order to examine the results, a standard Solr index was used as the baseline (P@20 = 0.760). Statistical significant difference at $p = 0.05$ or lower against the baseline (denoted by† in the tables) was calculated using Fisher's two-sided paired randomization test. The two-sided paired randomization test examines the significance of the difference between two sets of data by calculating the difference of each pair of the datasets and then passing them to a more common significance test such as a one-sample t-test.

As mentioned before, in addition to image retrieval, we tested the methods on broader text-based information seeking tasks, namely sentence paraphrasing and sentence-to-paragraph similarity tasks. For sentence paraphrasing, we use SemEval 2014 Multilingual Semantic Textual Similarity - Task 10 [1] (SemEval Task 10), the English subtask. The goal of this task is to measure the semantic similarity of two sentences. The participating systems are compared by their mean Pearson correlation between the system output and a human-annotated gold standard. For sentence-to-paragraph similarity, we select the collection of SemEval 2014 Cross-Level Semantic Similarity - Task 3 [13] (SemEval Task 3), the paragraph to sentence subtask. The test collection contains 500 sentence-paragraph pairs. Similar to the Task 10, Pearson correlation is used as evaluation metrics. Table 1 summarises the tasks and test collections used in the experiments.

Table 1. Tasks and test-collections.

Task	Test collection	Evaluation metric	Collection size
sentence-to-sentence	SemEval 2014 STS - Task 10 [1]	Pearson correlation	3750 sentence pairs
sentence-to-paragraph	SemEval 2014 STS - Task 3 [13]	Pearson correlation	500 sentence-paragraph pairs
document retrieval	MediaEval 2013/2014 retrieving diverse social images [10, 11]	P@20	309 topics - 60739 documents

We used the English Wikipedia text corpus to train our word representation models. For Word2Vec, we created models in 50, 100, 200, 300, 400, and 600 dimensions. We trained our Word2Vec word representation using Word2Vec toolkit[3] by applying CBOW approach of Mikolov et al. [18] with context

---

[3] https://code.google.com/p/word2vec/.

windows of 5 words and subsampling at $t = 1e^{-5}$. The Random Indexing word representations were trained using the Semantic Vectors package[4] with the default parameter settings of the package which considers the whole document as the context window. In all the models, we considered the words with frequency less than five as noise and filtered them out.

In the following, we define two text-to-text similarity methods and report and discuss the results of their evaluations on the mentioned tasks.

4.2 Combinatorial Method

The first algorithm, denoted as *SimCombi*, is based on the mean of words' similarity values. The algorithm first calculates the similarity of a given text (A) to another one (B) by simply aggregating the word-level similarity values that are greater than a given threshold (Algorithm 1). Then, to make the similarity symmetric, we repeat the same algorithm from B to A and return the mean of these two values as the similarity of the two texts. Although the algorithm is very simple, the choice of the best threshold is not obvious. By increasing the threshold, we remove more word pairs and therefore lose a part of the information. Decreasing the threshold adds more word pairs and therefore more noise to the calculation.

Algorithm 1: SimCombi

Input: text A and B, and threshold value t
Output: similarity of the text A to B
$meanList \leftarrow [];$
for $w \in A$ **do**
$\quad simList \leftarrow [];$
$\quad$ **for** $v \in B$ **do**
$\quad\quad$ **if** $\cos(w, v) >= t$ **then**
$\quad\quad\quad simList \leftarrow simList + \cos(w, v);$
$\quad meanList \leftarrow meanList + \text{mean}(simList)$
return mean($meanList$);

The performance for the three test collections for varying thresholds between 0 and 1 in 0.05 increments are shown in Figs. 2, 3, and 4. The best achieved results of the tasks are shown in Table 2. For the sentence paraphrasing task, the most impressive result is that the best result achieved an average correlation of 0.71 as the best overall performance. This represents rank 11th out of the 38 submitted runs. However, all 10 runs above use a knowledge base and/or NLPwhich would not generalize to other domains or languages. For the

---

[4] https://code.google.com/p/semanticvectors/.

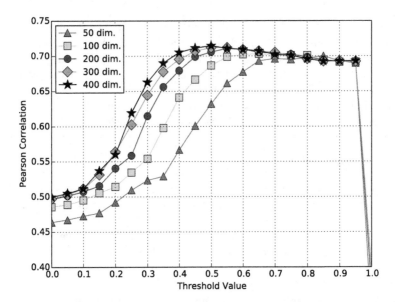

Fig. 2. Evaluation results of SemEval 2014 multilingual semantic textual similarity - Task 10 [1] English subtask

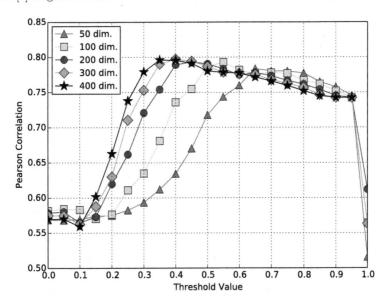

Fig. 3. Evaluation results of SemEval 2014 cross-level semantic similarity - Task 3 [13], paragraph to sentence subtask

MediaEval task, we observed that the best result of evaluating the SimCombi algorithm as a semantic-based similarity method outperforms the simple content-based approach.

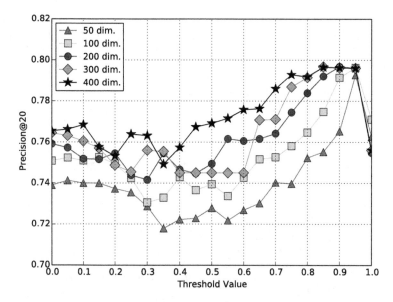

Fig. 4. Evaluation results of MediaEval 2013/2014 retrieving diverse social images Task [10,11]

As it is clear from the results, the choice of the threshold has an important effect on the effectiveness of the method. In order to effectively guess the parameters, for the SemEval tasks we can consider the following observations on the behavior patterns: (1) the performance is very low in smaller threshold values and increases steadily as the threshold increases until reaching a peak and then it slightly decreases. (2) Higher dimensions have overall better performance, while all the models finally converge. (3) The peak of performance is in lower similarity values for higher dimensions.

While the mentioned observations can be useful for parameter tuning of the SemEval tasks, it cannot be clearly extended to MediaEval (document retrieval). The reason could be due that the tasks are more complicated such that more factors confound the final performance. For example, the length of the documents are much more varied here than in the SemEval tasks.

In order to address the problem of parameter tuning in the SimCombi method, in the following we define a parameter-free semantic similarity method which shows very similar performance to the best results of the SimCombi method.

4.3   Greedy Method

The Greedy method, denoted *SimGreedy* [21], is inherited from the SimCombi method while applying a greedy approach in selecting the words. The algorithm measures the semantic-based text-to-text similarity by considering only the word with the highest similarity value in the B document to each word in the A

Table 2. Best results of mean Pearson correlation of SemEval 2014 Task 10 [1], SemEval 2014 Task 3 [13] paragraph to sentence subtask, and P@20 of MediaEval retrieving diverse social images Task 2013/2014 [10,11]. All the MediaEval results are significantly better than the Solr baseline

Dimension	SemEval task 3	SemEval task 10	MediaEval
50	0.783	0.700	0.792
100	0.792	0.703	0.796
200	0.793	0.710	0.796
300	0.797	0.712	0.796
400	0.795	0.714	0.796

document. The approach calculates the relatedness of document A to document B based on $SimGreedy(A, B)$ defined as follows:

$$SimGreedy(A, B) = \frac{\sum_{t \in A} idf(t) * maxSim(t, B)}{\sum_{t \in A} idf(t)} \tag{1}$$

where t represents a term of document A and $idf(t)$ is the Inverse Document Frequency of the term t. The function $maxSim$ calculates separately the cosine of the term t to each word in document B and returns the highest value. In this method, each word in the source document is aligned to the word in the target document to which it has the highest semantic similarity. Then, the results are aggregated based on the weight of each word to achieve the document-to-document similarity. $SimGreedy$ is defined as the average of $SimGreedy(A, B)$ and $SimGreedy(B, A)$. Considering n and m as the number of words in documents A and B respectively, the complexity of SimGreedy is of order $O(n * m)$.

We checked the effectiveness of SimGreedy by first evaluating the sentence paraphrasing (SemEval 2014 Task 10 [1]) and the paragraph to sentence similarity task (SemEval 2014 Task 3 [13]). Tables 3 and 4 show the mean Pearson correlations between the similarity methods and the gold standard. In both the tasks, SimGreedy exposes very similar results to the best performing results of SimCombi. It also appears that the effect of similarity method is more important than the number of dimensions of the vector representation such that after the dimension of 100 in both the tasks the results are very similar.

In the next step, we evaluated the SimGreedy method on MediaEval Retrieving Diverse Social Images Task 2013/2014 [10,11] as a more complicated task, shown in Table 5. We observed that using SimGreedy as a semantic-based similarity method outperforms the simple content-based approach while after the dimension of 100, its performance is very similar to the best results of the Sim-Combi method. Similar to the previous tasks, the number of dimensions does not have a significant effect on the result of the method.

In the following, we want to examine the effect of the word representation method on the performance of the semantic similarity method. To answer the question, we selected the models with 200 dimensions (as a generally good

Table 3. Mean Pearson correlation of SemEval 2014 Task 10 [1] using Word2Vec (W2V) [18] word representation

Dimension	SimGreedy	SimCombi (best)
50	0.697	0.700
100	0.707	0.703
200	0.712	0.710
300	0.713	0.712
400	0.714	0.714

Table 4. Mean Pearson correlation of SemEval 2014 Task 3 [13], paragraph to sentence subtask using Word2Vec (W2V) [18] word representation

Dimension	SimGreedy	SimCombi (best)
50	0.778	0.783
100	0.787	0.792
200	0.789	0.793
300	0.790	0.797
400	0.790	0.795

Table 5. MediaEval retrieving diverse social images Task 2013/2014 [10,11]. Models trained on Wikipedia using Word2Vec (W2V). The sign † denotes statistical significant difference

Dimension	SimGreedy	SimCombi (best)
50	0.766	†0.792
100	†0.787	†0.796
200	†0.795	†0.796
300	**†0.801**	†0.796
400	†0.799	†0.796
Solr (Baseline)		0.760

performance model) together with 600 as a much higher dimension and evaluated the MediaEval tasks on the models created with Word2Vec and Random Indexing methods. As shown in Table 6, Word2Vec shows slightly better results than Random Indexing while Random Indexing is still significantly better than the baseline. We can then conclude that the similarity method has more effect on the results than the number of dimensions or word representation method.

In order to compare the results with the participating systems in the task, we repeated the experiment on 2014 test dataset. As it is shown in Table 7 using SimGreedy and Word2Vec, we achieved the state-of-the-art result of 0.842 for

Table 6. MediaEval retrieving diverse social images Task 2013/2014 [10,11]. Models trained on Wikipedia using Random Indexing (RI) and Word2Vec (W2V). The sign †denotes statistical significant difference

Representation	Dimension	SimGreedy
Word2Vec	200	†**0.795**
Word2Vec	600	†0.793
Random Indexing	200	†0.788
Random Indexing	600	†0.787
Solr (Baseline)		0.760

P@20 between 41 runs including even the ones which used image features but not external resources.

Table 7. MediaEval retrieving diverse social images Task 2014 Results using query expansion. Models are trained on Wikipedia corpus with 200 and 600 dimensions. Our semantic-based approach only uses the textual features. *Best* indicates the state-of-the-art performing system in the 2014 task for different runs

Representation	Dimension	P@20
Word2Vec	200	0.833
Word2Vec	600	**0.842**
Random Indexing	200	0.813
Random Indexing	600	0.817
Best text (Run1)		0.832
Best text-visual (Run3)		0.817
Best all resources (Run5)		0.876

Considering the achieved results, in the next section we focus on optimizing the performance of the SimGreedy algorithm, to face the practical requirements of real-world application problems.

5   Optimizing Semantic Text Similarity

Although SimGreedy performs better in comparison to the content-based approach, based on the time complexity discussed before, it has a much longer execution time. We observed that SimGreedy is approximately 40 times slower than Solr so that SimGreedy generally has the query processing time of about 110 to 130 minutes while it takes about three minutes for Solr. The method can be especially inefficient when the documents become longer. Therefore, we apply two optimization techniques for SimGreedy to achieve a better execution time without degrading its effectiveness.

5.1   Two-Phase Process

In the first approach, we turn the procedure into a two-phase process [6]. In order to do this, we choose an alternative method with considerably less execution time in comparison to SimGreedy such as using Solr. Then, we apply the faster algorithm to obtain a first ranking of the results and afterwards, the top n percent of the results is re-ranked by applying SimGreedy. Therefore, the SimGreedy algorithm computes only on a portion of the data which is already filtered by the first (faster) one.

Considering that the alternative algorithm has the execution time of t and is k time faster than SimGreedy, applying this approach takes $t+t\cdot k\cdot n/100$ where n is the percentage of the selected data. In fact, this approach is $k/(1+k\cdot n/100)$ times faster than running the SimGreedy algorithm standalone. While achieving better execution time, the choice of the parameter n can reduce the effectiveness of the SimGreedy method. Finding the optimal n such that performance remains in the range of significantly indifferent to the non-optimized SimGreedy is a special problem of this method.

Table 8. Execution time in minutes of the standard, Two-Phase, and Approximate Nearest Neighbor (ANN) approaches of SimGreedy. Models are trained on the Wikipedia corpus with 200 dimensions. There is no statistically significant difference between the achieved results of the evaluation metric (P@20).

Repres	Algorithm	Indexing time	I/O	Query time	Overall	P@20
W2V	SimGreedy	-	0:16	1:50	2:06	0.795
	SimGreedy + Two-Phase	-		0:50	1:06	0.772
	SimGreedy + ANN	0:28		0:17	1:01	0.782
RI	SimGreedy	-	0:14	2:07	2:24	0.788
	SimGreedy + Two-Phase	-		1:00	1:14	0.770
	SimGreedy + ANN	0:21		0:19	0:54	0.782

To apply this technique on the MediaEval collection, we selected Solr as the first phase. SimGreedy as the second phase uses vector representations trained on Wikipedia by Word2Vec and Random Indexing methods, both with 200 dimensions. For all the integer values of n from 1 to 100, we found an extremely similar behaviour between the two methods summarized in Fig. 5. To find the best value for n as the cutting point, we identified the highest precision value that is not significantly different (using Fisher's two-sided paired randomization test with $p = 0.05$) from the best one (i.e. when n is 100%). This corresponds to $n = 49$. Giving the second phase (SimGreedy) is about 40 times slower than the first

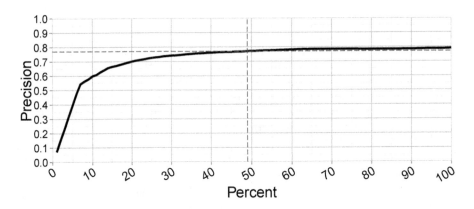

Fig. 5. Average performance of the two-phase approach with best value at around 49%

(Solr), using this approach improves the execution time to almost two times (48%) while the performance remains the same.

5.2 Approximate Nearest Neighborhood

In this technique, we exploit the advantages of Approximate Nearest Neighbor (ANN) methods [2]. Similar to Nearest Neighbor search, ANN methods attempt to find the closest neighbors in a vector space. In contrast to the Nearest Neighbor method, ANN approaches approximate the closest neighbors using pre-trained data structures, while in a significantly better searching time. Considering these methods, we can adapt the *maxSim* function of *SimGreedy* to an approximate nearest neighbor search where it attempts to return the closest node to a term. Therefore in this approach, first we create an optimized nearest neighbor data structure (indexing process) for each document and then use it to find the most similar terms.

The overhead time of creating the semantic indices depends on different factors such as the vector dimension, the number of terms in a document, and the selected data structure. While this excessive time can influence the overall execution time, it can be especially effective when the indices are used frequently by many queries.

We apply this technique on MediaEval by first creating an ANN data structure—denoted as semantic index—for each document using the scikit-learn library[5]. Due to the high dimension of the vectors (>30), we choose the Ball-Tree data structure with the leaf size of 30. The Ball-Tree data structure recursively divides the data into hyper-spheres. Such hyper-spheres are defined by a centroid C and a radius r so that points with a maximum leaf size are enclosed. With this data structure, a single distance calculation between a test point and the centroid is sufficient to determine a lower and upper bound on the distance

---

[5] http://scikit-learn.org/stable/.

to all points within the hyper-sphere. Afterwards, we use the semantic indices to calculate the SimGreedy algorithm. We run the experiment using vector representations with 200 dimensions using both Word2Vec and Random Indexing methods trained on Wikipedia.

Table 8 shows the results compared with the original SimGreedy as well as Two-Phase algorithm. The I/O time consists of reading the documents, fetching the corresponding vector representations of the words and writing the final results which is common between all the approaches. Although the ANN approach has the overhead of indexing time, its query time is significantly less than the original SimGreedy and also Two-Phase approach. We therefore see an improvement of approximately two times in the overall execution time in comparison to the original SimGreedy method. In spite of the time optimization, there is no significant difference between the evaluation results of the methods.

It should also be noted that since in MediaEval task, each topic has its own set of documents, the semantic index of each document is used only one time by its topic. Considering this fact, we expect a larger difference between the overall execution times when the indexed documents are used by all the topics as is the normal case in many information retrieval tasks.

6 Conclusions and Future Work

We explored the effect of textual semantic and optimization methods in the social media domain as an example of a semantic index. In addition, we checked the sanity and effectiveness of the methods on two information seeking tasks, namely sentence paraphrasing and sentence-to-paragraph similarity. We ran experiments on the MediaEval Retrieving Diverse Social Images Task 2013/2014 using Word2Vec and Random Indexing vector representations. Beside achieving state-of-the-art results, we show that SimGreedy—a semantic-based similarity method—outperforms a term-frequency-based baseline using Solr. We then focused on two optimization techniques: Two-Phase and Approximate Nearest Neighbor (ANN) approaches. Both the methods reduced the processing time of the SimGreedy method by half while keeping precision within the boundary of statistically insignificant difference.

Although these techniques similarly optimize the processing time, they show different characteristics in practice. While the Two-Phase approach needs pre-knowledge on the performance of the other search methods for setting the parameters, the ANN method can easily be applied on new domains with no need for parameter tuning. In addition, in the ANN approach, despite the overhead time of creating semantic-based data structures, the query time is significantly faster which is a great benefit in real-time use cases.

In future work, we will exploit the semantics of different facets (e.g. text, image, etc.) by first indexing and then combining them in the scoring process of our multimodal information retrieval platform. The concept index is achieved differently for text and image: For image facets, it represents the probability of a visual concept that has been learned from an image (e.g. from a visual classifier).

For text facets, it represents the probability of a term being conceptually similar to its context (e.g., document, window of the terms, and etc.). Despite the effectiveness of SimGreedy (as an approach for semantic similarity), for each term in the source document, it only finds the highest similar term in the destination and ignores the others with less similarity value. We therefore want to study new, alternative similarity measures that match terms with groups of related terms.

References

1. Agirrea, E., Baneab, C., Cardiec, C., Cerd, D., Diabe, M., Gonzalez-Agirrea, A., Guof, W., Mihalceab, R., Rigaua, G., Wiebeg, J.: Semeval-2014 task 10: multilingual semantic textual similarity. In: SemEval (2014)
2. Arya, S., Mount, D.M., Netanyahu, N.S., Silverman, R., Wu, A.Y.: An optimal algorithm for approximate nearest neighbor searching fixed dimensions. J. ACM (JACM) 45(6), 891–923 (1998)
3. Baroni, M., Dinu, G., Kruszewski, G.: Don't count, predict! a systematic comparison of context-counting vs. context-predicting semantic vectors. In: Proceedings of the 52nd Annual Meeting of the Association for Computational Linguistics, vol. 1, pp. 238–247 (2014)
4. Clinchant, S., Ah-Pine, J., Csurka, G.: Semantic combination of textual and visual information in multimedia retrieval. In: Proceedings of the 1st ACM International Conference on Multimedia Retrieval (2011)
5. Csurka, G., Dance, C.R., Fan, L., Willamowski, J., Bray, C.: Visual categorization with bags of keypoints. In: Workshop on Statistical Learning in Computer Vision (at ECCV) (2004)
6. Dang, V., Bendersky, M., Croft, W.: Two-stage learning to rank for information retrieval. In: Proceedings of European Conference on Information Retrieval (2013)
7. Deerwester, S.C., Dumais, S.T., Landauer, T.K., Furnas, G.W., Harshman, R.A.: Indexing by latent semantic analysis. J. Am. Soc. Inf. Sci. (JASIS) 41, 391 (1990)
8. Depeursinge, A., Müller, H.: Fusion techniques for combining textual and visual information retrieval. In: Müller, H., Clough, P., Deselaers, T., Caputo, B. (eds.) ImageCLEF, vol. 32, pp. 95–114. Springer, Heidelberg (2010)
9. Eskevich, M., Jones, G.J., Aly, R., et al.: Multimedia information seeking through search and hyperlinking. In: Proceedings of the Annual ACM International Conference on Multimedia Retrieval (2013)
10. Ionescu, B., Popescu, A., Lupu, M., Gînsca, A.L., Boteanu, B., Müller, H.: Div150cred: a social image retrieval result diversification with user tagging credibility dataset. In: ACM Multimedia Systems Conference Series (2015)
11. Ionescu, B., Radu, A.-L., Menéndez, M., Müller, H., Popescu, A., Loni, B.: Div400: a social image retrieval result diversification dataset. In: Proceedings of ACM Multimedia Systems Conference Series (2014)
12. Jia, Y., Shelhamer, E., Donahue, J., Karayev, S., Long, J., Girshick, R., Guadarrama, S., Darrell, T.: Caffe: convolutional architecture for fast feature embedding. In: Proceedings of the ACM International Conference on Multimedia, pp. 675–678. ACM (2014)
13. Jurgens, D., Pilehvar, M.T., Navigli, R.: Semeval-2014 task 3: cross-level semantic similarity. In: SemEval 2014, p. 17 (2014)

14. Liu, C., Wang, Y.-M.: On the connections between explicit semantic analysis and latent semantic analysis. In: Proceedings of Conference on Information and Knowledge Management, New York, USA (2012)

15. Liu, N., Dellandréa, E., Chen, L., Zhu, C., Zhang, Y., Bichot, C.-E., Bres, S., Tellez, B.: Multimodal recognition of visual concepts using histograms of textual concepts and selective weighted late fusion scheme. Computer Vision and Image Underst. **117**, 493–512 (2013)

16. Magalhaes, J., Rüger, S.: Information-theoretic semantic multimedia indexing. In: Proceedings of the 6th ACM International Conference on Image and Video Retrieval, pp. 619–626. ACM (2007)

17. Manyika, J., Chui, M., Brown, B., Bughin, J., Dobbs, R., Roxburgh, C., Byers, A.H.: Big data: the next frontier for innovation, competition, and productivity. McKinsey Global Institute (2011)

18. Mikolov, T., Chen, K., Corrado, G., Dean, J.: Efficient estimation of word representations in vector space. arXiv preprint 2013 arXiv:1301.3781

19. Paramita, M.L., Grubinger, M.: Photographic image retrieval. In: Müller, H., Clough, P., Deselaers, T., Caputo, B. (eds.) ImageCLEF, vol. 32, pp. 141–162. Springer, Heidelberg (2010)

20. Pham, T.-T., Maillot, N., Lim, J.-H., Chevallet, J.-P.: Latent semantic fusion model for image retrieval and annotation. In: Proceedings of Conference on Information and Knowledge Management (2007)

21. Rekabsaz, N., Bierig, R., Ionescu, B., Hanbury, A., Lupu, M.: On the use of statistical semantics for metadata-based social image retrieval. In: Proceedings of the 13th International Workshop on Content-Based Multimedia Indexing (CBMI) (2015)

22. Sabetghadam, S., Lupu, M., Bierig, R., Rauber, A.: A combined approach of structured and non-structured IR in multimodal domain. In: Proceedings of ACM International Conference on Multimedia Retrieval (2014)

23. Sahlgren, M.: An introduction to random indexing. In: Methods and Applications of Semantic Indexing Workshop in the Proceedings of Terminology and Knowledge Engineering (2005)

24. Thomee, B., Popescu, A.: Overview of the ImageCLEF 2012 Flickr photo annotation and retrieval task. In: Proceedings of Cross-Language Evaluation Forum (CLEF) (2012)

Improving Document Retrieval in Large Domain Specific Textual Databases Using Lexical Resources

Ranka Stanković[1]($\boxtimes$), Cvetana Krstev[2], Ivan Obradović[1], and Olivera Kitanović[1]

[1] Faculty of Mining and Geology, University of Belgrade, Belgrade, Serbia
{ranka,ivan.obradovic,olivera.kitanovic}@rgf.bg.ac.rs
[2] Faculty of Philology, University of Belgrade, Belgrade, Serbia
cvetana@matf.bg.ac.rs

Abstract. Large collections of textual documents represent an example of big data that requires the solution of three basic problems: the representation of documents, the representation of information needs and the matching of the two representations. This paper outlines the introduction of document indexing as a possible solution to document representation. Documents within a large textual database developed for geological projects in the Republic of Serbia for many years were indexed using methods developed within digital humanities: bag-of-words and named entity recognition. Documents in this geological database are described by a summary report, and other data, such as title, domain, keywords, abstract, and geographical location. These metadata were used for generating a bag of words for each document with the aid of morphological dictionaries and transducers. Named entities within metadata were also recognized with the help of a rule-based system. Both the bag of words and the metadata were then used for pre-indexing each document. A combination of several *tf_idf* based measures was applied for selecting and ranking of retrieval results of indexed documents for a specific query and the results were compared with the initial retrieval system that was already in place. In general, a significant improvement has been achieved according to the standard information retrieval performance measures, where the InQuery method performed the best.

1 Introduction

Advancements in database technology provide nowadays for management of large quantities of heterogeneous data. However, besides this engineering challenge—efficient management of such data, the "exploding world of Big Data" poses yet another, semantic challenge—finding and meaningfully combining information that is relevant to a user query [1]. Large textual databases, that is, large collections of textual documents are an example of big data, which pose three basic problems to Information Retrieval (IR): the representation of document content, the representation of user information needs and the comparison of these two representations.

© Springer International Publishing AG 2017
N.T. Nguyen et al. (Eds.): TCCI XXVI, LNCS 10190, pp. 162–185, 2017.
DOI: 10.1007/978-3-319-59268-8_8

In general, if the response to a user query related to a collection of documents is performed by keyword search of these documents, then a preprocessing phase for additional representation of document content is not necessary. However, when these collections reach a certain volume, simple keyword search through the entire collection becomes time consuming and inefficient, as the recall grows but precision is likely to drop considerably. Thus in the case of large collections, an additional representation of the document content is generated, formally referred to as the document surrogate, with the aim of increasing document retrieval efficiency, through a better matching of user needs and retrieval results.

Document surrogates typically consist of metadata about the document, such as title, abstract, author and the like, as well as of keywords which denote document content. Surrogates can also contain an abstract and/or a snippet, a relevant text fragment. The content of a document surrogate, or its part, can be generated automatically by extracting and selecting specific terms (words) from the document text. Language processing methods and techniques developed within the field of digital humanities are used for completing this task. They provide for determining the boundaries of sentences within the document text, tokenization, stemming, tagging, recognition of nominal phrases and named entities and, finally, parsing [10].

Based on document representations by surrogates in large collections of textual documents, a preprocessing of documents usually takes place, in which an index of the collection of documents is formed, to be used for search and retrieval purposes. Relevant documents are retrieved and ranked upon a user query on basis of this index, using an approximate matching model, such as the vector space model, based on weight coefficients of terms, or the probabilistic model, based on relevance feedback [22].

When language processing methods and techniques are used for generating a document surrogate, they rely heavily on lexical resources, which is especially important in the case of languages with rich morphology, such as Serbian, and South-Slavic languages in general. Although Serbian belongs to the group of less-resourced languages, in which comprehensive lexical resources and language technology tools are still lacking or have not reached full maturity, it is safe to say that the current level of achievement is not negligible. According to the META-NET extensive survey performed in [20], some important lexical resources for Serbian were developed (corpora and e-dictionaries), as well as applications for basic language processing (tokenization, Part-Of-Speech (POS) tagging, morphological analysis), information retrieval and extraction [26].

Several successful applications of Serbian language resources and tools in tasks related to document indexing, retrieval and classification have been reported. A system for PhD dissertation metadata and full-text search was developed at the University of Novi Sad. It uses an index based on Lucene that integrates a Porters stemmer for Serbian [9]. Furlan and associates [5] also use Porter's stemmer and min-max normalization for logarithm of tf_{log} (the log-number of times the given word appears in a document) for calculating semantic similarity of short texts. Graovac [6] applies lexical resources for

Serbian—morphological dictionaries and the WordNet—for text categorization. Mladenović and associates [18] use the same resources for document-level sentiment polarity classification using maximum entropy modeling. Zečević and Vujičić-Stanković [27] apply various language-identification tools to distinguish Serbian among other closely related languages.

In this paper we describe an application of lexical resources and language tools for solving a big data problem, namely improvement of document retrieval from the database of geological projects financed by the Republic of Serbia. To that end documents in this large textual database are indexed using simultaneously two methods: by generating a bag-of-words and by named entity recognition for each document. In the next section we give an outline of the textual database of geological projects and the initial document retrieval system based on text scanning, along with its shortcomings. The improved system developed using lexical resources and language tools is described in Sect. 3, while the evaluation of this improvement is given in Sect. 4, followed by some concluding remarks.

2   The Database of Geological Projects

2.1   Motivation

Although the volume of geological data and related information on various geological phenomena in Serbia has been growing rapidly in the last decades, it was not accompanied by an adequate development and implementation of modern information technologies. Until recently, management of this growing body of geological documentation relied on traditional methods based on libraries and archives, which often made the task of obtaining specific information difficult or time consuming. Geological data have been collected for years, using different methods, and stored in various formats, seldom structured, most often in textual form. A very small part of these data was transformed in machine readable and structured format. The better part is still in paper form, and thus subject to decay or loss. An analysis of the way geological research results, stored in numerous archives and document libraries, were used, showed that this usage was inefficient, due to inadequate organization, limited access and general lack of readiness for introducing modern information technology. Thus a comprehensive digitalization is needed, which is expected to be intensified in the forthcoming years [23].

As a result of this analysis, the then Ministry of Natural Resources and Environment Protection (now Ministry of Mining and Energy of the Republic of Serbia), launched in 2004 the project of the Geological Information System of Serbia (*GeolISS*), which has been developed in several phases over the past decade. The aim of this information system was primarily to establish an object-oriented database for digital archiving of geologic data in the field of general geology, exploration of mineral deposits, hydrogeology and engineering geology, as a modern and efficient information basis for planning, design and decision-making in the geological domain.

Within the *GeoISS* project a web portal[1] was developed with the aim to provide quicker and easier access to geological data and information. Users, both professional and lay, can use this geo-portal to search and access information available within *GeoISS* database. The content on the portal is grouped into several categories: cartographic content, multimedia, dictionaries and textual databases. The "core" of *GeoISS* is the Geological Dictionary (Thesaurus) containing 5,152 geological terms described by definitions, of which 4,839 have a translation into English. The cartographic content includes a general geological map, maps of national parks, map of endangered groundwater bodies, geo-morphological map, map of exploration-mining fields, while the most prominent multimedia content are the gallery of photos and movies, geoheritage, BEWARE GIS web portal for interactive landslide data management, hazard and risk analysis, and jeweler mineral resources. Textual databases, also known as catalogs, consist of projects, archival documents and bibliographies, library of geological projects documentation and exploration-exploitation approvals for water and solid mineral resources. Within the geo-portal access to applications for document search and retrieval is available.

A textual database of special importance is the database of documentation related to over 5,500 geological projects financed by the Republic of Serbia from 1956 to the present day.[2] For each project a structured description is available in the form of a project summary containing the following metadata: title, year, project location, company that developed the project, authors, abstract, keywords, geological field, prospects, application of mineral resource and possibilities for its use, field works, geomechanics, mining works, geodesic works, and prospective exploration. Each project summary also contains approximately 30% of the content of the projects itself, obtained basically by removing pictures, maps, tables, and the like, offering thus a reasonably accurate representation of the textual content of the geological project. Future plans include digitalization and full text archiving of the project content, followed by the implementation of the approach described in this paper to this future full text database.

2.2   The Initial Solution for Document Retrieval

The initial solution for searching the textual databases in *GeoISS* (which is in use for several years) is based on user queries consisting of keywords, single or multi-word units (MWU), which can be combined into Boolean expressions. When a MWU is used as a keyword, it must be entered under quotation marks in order to be treated as a whole. A general search, which looks for keyword matches in all metadata fields in the summary report is available, but the user can also perform a faceted search using additional criteria. These criteria restrict

---

[1] http://geoliss.mre.gov.rs; search of fund documentation http://geoliss.mre.gov.rs/index.php?page=fodib.

[2] Actually, almost 9,000 geological projects were financed in this period, but some of them were lost, some are not open to general public, and for some only basic data exists.

the search to specific metadata fields. For example, if the user chooses the facet *mineral resource* then only the following fields in the database are taken into consideration: title, field, keywords, and abstract. Likewise, the *location* facet searches for keyword matches in another group of fields: municipality, county, name of the cartographic sheet, location and chronological number of the document, and the sheet signature. When a match is found, the search system registers the corresponding metadata field, and this information is subsequently used for document ranking.

Fig. 1. A search for documents dealing with "lignite coal in Tamnava region" by GeoliSS

When performing faceted search, the users express their information need by selecting the facets and appropriate keywords, and they can combine any number of facets. Different facets are linked by conjunction, whereas for more than one keyword within a single facet a disjunction is generated. For example, if the user is interested in projects that deal with the research of "lignite coal in Tamnava region", then *mineral resource* is selected as one facet and the words *lignit* 'lignite' and *ugalj* 'coal' are defined for keyword search, and the system will search for any of these two words in appropriate fields. The second facet is *location*, and the corresponding keyword is *Tamnava*. This query and the documents retrieved are depicted in Fig. 1. The panel shows that the system found 4 results, and appropriate document snippets are displayed. For each document there is also a link enabling the user to look into further details on the retrieved document. The user can chose the maximum number of retrieved documents to be displayed on one page, and if the recall exceeds this number, a pagination is generated and the user can review the recall page by page.

A specific feature of Serbian is the common use of two alphabets: Cyrillic and Latin, and consequently the system allows the user to initiate her/his search in either of them, automatically expanding the search query with the other. However, search results are displayed in the original alphabet used in the documents, and that is Cyrillic.

Keyword search in the initial system is performed by scanning the text of appropriate fields with given keywords in which word boundaries are not taken into consideration. This partially solves the problem of rich morphology that is characteristic for Serbian. For instance, scanning with *lignit* will also retrieve inflected forms *lignita, lignitu, lignitom*, etc. However, this solution is also a source of many false retrievals, especially when keywords are very short and can be found as substrings in many unrelated document words, like acronyms (e.g. *SO* derived from *skupština opštine* 'municipality council') and symbols of chemical elements (e.g. *Ca* for calcium).

For each field searched within a specific facet, a weight factor is assigned. For example, when the facet 'location' is used in a query, the weights of corresponding metadata fields are: Municipality 8, County 7, Title 4, Keywords 3, Abstract 2, Appendices 1, whereas for the facet "mineral resource", the fields searched and their weights are the following: Title 8, Signature 6, Keywords 4, Abstract 2, Appendices 1. System administrators have the possibility of adjusting these parameters, which are not hardcoded in the software solution, but rather registered in a database and accessible to users.

Table 1. A matrix of key words, fields that are searched, and weight factors for query "lignite coal in Tamnava region".

DocId	Abstract	Appendices	Keywords	Municipality	Title	Total
577			4	8	12	24
lignit					8	8
Tamnava				8	4	12
ugalj			4			4
578			3	8	8	19
Tamnava			3	8		11
ugalj					8	8
8823				8	8	16
Tamnava				8		8
ugalj				8		8
6255	2		4			6
Tamnava	4					2
ugalj			4			4

Query processing on the server side expands the faceted query by creating a matrix of key words, fields that are searched, and weight factors (see Table 1), and then translates this query into SQL (Structured Query Language) form. The query generated in such a way searches the text of the subset of attributes in the database that correspond to the selected search facets. Ranking of retrieved documents is performed in descending order of the total sum of weight factors for all fields in which the keywords from the faceted search were found. The keyword matrix and the ranking of retrieved documents for the faceted query related to "lignite coal in Tamnava region" are depicted in Table 1.

The initial system achieved good results with faceted search in which keywords in metadata fields appeared in the same form in which they were used in the query (usually the nominative singular), but a large number of other forms could not be found. For example, if the keyword *Tamnava* (used in the nominative) appeared in the database in the locative form as in *u Tamnavi* 'in Tamnava' then the initial system would not be able to recognize it. As already mentioned, the initial system did not match whole words precisely in order to recognize at least some inflectional forms. However, we also pointed out that this became a serious disadvantage affecting precision when short words that could be parts of other words were used in a search. In order to improve the way the search mechanism copes with Serbian rich morphology an upgrade of the initial system was developed.

3   The Improved Solution

The initial solution has been used from 2008, while the development of the improved solution started at the beginning of 2015 and is available for use since June 2015. Besides tackling the problem of morphology this new solution also offers new features that enable the user to evaluate the retrieved documents.

As we have already pointed out, a Serbian keyword in a search query is almost always entered in the nominative singular, while in the texts that are searched it can occur in different inflectional forms. Thus, for languages such as Serbian, some kind of normalization of morphological forms has to be performed both for document indexing and query processing. One solution is to use stemmers. For Serbian, work on several stemmers was reported: a stemmer as a part of a larger system for information retrieval, PoS tagging, shallow parsing and topic tracking [15], a stemmer and lemmatizer based on suffix stripping [11], the same basic idea being used in the stemmer presented in a later paper [17].

The only stemmer available for practical use is the last one since its code is available from the paper itself. However, although the author claims accuracy of 92% it was evaluated on a very small text (522 words) so its reliability is not confirmed. Also, as Hiemstra states [8] "Stemming tends to help as many queries as it hurts." The other possibility is statistical lemmatization for which TreeTagger trained for Serbian is available, already used for lemmatization of the Corpus of Contemporary Serbian [25]. However, this lemmatizer was trained on a general corpus that differs significantly from domain corpora, such as our textual database of geological projects, and additionally it does not take into account MWUs.

The approach to lemmatization in developing an improved solution for searching the textual database of geological projects described in this paper is based on morphological electronic dictionaries and finite-state transducers for Serbian [12].

3.1   Used Resources

Lexical Resources. The resources for natural language processing of Serbian consisting of lexical resources and local grammars are being developed using the finite-state methodology as described in [3,7]. The role of electronic dictionaries, covering both simple words and multi-word units, and dictionary finite-state transducers (FSTs) is text tagging. Each e-dictionary of forms consists of a list of entries supplied with their lemmas, morphosyntactic, semantic and other information. The forms are, as a rule, automatically generated from the dictionaries of lemmas containing the information that enable production of forms. For this purpose almost 1,000 inflectional transducers were developed. The system of Serbian e-dictionaries covers both general lexica and proper names and all inflected forms are generated from 135,000 simple forms and 13,000 MWU lemmas. Approximately 28.5% of these lemmas represent proper names: personal, geopolitical, organizational, etc.

Named Entity Recognition. According to [19] the term "Named Entity" (NE) usually refers to names of persons, locations and organizations, and numeric expressions including, time, date, money and percentage. Recently other major types are being included, like "products" and "events", but also marginal ones, like "e-mail addresses" and "book titles".

The NE hierarchy in our Named Entity Recognition (NER) system consists of five top-level types: persons, organizations, locations, amounts, and temporal expressions, each of them having one or more levels of sub-types. Our tagging strategy allows nesting, which means that a named entity can be nested within another named entity, e.g. a toponym within an organization name, like in *<org>Institut za gradjevinarstvo<top>Subotica</top></org>* 'Institute for civil engineering Subotica'.

The Serbian NER system is a handcrafted rule-based system that relies on comprehensive lexical resources for Serbian. For recognition of some types of named entities, e.g. personal names and locations, e-dictionaries and information within them is crucial; for others, like temporal expressions, local grammars in the form of FSTs that try to capture a variety of syntactic forms in which a NE can occur had to be developed. However, for all of them local grammars were developed that use wider context to disambiguate ambiguous occurrences as much as possible [13]. These local grammars were organized in cascades that further resolve ambiguities [16]. NER system was evaluated on a newspaper corpus and results reported in [13] showed that F-measure of recognition was 0.96 for types and 0.92 for tokens.[3]

---

[3] Tokens are all occurrences (in this case, NEs) in a given texts, types are different occurrences.

Table 2. Distribution of three top-level NEs: persons, locations and organizations.

NE type	Frequency	Average per doc	% of the text
Person	14.817	2.69	1.14
Location	65.724	11.93	5.05
Organization	3.492	0.63	0.27
Total	84.003	15.25	6.45

For the purpose of indexing, we applied our NER system to title and abstract fields of our geological structured data. The whole collection consisted of 5,510 documents (1,302,521 simple word forms). Almost all documents contained at least one NE—in only 71 (1.29%) not a single NE was recognized. On the average, 11 NEs of all types were recognized per document, with as many as 102 NEs for one of them. One of documents contained 25 different NEs. For indexing we used only three top level types: personal names, locations and organizations and their distribution is presented in Table 2. Nested NEs were also used for indexing, e.g. toponym *Subotica* in "Institute for civil engineering Subotica".

3.2   The Architecture of the New System

Indexing of documents on geological projects is done so that for each document a text is generated of all the fields and records in the project summary database, where the title and geological subdomain are given extra weight, 3 and 2, respectively. Two types of "representative items" or indexes that are used for search are generated: a bag of words and named entities, which are equally treated in document indexing. Figure 2 presents the architecture of the new system, where the left side depicts the preprocessing phase for document indexing, based on lexical resources and language technology tools, and the right side the query processing including calculation of similarity between information need represented by user query and document representations. The bag of words implies the representation of the document by a set of ungrammatical words—in our case nouns, adjectives, adverbs and acronyms—followed by their frequencies. Thus, the text generated for each document is lemmatized and noun lemmas (simple and multi-word) are extracted and their frequency is calculated. In that way a total of 12,790 simple lemmas (with 647,303 occurrences) and 271 MWUs (with 9,219 occurrences) were extracted from all documents on geological projects. The bag of words generated for each particular document represents its first index.

The second index is generated from recognized NEs that belong to 3 selected types—location, organization and persons. Figure 3 represents one document from our collection in which recognized NEs are highlighted—toponyms are underlined, personal names (with roles) are underlined with a double line, organization names are framed. Determination of weights for terms within the indexes of a document is a complex process and there are numerous models, the most used being: *tf* based on the term frequency in the document index, *idf* which

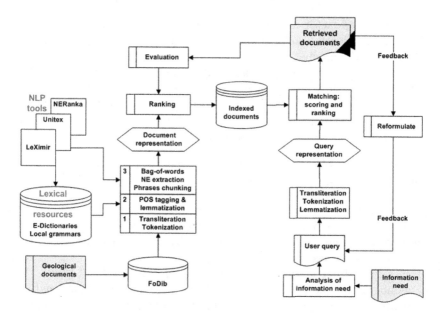

Fig. 2. The architecture of the improved system.

Прелиминарна техноекономска студија услова и могућности експлоатације лежишта угља Черевић Нови Сад, Фрушка Гора, Рударски институт Београд. Ову студију је требало урадити на основу података из Елабората о прорачуну резерви угља Ц2 категорије између Беочина и Баноштора. Институт за грађевинарство Суботица, Миливој Макар, дипл. инж. руд. Беочин. Истраживано подручје налази се на северним падинама Фрушке Горе, између Беочина на истоку и Баноштора на западу. Угљени слојеви се даље настављају према западу до Корушке. Студија о хидрогеолошким истраживањима у зони између Параћина и Главице у циљу отварања новог изворишта (I фаза). Београд Др Војислав Томић, доцент, Невен Крешић, дипл.инж.

Fig. 3. A document showing NER results.

takes into account the number of documents in which the term appears, tf_idf which is the combination of these two, probabilistic, which includes in addition relevance weights, tfc_tfc which modifies the formula for ranking with cosine normalization, tfc_nfc which uses a normalized tf factor for terms of the query (as different mapping of the vector space of documents and queries is more efficient), lnc_ltc where the linear function is replaced by the logarithm, and finally the lnu_ltu which uses the document length and the average length of documents instead of cosine measure for normalizing length [8].

The improved system ranking uses several measures, starting with tf_idf measure based on frequencies of words allocated to the text, text length, and the document frequency [14]. Further development included modification of tf_idf with cosine normalization (tfc_tfc), tfc_nfc term weighting algorithm with normalized tf factor for the query term weights, lnc_ltc measure where l stands for weights with a logarithmic tf component, lnu_ltu where normalization is based on the number of unique words in text, as well as several measures used in InQuery and Okapi systems.[4] Authors in [4] report on term weighting experiments with a linear combination of retrieval clues, one of the form $\alpha + \beta \cdot tf + \gamma \cdot idf + \delta \cdot tf \cdot idf$. The best performance was achieved when $\alpha = 0.4$, $\beta = \delta = 0$ and $\gamma = 0.6$.

Indexing is performed in the following steps:

1. Generating a text (D_i) from records and fields of the project summary related to a particular project document, where $i = 1, \ldots N$ and N is the size of the document collection;
2. Lemmatizing and POS tagging of all D_i texts;
3. Recognizing NEs and assigning the chosen types to documents;
4. Selecting ungrammatical words t_{ij} for each D_i and calculating:
   (a) n_{ij} as frequencies of t_{ij},
   (b) average and maximum term frequency (avg_tf_i, max_tf_i),
   (c) number of unique words in document (no_uw_i) and document length (l_i),
   (d) relative frequency tf_{ij} for each term t_{ij} in a text D_i as n_{ij}/l_i where l_i is the length of the text in the number of simple words,
   (e) normalized term frequency $ntf = \log(tf + 0.5)/\log(max\_tf + 1)$,
   (f) $H\_inquery = (max\_tf \leq 200 ? 1 : 200/max\_tf)$, penalty for long documents,
   (g) $K\_okapi = k_1 \cdot ((1 - k_2) + k_2 \cdot l_i/avg\_dl)$ where avg_dl is the average document length, $k_1 = 1.2$, $k_2 = 0.75$ length normalisation;
5. Creating a dictionary of the whole document collection from all words selected in Step 4. For each term T_k in the document collection, $k = 1, \ldots M$, where M is the size of the dictionary of document collection:
   (a) calculating document frequency df_k as the number of documents in the collection in which the term T_k appears,
   (b) calculating the acceptable indicator idf_k of term value as a document discriminator as $\log(N/df_k)$ (lnc_ltc algorithm uses for ltc expression $idf1_k = \log((N + 1)/df_k)$),
   (c) $nidf_k = idf_k/\log(N)$,
   (d) $idf\_okapi = \log((N - df_k + 0.5)/(df_k + 0.5))$);
6. Calculating the document vector combined measure:
   (a) $tf\_idf = tf \cdot idf$, and vector intensity int_tf_idf,
   (b) $ltf = 1 + \log(tf)$ and vector intensity int_ltf,
   (c) $tfc = tf\_idf/int\_tf\_idf$,
   (d) $lnc = ltf/int\_ltf$,

---

[4] InQuery, an indexing and retrieval "engine" is developed at the Center for Intelligent Information Retrieval (CIIR), College of Information and Computer Sciences, University of Massachusetts Amherst [2]. The Okapi system was originally developed at the Polytechnic of Central London in the early 1980's and later developed at City University London and Microsoft Research [21].

(e) $lnu = (ltf/(1 + log(avg\_tf)))/((1 - s) + s \cdot (no\_uw))$, with the constant value $s = 0.25$,

(f) $w\_inquery = 0.4 + 0.6 \cdot (b \cdot H\_inquery + (1 - b) \cdot ntf) \cdot nidf$, $b = 0.5$,

(g) $w\_okapi = (k_1 + 1) \cdot tf/(K\_okapi + tf)$.

In the search stage the similarity of the search query vector and the document are determined as follows:

1. the query is analyzed, tokenization is performed (separating into words, where a MWU within quotation marks is treated as one word) followed by calculating:
   (a) maximum term frequency max_tf and number of unique words no_uw from query,
   (b) $nfc = (0.5 + 0.5 \cdot tf/max\_tf) \cdot lema\_idf$,
   (c) $ltc = (1 + log(tf)) \cdot lema\_idf1$,
   (d) $ltu = ltc/((1 - s) + s \cdot no\_uw)$;
2. for each document and for each word in the query depending on the selected method the weight is calculated, where d stands for document and q for query:
   (a) 'tfc_nfc': $d\_tfc \cdot q\_nfc$,
   (b) 'lnc_ltc': $d\_lnc \cdot q\_ltc$,
   (c) 'lnu_ltu': $d\_lnu \cdot q\_ltu$,
   (d) '$inquery$': $d\_w\_inquery \cdot q\_tf$,
   (e) '$okapi$': $d\_w\_okapi \cdot q\_idf\_okapi$.
3. the similarity between the query and the document is ranked based on the sum of weights for all words in the query.

Документациони елаборат геолошких истраживања лежишта лигнита "Тамнава - запад". Обреновац 1:100 000 "Тамнава - запад" лок. Каленић, Мали Борак, Рад РО "Колубара-пројект", ООУР Биро за пројектовање и инжењеринг из Лазаревца... исклињавања слојева угља, јер су растојања између истражних радова била два пута мања од растојања дата за поједине категорије резерви угља. Током 1983-84. год. изведене су укупно 62 бушотине, просечне дубине 82,11 м. Извештај о резултатима истражних радова минералних сировина у Тамнавском басену - шира околина Уба за 1984. годину - У6 Бој Брдо и Гредина.

Fig. 4. Examples of sources of erroneous hits.

Document in Fig. 4 has been retrieved for the faceted query with keywords "Tamnava OR Ub" (two mining sites) in the *location* facet and "ugalj OR lignit" (coal or lignite) keywords in the *mineral resource* facet. The initial system would identify *lignita* (as a substring of the genitive form of *lignit*) and *Tamnava* as matches (underlined by a thicker single line) but would fail to identify *uglja* (genitive form of *ugalj* underlined by a double line), which is, however, identified by the improved system. As we have already mentioned, the initial system identification method was based on 'like' function, which means that it searched the entire content within a field, regardless of the position of the search string, which solves some problems but introduces other. Thus, for example, the initial system falsely matched the keyword *Ub* in the words *Kolubari* and *dubini* (the substring *ub* is framed in these words). As a result, in the first 50 matches offered by the initial system only the first document pertains to *Ub*, six pertain to *Tamnava*, and all the rest are a result of "false matches" of the keyword *Ub*. Such errors do not occur in the improved system, but "false matches" cannot be completely avoided, as for example in the case of *so* 'salt', which is a mineral resource, but also the acronym for *skupština opštine* 'municipality council', which appears in a number of documents. However, the initial system finds a string *so* in as many as 1,842 documents since it is a frequent syllable in Serbian, while the faceted search retrieves only 169 of them, some of which refer to a municipality council, others to salt. Faceted search in general improves ranking within the initial system. Namely, if a "general search" is performed instead of a faceted search for the query "Tamnava or Ub and coal or lignite" the document "Coal of the Tamnava basin in the vicinity of Ub", which was ranked first in the faceted search, drops to the 21st place, with irrelevant documents being better ranked due to "false match" in a greater number of fields, given that the general search looks into all fields in the database, not only those related to a specific facet.

4   Evaluation

The improved system includes an evaluation module, which allows a logged user to evaluate the relevance of retrieved documents after the search has been completed.[5] Figure 5 depicts the evaluation panel: when the query and the search

Fig. 5. The web panel for evaluation of retrieved documents by different methods.

---

[5] Available at http://geoliss.mre.gov.rs/fodibevaluacija/.

method are specified, results of a previous search can optionally be filtered. In order to alleviate this task, the system highlights the text in which keywords from the search were found.

From the same web page access is being enabled to pages with statistical data pertaining to evaluation, such as the precision-recall curve or 11-point Interpolated Average Precision for the query [22]. Comparison of several queries cross linked with different ranking methods can also be represented with the Average Precision graph. In this section we will present and describe these graphs.

The goal of evaluation was to assess and compare the efficiency of the initial and improved search methods. The evaluation was performed over the entire collection of documents and a set of 55 information needs, represented by respective queries. For query selection the log of the existing system was used, while also consulting geologist about their most common information needs. It turned out that most frequent requests are for a mineral resource type like copper, gold, coal, optionally at some location, or a geological event like landslide or earthquake. For evaluation standard measures were used, namely precision $P = tp/(tp + fp)$, recall $R = tp/(tp + fn)$, and $F1$-measure $F = 2 \cdot P \cdot R/(P + R)$, where $tp - $ *true positive* is the number of relevant documents retrieved, $fp - $ *false positive* is the number of non-relevant documents retrieved, and $fn - $ *false negative* is the number of relevant documents that were not retrieved. During the evaluation ranked responses were offered to users, and the measures P and R were calculated for sets containing the first i choices offered, where $i \in [1, 50]$ [14]. In this way, curves showing the dependency between precision and recall for all 55 queries were obtained, as illustrated in Fig. 6 for the query "geothermal energy in spas". It should be noted that results in this section are presented and

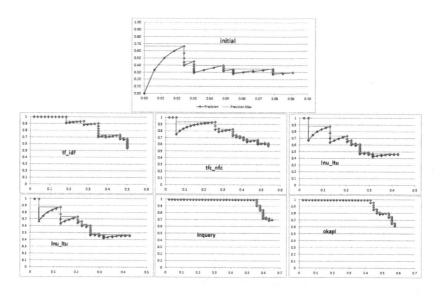

Fig. 6. Precision-recall curve for the query "geothermal energy in spas".

discussed for six out of seven available indexing methods. Namely the results of the tfc_tfc method were omitted as they were identical to the results of the tfc_nfc method. The precision of the initial system is in general better among first-ranked documents than in the case of the improved system, with the exception of the InQuery method, while the recall is better with the improved system.

Although the precision-recall curves offer a pretty good insight into system performance, it is often necessary to generate some sort of concise information, or even a single number. The usual approach is the 11-point Interpolated Average Precision, obtained by calculating the interpolated precision for each query over 11 recall values of $0.0, 0.1, 0.2, \ldots, 1.0$, and then calculating their average. When the Interpolated Average Precision for 11 levels of recall is calculated, a comparative graph is obtained of the relationship between precision and recall. The procedure was applied for all 55 information needs (queries). This set of queries has then been sorted in ascending order of the difference between the best performing ranking method for indexed documents InQuery and the performance of the initial method, and the results are depicted in Fig. 7.

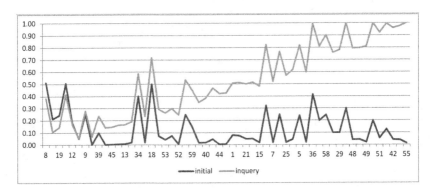

Fig. 7. Differences between initial method and InQuery indexing sorted in ascending order.

We shall now discuss two sets of five queries each, where differences between the initial and improved system are greatest, once in favor of the former and once in favor of the latter, as well as a set of 10 queries where the improvement is achieved, but on a moderate scale. The results will be presented in tables, showing the information need in the first column, the corresponding faceted query keywords in the second and the query surrogate, that is, linguistically preprocessed information need in the third. For example, within this preprocessing, the information need *kvalitet podzemnih voda u Beogradu* 'quality of underground waters in Belgrade' is transformed by the improved indexed based system into a set of lemmas, recognized by lexical analysis. Prepositions, conjunctions and the like are omitted, e.g. the preposition *u* 'in' in this query. The noun *kvalitet* 'quality', adjective *podzemni* 'underground' and toponym *Beograd* have unambiguous lemmas, whereas *voda* can correspond to nouns 'water' and 'platoon', but also to a form of the verb *vodati* 'to lead someone'. The system also recognizes the MWU *podzemne vode* 'underground waters'.

Table 3. Five queries for which the initial system performed better than the improved.

8 **information need:** *geofizički karotaž Naftagas* — **faceted query:** *geofizički karotaž*; *Naftagas* — **indexed query:** *geofizički*; *karotaž*; *NAFTAGAS* — 'geophysical logging Naftagas'

22 **information need:** *dolomit "Institut za puteve" "Institut za istraživanja i ispitivanja"* — **faceted query:** *Dolomit*; *Institut za puteve*; *Institut za istraživanja i ispitivanja* — **indexed query:** *dolomit;istraživanje* — 'dolomite "The Highway Institut"'

19 **information need:** *Dunav Sava podzemna* — **faceted query:** *Dunav Sava*; *podzemna* — indexed query: *Dunav;Sava;Savo*; *podzemni* — 'Danube Sava underground'

14 **information need:** *rezerve uglja u Sjeničkom basenu* — **faceted query:** *rezerve uglja*; *Sjenički basen* — **indexed query:** *rezerva*; *ugalj*; *uglja*; *sjenički*; *basen* — 'coal reserves in Sjenica basin'

12 **information need:** *izvorište zagadjenja Obrenovac Lazarevac Lajkovac* — **faceted query:** *izvorište zagadjenja*; *Obrenovac Lazarevac Lajkovac* — **indexed query:** *izvorište*; *zagadjenje*; *Obrenovac*; *Lazarevac*; *Lajkovac* — 'source of pollution Obrenovac Lazarevac Lajkovac'

Table 3 shows examples of queries in which the initial system performed better than the improved. This is mostly due to the fact that the improved system often erroneously selects documents in which a toponym is specified, by failing to discern between toponyms in names of institutions that have produced the document, e.g. *Rudarski institut Beograd* 'Mining Institute in Belgrade' and toponyms pertaining to the location of the geological site to which the document refers. In the initial version of the improved system a problem was also encountered related to the lack of domain specific geologic terms, such as *karotaž* 'logging'. This problem is being solved by continuous enrichment of e-dictionaries.

In the columns of Table 4 the Average Precision $AP = \sum_{k=1}^{n} P(k)\Delta(k)$ is given for queries in Table 3 using the current system and all indexing methods except tfc_tfc, where $n = 50$ is the number of retrieved documents, $P(k)$ is the precision in the intersection point k, and $\Delta(k)$ is the change in the recall from item $k - 1$ to item k. The comparison of all applied methods for 5 queries for which the initial method achieved better results is given in Fig. 8.

Table 5 depicts a set of queries in which a moderate improvement has been achieved in comparison to the initial system, ranging from 0.36 to 0.46 (Table 6, Fig. 9). It should be noted that for the query *ležište bakra* 'copper deposit' the improved system assigns two nouns, *bakar* 'copper' and *bakra* 'copper cauldron', but the results are nevertheless better in comparison to the initial system, which does not recognize *bakra* as the genitive of *bakar* at all.

Table 4. Comparison of indexing methods for queries in Table 3.

Id	Difference inquery initial	initial	tf_idf	tfc_nfc	lnc_ltc	lnu_ltu	inquery	okapi
8	−0.13	0.51	0.232	0.144	0.158	0.128	0.381	0.315
22	−0.11	0.21	0.124	0.19	0.108	0.131	0.108	0.137
19	−0.10	0.24	0.168	0.176	0.268	0.235	0.146	0.168
14	−0.09	0.51	0.087	0.233	0.168	0.05	0.414	0.249
12	−0.01	0.18	0.197	0.02	0.049	0.015	0.168	0.169

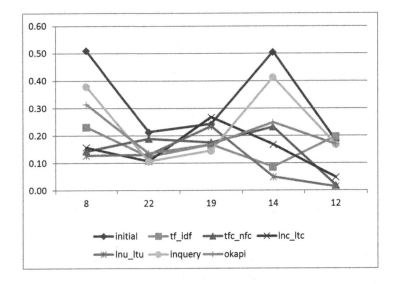

Fig. 8. Comparison of all indexing methods for queries in Table 3.

Finally, Table 7 outlines a set of queries for which a considerable improvement has been made in comparison to the initial system ranging from 0.87 to 0.99 (Table 8, Fig. 10). In the query *ispitivanje tla u Nišu* 'soil analysis in Niš' linguistic preprocessing eliminates the preposition *u* 'in' unambiguously recognizes the nouns *ispitivanje* 'analysis' and *tlo* 'soil', whereas *Nišu* is recognized as the genitive of the toponym *Niš*, but also the accusative of the noun 'niche' and the third person plural of the verb 'to swing'. Nevertheless, the obtained results are considerably better than the results of the initial method.

Figure 11 depicts the MAP for all 55 queries over the six ranking methods for indexed documents and the initial method. The worst performing ranking method *lnu_ltu* has an almost three times better performance than the initial method, whereas the results for the best performing method InQuery are over four times better than for the initial method.

Table 5. Five queries for which the improved system achieved a moderate improvement.

40 **information need:** *nafta bušotina Braničevo* — **faceted query:** *nafta; bušotina; Braničevo* — **indexed query:** *nafta; bušotina; Braničevo* — 'oil drill-hole Braničevo'

27 **information need:** *gravimetrija geofizika* — **faceted query:** *Gravimetrija; geofizika* — **indexed query:** *Gravimetrija; geofizika* — 'gravimetry geophysics'

44 **information need:** *istraživanja u kolubarskom basenu* — **faceted query:** *istraživanje; "kolubarski basen"* — **indexed query:** *istraživanje; kolubarski;basen* — 'exploration in Kolubara basin'

35 **information need:** *rudno telo* — **faceted query:** *"rudno telo"* — **indexed query:** *rudni; Rudno; telo* — 'ore body'

1 **information need:** *zlato Au Bor Borski okrug* — **faceted query:** *zlato; Bor; "Borski okrug"* — **indexed query:** *zlato; Bor; Borski okrug* — 'gold Au Bor Bor region'

46 **information need:** *ležiste* — **faceted query:** *"ležiste bakra"* — **indexed query:** *ležište; bakar; bakra* — 'deposit'

21 **information need:** *klizište Umka Geozavod* — **faceted query:** *"klizište Umka"; GEOZAVOD* — **indexed query:** *klizište; Umka; GEOZAVOD* — 'landslide Umka Geozavod'

37 **information need:** *arteski bunar* — **faceted query:** *"arteski bunar"* — **indexed query:** *arteski; bunar* — 'Artesian well'

15 **information need:** *kvarcni pesak bušotine* — **faceted query:** *"Kvarcni pesak"; bušotina* — **indexed query:** *kvarcni; pesak; bušotina* — 'quartz sand drill-hole'

4 **information need:** *poplava plavljenje izlivanje* — **faceted query:** *poplava; plavljenje; izlivanje* — **indexed query:** *poplava; plavljenje; izlivanje* — 'flood flooding outpouring'

Table 6. Comparison of indexing methods for queries in Table 5.

Id	Difference inquery initial	initial	tf_idf	tfc_nfc	lnc_ltc	lnu_ltu	inquery	okapi
40	0.36	0.02	0.352	0.255	0.394	0.337	0.383	0.263
27	0.42	0.05	0.351	0.407	0.459	0.409	0.466	0.468
44	0.42	0.00	0.202	0.406	0.417	0.364	0.423	0.458
35	0.42	0.00	0.329	0.346	0.462	0.310	0.426	0.479
1	0.43	0.08	0.133	0.105	0.306	0.164	0.508	0.465
46	0.44	0.08	0.307	0.240	0.400	0.269	0.513	0.344
21	0.45	0.05	0.020	0.055	0.082	0.098	0.500	0.536
37	0.46	0.05	0.171	0.449	0.373	0.090	0.514	0.511
15	0.46	0.02	0.371	0.426	0.385	0.321	0.483	0.38
4	0.50	0.32	0.802	0.834	0.845	0.843	0.822	0.856

The evaluation, as well as the analysis of the results confirmed that the initial system achieves good results when searching with terms that occur as discipline

Table 7. Five queries for which the improved system achieved a considerable improvement.

51 **information need**: *ispitivanje tla u Nišu* — **faceted query**: *"ispitivanje tla";Niš* — **indexed query**: *ispitivanje*; *tle*; *tlo*; *nihati*; *Niš*; *niša* — 'soil analysis in Niš'

47 **information need**: *konturno bušenje* — **faceted query**: *"konturno bušenje"* — **indexed query**: *konturni*; *bušenje* — 'contour drilling'

42 **information need**: *životna sredina zaštita* — **faceted query**: *"životna sredina"*; *zaštita* — **indexed query**: *životan*; *sredina*; *zaštita* — 'environment protection'

33 **information need**: *klizište Barajevo* — **faceted query**: *"klizište Barajevo"* — **indexed query**: *klizište*; *Barajevo* — 'landslide Barajevo'

55 **information need**: *gama zračenje* — **faceted query**: *"gama zračenje"* — **indexed query**: *gama*; *zračenje* — 'gamma radiation'

Table 8. Comparison of indexing methods for queries in Table 7.

Id	Difference inquery initial	initial	tf_idf	tfc_nfc	lnc_ltc	lnu_ltu	inquery	okapi
51	0.87	0.05	0.678	0.642	0.704	0.301	0.922	0.766
47	0.87	0.13	1.000	1.000	1.000	0.994	0.996	0.998
42	0.92	0.04	0.594	0.584	0.741	0.408	0.959	0.948
33	0.94	0.04	0.588	0.734	0.793	0.464	0.976	0.892
55	0.99	0.01	0.860	0.986	0.986	0.952	1.000	1.000

and mineral resources facets, which are thus listed in the appropriate fields in the same form in which the users formulate their query (e.g. the nominative singular). It also confirmed the disadvantage of the system based on text scanning which affects the precision when short words that could be parts of other words are used in a search, such as the acronym of company "NIS". The average precision for query "geophysical logging Naftagas NIS" (obtained by adding "NIS" the acronym of the Naftagas company to query "geophysical logging Naftagas"), drops from 0.512 to 0.255 for the initial solution, while results for methods based on indexing are improved. The opposite happens for queries that contain terms that are missing from e-dictionaries, e.g. *karotaž* 'logging' or terms for which inflected forms are missing, e.g. the plural form *ugljevi* of *ugalj* 'coal' that is specific to the mining terminology. The graph presented in Fig. 12 gives average precisions for one query ("geothermal energy in spas"). The comparison of current system and new indexing methods shows that the InQuery method is superior for majority of queries over current system and other indexing methods.

The comparison of several methods for queries with greatest difference between highest and lowest value (in favor of improved methods) is given in Fig. 10. It is obvious that for the selected queries the performance of the initial method is significantly worse, whereas among the methods of the improved system InQuery is the most successful one. InQuery also gave best results measured by "Precision at k". This measure, giving precision at specific levels of retrieved

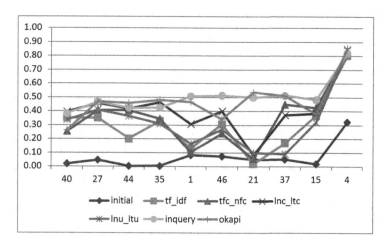

Fig. 9. Comparison of all indexing methods for queries in Table 5.

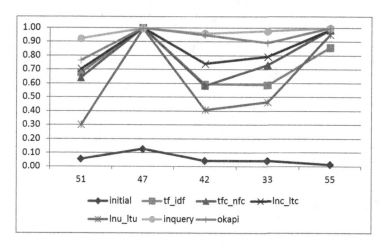

Fig. 10. Comparison of all indexing methods for queries in Table 7.

results (e.g. first 5, 10, 20, etc.) is also often taken into account, as users often look only at the certain number of best ranked results. It is especially the case when web search is performed, where a certain number of retrieved documents is given on each page, and users take only the first page into consideration. The advantage of this measure is that it does not require an estimate of the size of the set of relevant documents, but its disadvantage is that it is the least stable of the commonly used evaluation measures and that it does not average well, since the total number of relevant documents for a query has a strong influence on "Precision at k". [14] Fig. 13 depicts the average precision for the first 5, 10, 20, 30, 40, and 50 retrieved documents for all 55 queries, or information needs, where InQuery performs best, followed by Okapi.

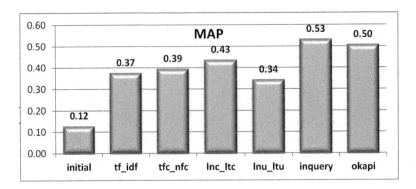

Fig. 11. Mean Average Precision (MAP) of all 55 queries for the initial and improved system with different ranking methods.

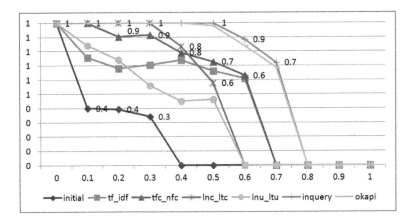

Fig. 12. Average precision for the query "geothermal energy in spas".

Evaluation results presented here are publicly available.[6] According to one of the evaluators the initial system only "looks nice" but its evaluation is cumbersome, and the improved system is by all means more precise. Another evaluator remarked that although the initial system performs well for some simple queries, it often gives completely erroneous results for complex ones. If assessed, the initial system would have a mark of 2 and the improved a 6, in comparison to Google Search with a mark of 10.

---

[6] For the initial system at http://geoliss.mre.gov.rs/fodibevaluacija/statistika.php, the improved system at http://geoliss.mre.gov.rs/fodibevaluacija/statistika-index. php for individual queries, and for the entire sets of queries at http://geoliss.mre. gov.rs/fodibevaluacija/statistika-all-methods.php.

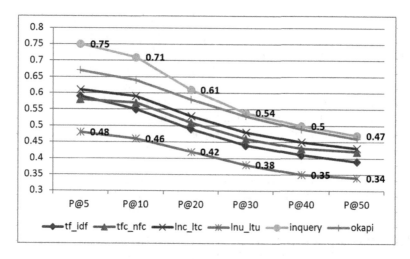

Fig. 13. The average precision for levels of recall ranging from 5 to 50 for all 55 queries.

5 Conclusion and Future Work

The evaluation results show that an improvement has indeed been achieved by introducing document indexing in the system. However, the initial solution, besides being simple to apply, outperformed the improved system for certain types of queries. Hence, future research should look into possibilities of combining these two methods, namely faceted search with linguistic preprocessing of queries and document indexing.

There are also several other courses of action towards further improvement. In order to minimize the number of unrecognized words within a query, morphological e-dictionaries of simple words and MWUs must be continuously updated with new geological terms. As for named entities, they will be adequately introduced into faceted search, along with the implementation of their normalization. The name entity recognition system will be improved to perform better in the geological domain, as it was initially developed for recognizing named entities in journal articles. Various combinations of weight measures for terms will be explored in order to reach an optimal combination. Finally, presentations of the information need and the document will be revisited, looking for the most efficient ways they can be matched.

Other textual as well as spatial databases and data collections will be used in the future for assessing the flexibility of the proposed solution, along with the introduction of geodatabases for visualization recognized toponym locations. Query expansion is also under consideration, where query terms would be supplemented with related terms, such as hyponyms or hypernyms, with the help of available resources, such as the geologic dictionary [24] for terms from domain terminology and WordNet for more general terms.

One of the shortcoming of the improved system is the absence of the possibility for fine-tuning the search, based on an analysis of results with or without specific keywords. Improvement of the software solution for filtering and extraction of search result is also needed. Another possible improvement would be the use of relevant queries for re-ranking the retrieved documents, where the weights of relevant documents would be included in the metrics. This is a variation of the Okapi method, which is pretty demanding for the average user, but makes sense for some frequently repeated queries, or queries that are repeated at certain time intervals.

Acknowledgement. This research was supported by the Serbian Ministry of Education and Science under the grant #47003 and KEYSTONE COST Action IC1302. The authors would like to thank the anonymous reviewers for their helpful and constructive comments. We are also grateful for the time and effort our young colleagues from the Faculty of Mining and Geology Biljana Lazić, Dalibor Vorkapić and Nikola Vulović invested in evaluating the document retrieval results.

References

1. Bizer, C., Boncz, P., Brodie, M.L., Erling, O.: The meaningful use of big data: four perspectives-four challenges. ACM SIGMOD Rec. **40**(4), 56–60 (2012)
2. Callan, J., Croft, W.B., Harding, S.: The inquery retrieval system, pp. 78–83 (1992)
3. Courtois, B., Silberztein, M.: Dictionnaires électroniques du français. Larousse, Paris (1990)
4. Croft, W.B., Smith, L.A., Turtle, H.R.: A loosely-coupled integration of a text retrieval system and an object-oriented database system. In: Proceedings of the 15th Annual International ACM SIGIR Conference on Research and Development in Information Retrieval, pp. 223–232. ACM (1992)
5. Furlan, B., Batanović, V., Nikolić, B.: Semantic similarity of short texts in languages with a deficient natural language processing support. Decis. Support Syst. **55**(3), 710–719 (2013)
6. Graovac, J.: Wordnet-based serbian text categorization. INFOtheca **14**(2), 2a–17a (2013)
7. Gross, M.: The use of finite automata in the lexical representation of natural language. In: Gross, M., Perrin, D. (eds.) LITP 1987. LNCS, vol. 377, pp. 34–50. Springer, Heidelberg (1989). doi:10.1007/3-540-51465-1_3
8. Hiemstra, D.: Using language models for information retrieval. Taaluitgeverij Neslia Paniculata (2001)
9. Ivanović, D., Milosavljević, G., Milosavljević, B., Surla, D.: A CERIF-compatible research management system based on the MARC 21 format. Inf. Knowl. Manag. **44**(3), 229–251 (2010)
10. Jackson, P., Moulinier, I.: Natural Language Processing for Online Applications: Text Retrieval, Extraction and categorization, vol. 5. John Benjamins Publishing, Amsterdam (2007)
11. Kešelj, V., Šipka, D.: A suffix subsumption-based approach to building stemmers and lemmatizers for highly inflectional languages with sparse resources. INFOtheca **9**(1–2), 23a–33a (2008)
12. Krstev, C.: Processing of Serbian - Automata. University of Belgrade, Belgrade, Texts and Electronic Dictionaries. Faculty of Philology (2008)

13. Krstev, C., Obradović, I., Utvić, M., Vitas, D.: A system for named entity recognition based on local grammars. J. Logic Comput. **24**(2), 473–489 (2014)
14. Manning, C.D., Raghavan, P., Schütze, H.: Introduction to Information Retrieval, vol. 1. Cambridge University Press, Cambridge (2008)
15. Martinović, M.: Transfer of natural language processing technology: experiments, possibilities and limitations case study: English to Serbian. INFOtheca **9**(1–2), 11a–21a (2008)
16. Maurel, D., Friburger, N., Antoine, J.Y., Eshkol, I., Nouvel, D., et al.: Cascades de transducteurs autour de la reconnaissance des entités nommées. Traitement Automatique des Langues **52**(1), 69–96 (2011)
17. Milosevic, N.: Stemmer for Serbian language. CoRR abs/1209.4471 (2012). http://arxiv.org/abs/1209.4471
18. Mladenović, M., Mitrović, J., Krstev, C., Vitas, D.: Hybrid sentiment analysis framework for a morphologically rich language. J. Intell. Inf. Syst. 1–22, to appear
19. Nadeau, D., Sekine, S.: A survey of named entity recognition and classification. In: Sekine, S., Ranchhod, E. (eds.) Named Entities: Recognition, Classification and Use, pp. 3–28. John Benjamins Publishing Company, Amsterdam (2009)
20. Rehm, G., Uszkoreit, H. (eds.): META-NET White Paper Series. Springer, Heidelberg (2012). http://www.meta-net.eu/whitepapers
21. Robertson, S.E., Walker, S.: Okapi/Keenbow at TREC-8. In: TREC, vol. 8, pp. 151–162 (1999)
22. Salton, G., McGill, M.J.: Introduction to modern information retrieval (1983)
23. Stanković, R., Prodanović, J., Kitanović, O., Nikolić, V.E.: Development of the Serbian geological resources portal. In: Proceedings of 17th Meeting of the Association of European Geological Societies, pp. 61–65 (2011)
24. Stanković, R., Trivić, B., Kitanović, O., Blagojević, B., Nikolić, V.: The development of the geolissterm terminological dictionary. INFOtheca **12**(1), 49a–63a (2011)
25. Utvić, M.: Annotating the corpus of contemporary Serbian. INFOtheca - J. Inform. Librariansh. **12**(2), 36a–47a (2011)
26. Vitas, D., Popović, L., Krstev, C., Obradović, I., Pavlović-Lažetić, G., Stanojević, M.: Srpski jezik u digitalnom dobu - The Serbian Language in the Digital Age. In: Rehm and Uszkoreit [20] (2012). http://www.meta-net.eu/whitepapers
27. Zečević, A., Stanković-Vujičić, S.: Language identification–the case of Serbian. In: Pavlović-Lažetić, G., Krstev, C., Vitas, D., Obradović, I. (eds.) Natural Language Processing for Serbian – Resources and Applications, pp. 101–112. Faculty of Mathematics, University of Belgrade. http://jerteh.rs/wp-content/uploads/2015/05/Zecevic.pdf

Domain-Specific Modeling: A Food and Drink Gazetteer

Andrey Tagarev[✉], Laura Toloşi, and Vladimir Alexiev

Ontotext AD, 47A Tsarigradsko Shosse, 1124 Sofia, Bulgaria
andrey.tagarev@ontotext.com

Abstract. Our goal is to build a Food and Drink (FD) gazetteer that can serve for classification of general, FD-related concepts, efficient faceted search or automated semantic enrichment. Fully supervised design of domain-specific models *ex novo* is not scalable. Integration of several ready knowledge bases is tedious and does not ensure coverage. Completely data-driven approaches require a large amount of training data, which is not always available. For general domains (such as the FD domain), re-using encyclopedic knowledge bases like Wikipedia may be a good idea. We propose here a semi-supervised approach that uses a restricted Wikipedia as a base for the modeling, achieved by selecting a domain-relevant Wikipedia category as root for the model and all its subcategories, combined with expert and data-driven pruning of irrelevant categories.

Keywords: Categorization · Wikipedia · Wikipedia categories · Gazetteer · Europeana · Cultural Heritage · Concept extraction

1 Introduction

Our work is motivated by the Europeana Food and Drink (EFD) project[1], which aims at categorizing food and drink-related concepts (FD), in order to digitalize, facilitate search and semantically enrich Cultural Heritage (CH) items pertaining to the 'food and drink' theme. For this purpose a maximally generic Food and Drink gazetteer needed to be created.

Modeling a domain from scratch requires interdisciplinary expertise, both in the particular domain and in knowledge-base modeling. Also, it is a tedious, time-consuming process. This might be unavoidable when working with narrowly-defined expert domains such as 'Art Nouveau' or 'Human Genes' but in this paper we describe a better approach for generating such gazetteers for broad or fuzzily-defined domains like 'Food and Drink', 'Arts', 'Sports', 'History', etc. While all examples in this paper deal with the specific FD application, the approach is easily generalizable to any domain with such an encyclopedic nature. In fact, the method presented in this paper is scalable, works with Linked Open

---

[1] http://foodanddrinkeurope.eu/.

© Springer International Publishing AG 2017
N.T. Nguyen et al. (Eds.): TCCI XXVI, LNCS 10190, pp. 186–209, 2017.
DOI: 10.1007/978-3-319-59268-8_9

Data and is semi-automated requiring only minimal input from domain-experts which makes it preferable for such applications.

To model encyclopedic domains we used the DBpedia project which is a great collection of general knowledge concepts extracted from the structured data of Wikipedia articles and categories. It is freely available and easily editable by anyone. The volume of information is enormous, e.g. the English wiki has a total of 35M pages, of which 30M are auxiliary (discussions, sub-projects, categories, etc.). Overall, Wikipedia has some 35M articles in over 240 languages. Multilingualism is a very important aspect that recommends the usage of Wikipedia, as CH objects in EFD come in eleven languages.

In this paper we give a detailed description of a method for generating gazetteers of broad domains, demonstrate the application of this method to generating a Food and Drink gazetteer, and present a critical discussion of the suitability of Wikipedia for this purpose. In Sect. 2, we describe the EFD application that motivated the creation of our method. In Sect. 3 contains a step-by-step description of the method itself. Section 4 presents some insightful (from both technical and application perspective) properties of the sub-hierarchy generated from the *Food and drink* root. Section 5 describes the supervised curation of the domain which narrows its focus and is the only human input required in the algorithm. Section 6 shows the results of the data-driven enrichment analysis. Section 7 demonstrates how automation can be extended beyond generating the gazetteer and into discovering documents belonging to the domain which can then be used to further refine the gazetteer. Section 8 presents a way of extending an existing gazetteer to other languages. Section 9 presents an annotator evaluation of the resulting gazetteer. Finally Sect. 10 concludes the paper with comments and discussion of possible future work.

Next, we mention previous work that has addressed domain-specific modeling in the past.

1.1 Related Work

Much work has been dedicated to building domain specific knowledge bases. Earliest approaches were fully supervised, domain experts defining *ex-novo* the classification model. With the development of modern NLP techniques such as concept disambiguation, concept tagging or relation extraction, semi-supervised and even unsupervised methods are emerging. For example, there are many methods for automated merging and integration of already existing ontologies [3,4,11]. In [10], a semi-supervised method for enriching existing ontologies with concepts from text is presented. More ambitious approaches propose unsupervised generation of ontologies [8,9], using deep NLP methods. In [5], a method is described, for generating lightweight ontologies by mapping concepts from documents to LOD data like Freebase and DBpedia and then generating a meaningful taxonomy that covers the concepts.

Classification of FD has been approached before. Depending on the purpose of the classification, there exist models for cooking and recipes, models for ingredients and nutrients, food composition databases (EuroFIR classification[2]), models that classify additives (Codex Alimentarius GSFA[3]), pesticides (Codex Classification of Foods and Feeds[4]), traded food and beverages nomenclature (GS1 standard for Food and Beverages[5]), national-specific classification systems, etc. [12] have proposed a cooking ontology, focused on: food (ingredients), kitchen utensils, recipes, cooking actions. BBC also proposed a lightweight food ontology[6], that classifies mainly recipes, including aspects like ingredients, diets, courses, occasions.

The purpose of the EFD project is to classify food and drink objects from a cultural perspective, which is not addressed by existing models.

2   Europeana Food and Drink

The EFD Classification scheme [2] is a multi-dimensional scheme for discovering and classifying Cultural Heritage Objects (CHO) related to Food and Drink (FD). The project makes use of innovative semantic technologies to automate the extraction of terms and co-references. The result is a body of semantically-enriched metadata that can support a wider range of multilingual applications such as search, discovery and browse.

The FD domain is generously broad and familiar, in the sense that any human can name hundreds of concepts that should be covered by the model: 'bread', 'wine', 'fork', 'restaurant', 'table', 'chicken, 'bar', 'Thanksgiving dinner', etc. In our particular application however, the model is required to cover a large variety of cultural objects related to FD, some of which exist nowadays only in ethnographic museums. These are described in content coming from a variety of CH organizations, ranging from Ministries to academic libraries and specialist museums to picture libraries. The content represents a significant number of European nations and cultures, it comprises objects illustrating FD heritage, recipes, artworks, photographs, some audio and video content and advertising relating to FD. It is heterogeneous in types and significance, but with the common thread of FD heritage and its cultural and social meaning. Metadata are available partly in English and native languages, with more than half of the metadata only available in native languages.

Content is heterogeneous and varied. Examples include [2]: books on Bovine care and feeding (TEL[7]), book on tubers/roots used by New Zealand aboriginals (RLUK[8]), self-portraits involving some food (Slovak National Gallery[9]), traditional recipes for Christmas-related foods (Ontotext), colorful pasta

---

[2] http://www.eurofir.org/.

[3] http://www.codexalimentarius.org/standards/gsfa/.

[4] ftp://ftp.fao.org/codex/meetings/ccpr/ccpr38/pr38CxCl.pdf.

[5] http://www.gs1.org/gdsn/gdsn-trade-item-extension-food-and-beverage/2-8.

[6] http://www.bbc.co.uk/ontologies/fo.

[7] http://www.theeuropeanlibrary.org/tel4/.

[8] http://www.rluk.ac.uk/.

[9] http://www.sng.sk/en/uvod.

arrangements (Horniman[10]), mortar used to mix lime with tobacco to enhance its psychogenic compounds (Horniman), food pounder cut from coral and noted for its ergonomic design (Horniman), toy horse made from cheese (Horniman), a composition of man with roosters/geese made from bread (Horniman), poems about food and love, photos of old people having dinner, photos of packers on a wharf, photos of Parisian cafes, photos of a shepherd tending goats, photos of a vintner in his winery, medieval cook book (manuscript), commercial label/ad for consommé, etc.

2.1   Wikipedia Categories Related to FD

Wikipedia categories live in the namespace 'https://en.wikipedia.org/wiki/ Category:' (note the colon at the end). We discovered a number of FD categories, amongst them: *Food and drink, Beverages, Ceremonial food and drink, Christmas food, Christmas meals and feasts, Cooking utensils, Drinking culture, Eating parties, Eating utensils, Food and drink preparation, Food culture, Food festivals, Food services occupations, Foods, History of food and drink, Holiday foods, Meals, Works about food and drink, World cuisine.* Other interesting categories: *Religious food and drink, Food law*: topics like halal, kashrut, designation of origin, religion-based ideas, fisheries laws, agricultural laws, food and drug administration, labeling regulations, etc., *Food politics, Drink and drive songs, Food museums.* We selected https://en.wikipedia.org/wiki/Category:Food_and_ drink as the root of our FD restricted model, considering that all the above-mentioned categories are its direct or indirect subcategories.

3   A Method for Domain-Specific Modeling

Wikipedia is loosely structured information. It has very elaborate editorial policies and practices, but their major goal is to create modular text that is consistent, attested (referenced to primary sources), relatively easy to manage. A huge number of templates and other MediaWiki mechanisms are used for this purpose. The structured parts of Wikipedia that can be reused by machines are: (*i*) Links (wiki links, inter-language links providing language correspondence, inter-wiki links, referring to another Wikipedia or another Wikimedia project e.g. Wiktionary, Wikibooks, external links), (*ii*) Informative templates, in particular Infoboxes; (*iii*) Tables; (*iv*) Categories; (*v*) Lists, Portals, Projects.

There are several efforts to extract structured data from Wikpedia. E.g. the Wikipedia Mining software[11] [6] allows extraction of focused or limited information. For our purpose, we prefer to use data sets that are already structured, like DBpedia. The data in RDF format is easily loaded in Ontotext GraphDB[12], which allows semantic integration of both Europeana and classification data, and easier querying using SPARQL.

---

[10] http://www.horniman.ac.uk/.

[11] http://sourceforge.net/projects/wikipedia-miner.

[12] http://ontotext.com/products/ontotext-graphdb/.

Table 1. Wikipedia: statistics concerning categories.

Wikipedia	art	cat	art→cat	cat per art	art per cat	cat→cat	cat per cat
English	4,774,396	1,122,598	18,731,750	3.92	16.69	2,268,299	2.02
Dutch	1,804,691	89,906	2,629,632	1.46	29.25	186,400	2.07
French	1,579,555	278,713	4,625,524	2.93	16.60	465,931	1.67
Italian	1,164,000	258,210	1,597,716	1.37	6.19	486,786	1.89
Spanish	1,148,856	396,214	4,145,977	3.61	10.46	675,380	1.7
Polish	1,082,000	2,217,382	20,149,374	18.62	9.09	4,361,474	1.97
Bulgarian	170,174	37,139	387,023	2.27	10.42	73,228	1.97
Greek	102,077	17,616	182,023	1.78	10.33	35,761	2.03

3.1 Wikipedia Categories

Category statistics for Wikipedia are presented in Table 1. The counts are obtained from DBpedia (see [2] Sect. 3.11.2). The columns have the following meaning:

- 'Wikipedia' specifies for which language the statistics are computed;
- 'art' is the number of content pages (articles);
- 'cat' is the number of category pages;
- 'art→cat' is the number of assignments of a category as parent of an article;
- 'cat per art' is the average number of category assignments per article, computed as art→cat/art;
- 'art per cat' is the average number of articles assigned per category, computed as art→cat/cat;
- 'cat→cat' is the number of assignments of a category as parent of another category;
- 'cat per cat' is the average number of parent categories per category, computed as cat→cat/cat.

As you can see, there is a great variety of categorization practices across languages. Polish uses a huge number of categories (relative to articles) and assignments. Dutch has a very small number of categories, and their application is not very discriminative ('art per cat' is very high).

Despite these differences, the categorization presents a wealth of information that our method uses for classification.

3.2 Method Overview

Our approach to domain-specific modeling is aimed at selecting a sub-hierarchy of Wikipedia, rooted at a relevant category, that covers well the domain concepts. Following Wikipedia, our model is hierarchical and parent-child relations follow SKOS principles [7]. The procedure follows the steps below:

1. Start by selecting the maximally general Wikipedia category that best describes the domain to ensure coverage. We will refer to this category as *root*.

2. Traverse Wikipedia by starting from the *root* and following `skos:broader` relations between categories to collect all *children* (i.e. sub-categories of the *root*). We also remove cycles to create a directed acyclic graph and calculate useful node metadata such as *level* (i.e. shortest path from root), number of unique subcategories, etc.
3. Top-down curation: perform manual curation by experts of the top (few hundred) categories to remove the ones irrelevant to the domain.
4. Bottom-up enrichment: map domain-related concepts to Wikipedia articles and evaluate enrichment in concepts mapped to each category. Thus, we automatically evaluate the relevance of categories, by direct evidence.

Technical details:

Step 1. Choose a *root* category that defines the domain.

Step 2. Breadth-first (BF) traversal selects all categories reachable from the root. In order to obtain the domain categorization, we keep all possible edges defined by the `skos:broader` relation, but remove edges that create cycles. Cycles are logically incompatible with the SKOS system, but are not forbidden and exist in Wikipedia (sometimes due to bad practices or lack of control). In order to remove cycles, we check that a potential child of the current node of the BF procedure is not also its ancestor before adding the connection. The average number of children of a category is 2.02, therefore we expect the number of categories to grow exponentially with each level until the majority of connections start being discarded for being cyclical.

Step 3. We generate a list of the few hundred most important categories (based on being close to the *root* and having many descendants) that are judged for relevance by an expert. Ones judged irrelevant are marked for removal. Removal of a category consists of a standard node-removal procedure in a directed graph, meaning that all node metadata including all incoming and outgoing edges are deleted and the node is marked as irrelevant in the repository (to be omitted in future builds). As a consequence, the sub-hierarchy may split into two or more connected components, one of which contains the root, the others being rooted at the children of the removed category. In such a case, we discard all connected components, except for the one starting at the initial *root*. The expert curation drastically reduces the size of the sub-hierarchy with minimal work, thus being an efficient early method for pruning.

Step 4. Moving away from the *root*, the number of categories of the domain hierarchy grows exponentially. Manually checking the validity of the categories w.r.t. the domain becomes infeasible. We propose a data-driven approach here: given a collection of documents, thesauri, databases, etc. relevant to the domain, we use a general tagging algorithm to map concepts from the collection to the hierarchy. Categories to which concepts are mapped are likely to belong to the domain, supported by evidence. For the categories to which no concepts have

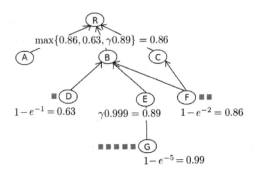

Fig. 1. Scoring categories bottom-up. Concepts mapped to categories are marked with red squares. Categories are marked with circles and named with capital letters. (Color figure online)

been mapped, we can infer their validity by using evidence mapped to children or even more distant descendants. For a leaf category (with no children) X with t concepts directly mapped to it, the score is computed as:

$$score(X) = 1 - e^{-t} \qquad (1)$$

For a category Y with children $Y_1, ..., Y_n$ and t directly mapped concepts, the score is computed as:

$$score(Y) = \max\{1 - e^{-t}, \max_{i=1}^{n}\{\gamma score(Y_i)\}\}, \qquad (2)$$

where $\gamma \in (0, 1)$ is a decay factor, that decreases the score of categories as they get further away from descendants with evidence (i.e. mapped concepts). Figure 1 illustrates an example, where the scores of leaf categories D, E, F are computed based on Eq. 1 and the scores of categories E and B are computed using Eq. 2. The scores can be used for automatically pruning categories that have a score under a certain threshold, where the threshold is level-specific.

4   Properties of the FD Classification Hierarchy

Following the method described in Sect. 3.2 we generated the *FD hierarchy*. We retrieved $887,523$ categories or about 80% of all categories in the English Wikipedia (see Table 1). The categories span 26 levels below the FD root. The distribution of the number of categories by level is unimodal, peaking at the 16th level, where we retrieve about $200,000$ categories (see Fig. 2). The average number of subcategories of a category is 2.36.

Most subcategories reachable from the selected root are *not relevant* to the domain. e.g. all the top 10 most populous categories at level 5 are irrelevant: Oceanography, Water pollution, Physical exercise, Bodies of water, Natural materials, Country planning in the UK, etc. We discuss below reasons and examples for such a disappointing initial hierarchy.

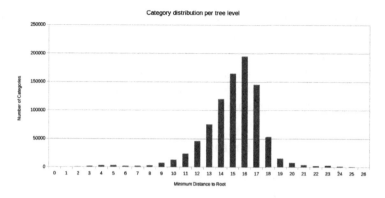

Fig. 2. Distribution of the shortest-path length from categories to the FD root category.

4.1   Reasons for Irrelevant Inclusions

Semantic Drift. The main reason for irrelevance is "semantic drift": since the meaning of the Wikipedia "parent category" relation is not well-defined, the longer path one follows, the harder it becomes to see any logical connection between the two categories (ancestor and descendant). E.g. following the chain
Food and drink → Food politics → Water and politics →
Water and the environment → Water management,
one quickly reaches into rivers, lakes and reservoirs. Luckily it is easy to cut off major irrelevant branches early in the hierarchy.

Wrong Hierarchy. We were surprised to reach football teams. This happens along this chain:
Food and drink → Food politics → Water and politics → Water and the environment → Water management → Water treatment → Euthenics → Personal life → Leisure → Sports → Sports by type → Team sports → Football.
The above chain contains a wrong supercategory assignment: *Euthenics* is the study of the improvement of human functioning and well-being by improvement of living conditions. *Personal life, Leisure* and *Sports* are correctly subcategories of *Euthenics*. But *Water treatment* should not be a supercategory of *Euthenics*. This issue was fixed on June 12, 2014 by removing *Euthenics* from *Water treatment*. However, similar problems still exist elsewhere.

Partial Inclusion. *Food and drink* has child *Animal products*. Only about half of the children of *Animal products* are relevant to the FD domain: *Animal-based seafood, Dairy products, Eggs (food), Fish products, Meat.* Some are definitely not appropriate to FD:
Animal dyes, Animal hair products, Animal waste products, Bird products, Bone products, Coral islands, Coral reefs, Hides.
Finally, there are some mixed subcategories that may include both relevant and irrelevant children: *Animal glandular products*: milk and its thousands of

subcategories is relevant, castoreum is not; *Insect products*: honey is relevant, silk is not; *Mollusc products*: clams and oysters are relevant; pearls are not.

Non-human Food or Eating. Food and drink explicitly includes animal feeding, thus not all are foods for humans, e.g. *Animal feed*. The subcategory *Eating behaviors* has some appropriate children, e.g. *Diets, Eating disorders*, but has also some inappropriate children, e.g. *Carnivory, Detritivores*.

5   Top-Down Expert Pruning

Supervised pruning of irrelevant categories becomes more efficient as experts are presented 'heavier' categories first; therefore we used a heuristic measure for the number of Wikipedia articles reachable from a certain category and provided them to the expert in descending order for judgment. This way, if an irrelevant category is removed, we can expect a drastic decrease of the number of nodes. The expert judged 239 of the top 250 categories in the list as irrelevant to the EFD topic. After removing them, we obtained a more focused hierarchy containing 17542 unique categories, therefore achieving a 50-fold decrease, with an hour effort from a human expert. At this step, we consider that a consensus among several experts is not needed, because only clean mismatches were removed. Examples of removed categories:
Natural materials, Natural resources, Water treatment, Education, Academia, Academic disciplines, Subfields by academic discipline, Scientific disciplines, Real estate, Civil engineering, Construction, Water pollution, Property, Land law, Intelligence, etc.
Some of these categories seem simply irrelevant, like *Civil engineering*, others could potentially lead to articles relevant to FD, like *Natural resources*. The path from FD to *Natural resources* goes through *Agriculture, Agroecology, Sustainable gardening Natural materials* (length 5). However, the category is too broad and too distant to matter, and whatever relevant articles it would link to, should be retrievable by alternative, shorter paths from the FD root. For example, *Natural resources* leads to Salt via *Minerals* and *Sodium minerals*. However, there is a shortcut from FD directly to Salt via *Foods, Condiments, Edible salt*, so there is no need to pass by *Natural resources*, which in turn adds to the hierarchy many irrelevant subcategories.

The new cardinalities per level are shown in (Fig. 3a). (Figure 3b) reveals the levels at which the curation has the largest effect: starting with level 8, the decrease is larger than 50% and from level 11, the decrease is larger than 90%.

The refinement of the FD hierarchy was performed by an expert using the specially designed drill-down UI shown in Fig. 4. It starts with the *root* category and displays a node's child categories ordered by our heuristic measure of weight and all articles directly linked to the node. The user can drill-down on categories to expand them in the same way and quickly mark them as irrelevant which removes them from the repository and UI.

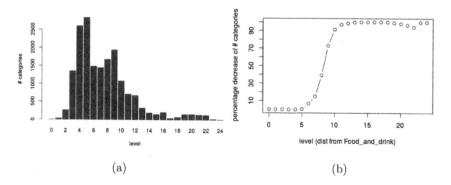

Fig. 3. (a) Number of categories per level after expert curation. (b) Decrease of number of categories per level after expert curation.

6 Bottom-Up Data-Driven Enrichment

A data-driven approach for estimating category relevance was described at Step 3 of our method (see Sect. 3.2). To demonstrate the approach, we considered the Horniman Objects Thesaurus, consisting of about 1500 concepts used for describing Horniman museum artefacts (700 are currently used in objects).

The Horniman thesaurus is a shallow hierarchy consisting of four levels. At the second level, the classification is most informative: *agriculture and forestry, domestication of animals, food processing and storage, food service, hunting, fishing and trapping, narcotics and intoxicants: drinking.* For example, the object *shark hook* (Fig. 5) belongs to the following path: *tools and equipment: general, hunting, fishing and trapping, fish hooks, shark hooks.*

6.1 Mapping the Horniman Thesaurus to Wikipedia Articles

We use an Ontotext general-purpose concept extractor[13] that identifies Wikipedia concepts in general text. For the purpose, we concatenated all thesaurus terms into several pseudo-documents, grouped by the second level category. The concept extractor relies on the context of each candidate for disambiguation, in the sense that the word 'mate' form the thesaurus entry 'mate teapot' would be mapped to http://en.wikipedia.org/wiki/Mate_(beverage), in the context of other terms regarding drinking, and not to other senses, listed in the disambiguation page http://en.wikipedia.org/wiki/Mate. In order to create context, we delimited the thesaurus terms in the pseudo-documents by comma (','). e.g., the pseudo-document for 'hunting, fishing and trapping' starts with:

'*hunt and fishing trap, fishing net, spring trap, mantrap, mole trap, spear, fish spear, eel spear, elephant spear, spike wheel trap, spindle, snare trap, marmot snare, bird snare, sinker, net sinker, sheath, hunting knife sheath, shellfish rake, clam digger, sample, arrow poison, reel, quiver, poison, no-return trap, fish trap, nose clip, net,*

---

[13] Customized version of http://tag.ontotext.com/.

Fig. 5.   Shark   hook, an   object   from   the Horniman   Museum http://www.horniman. ac.uk/collections/ browse-our-collections/ object/136887.

Fig. 4. Visualization interface for the FD categorization.

hunting net, hand net, fishing net, dip net, pig net, pigeon net, scoop net, line, fish line, lure, fly, cuttlefish lure, knife, hunting knife, keep, rat trap, fishing rod, float, line float, net float, fishing float, fish hook, ice-hole hook, halibut hook, gorge, pike hook, salmon hook, shark hook...'

Evaluation. The concept extractor returned 337 unique Wikipedia concepts, with an estimated precision 0.91 of and estimated recall of 0.7. For example, *shellfish rakes*: correctly identifies https://en.wikipedia.org/wiki/Shellfish, but incorrectly returns the redirect https://en.wikipedia.org/wiki/Train for rake, instead of https://en.wikipedia.org/wiki/Rake_(tool).

6.2   Scoring FD Categories w.r.t. Mapped Horniman Concepts

Of all 337 concepts, 219 are in the FD hierarchy. Using our scoring scheme, we 'activated' 451 categories on the path to the FD root. The highest-scoring are shown in Table 2.

Table 2. The highest scoring categories w.r.t. the proposed scoring scheme.

Category	Score	Category	Score
Cooking utensils	1.00	*Crops*	0.99
Teaware	0.99	*Spices*	0.98
Serving and dining	0.99	*Agricultural machinery*	0.98
Cooking appliances	0.99	*Commercial fish*	0.98
Drinkware	0.99	*Eating utensils*	0.98
Staple foods	0.99	*Food storage containers*	0.98
Tropical agriculture	0.99	*Serving utensils*	0.98
Gardening tools	0.99	*Animal trapping*	0.98
Fishing equipment	0.99	*Food and drink*	0.95
Cooking techniques	0.99	*Recreational fishing*	0.95
Cookware and bakeware	0.99	*Breads*	0.95
Crockery	0.99	*Hunting*	0.95
Kitchenware	0.99	*Dairy products*	0.95
Spoons	0.99	*Food ingredients*	0.95
Fishing techniques and methods	0.99	*Food preparation appliances*	0.95

Qualitative evaluation of the scoring system: note that we retrieve Wikipedia categories concerning the broad topics of the Horniman thesaurus that were not explicitly input to our method: agriculture, domestic animals, food processing and storage, hunting and fishing, drinking. Figure 6 shows all the categories up to the FD root that get 'activated' by the bottom-up scoring, meaning that they get a positive score.

Category scoring is also useful for ranking results of a semantic search, provided that enough relevant data is collected and mapped onto the hierarchy. If a user queries a concept, the tool can return a list of Wikipedia categories relevant to the concept, ranked by relevance to the FD domain. For example, if a user searches for 'fork', the category 'Gardening tools' 0.998 will appear higher in the results than *Eating utensils* 0.982, because more concepts from the Horniman museum are mapped to *Gardening tools*.

6.3   Other CHO Collections: Alinari, TopFoto and Wolverhampton

In addition to Hornimann, we performed enrichment on three more data providers' Cultural Heritage Objects. These providers were *Fratelli Alinari, Top-Foto Partners LLP* and *Wolverhampton Arts and Museums*. The former two provided primarily visual archives with some description of the photographs' contents while the latter provided descriptions of physical objects which often but not always came with a picture of the object.

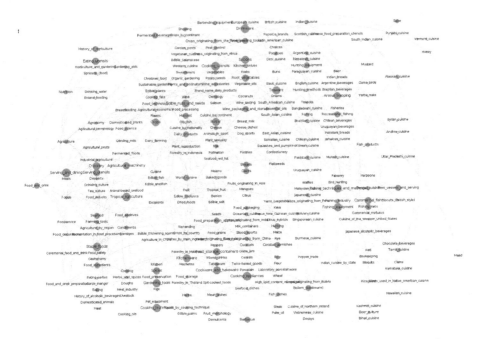

Fig. 6. Paths to *Food and drink*, activated by the bottom-up scoring scheme. Larger image available at ftp://ftp.ontotext.com/pub/EFD/Horniman3.png

Table 3. Enrichment comparison between providers

Provider	CHOs	% of Total	Enriched CHOs	Coverage	Enrichments	per CHO
Horniman	4351	61.3%	4351	100%	40096	9.2
Alinari	498	7.0%	187	37.6%	540	1.1
TopFoto	1814	25.5%	1780	98.1%	14052	7.7
Wolverhampton	438	6.2%	405	92.5%	4161	9.5
All	7101	100%	6723	94.7%	58849	8.3

In Table 3 we can see a summary of the results we obtained from the four different data providers. In the table the first column lists the institution's name; the second is the total number of Cultural Heritage Objects provided; the third shows what fraction of the total CHOs that represents; the fourth shows the number of CHOs that have been enriched with at least one Food and Drink concept; the fifth shows what percentage of the CHOs have been enriched; the sixth shows the total number of concepts discovered in CHOs; the final column shows how many concepts have been discovered on average per CHO.

Unsurprisingly, our Food and Drink gazetteer performs exceptionally well on the Horniman data as we can see every object in the collection has been tagged with at least one concept and on average we discovered over nine objects per CHO. The good news is that the gazetteer has generalized very well and we can observe over 90% coverage for both *TopFoto* and *Wolverhampton* as well as nearly 95% coverage on the full data set.

The data provider we observe the worst results on is Alinari. Further exploration reveals that the reason for that is the quality of the metadata. Namely, the description field of many of their objects (which should be reserved for a description of the photo's contents and should be the most likely source of Food and Drink concepts) very often simply consists of an identical administrative message with no relation to the specific photograph or Food and Drink in general.

The conclusion is that the Food and Drink gazetteer we have produced is very well suited to our purposes so far. We intend to enrich more data provider collections in the future for further corroboration but this is solid evidence for the method's effectiveness.

7   A Food and Drink Statistical Classifier

The Food and drink hierarchy naturally provides with data for training a statistical classifier that is able to discriminate between food-and-drink and non-food-and-drink documents. Specifically, we constructed two sets of documents, *positives* and *negatives*, as follows. The *positives* are the abstracts of all Wikipedia concepts that are in the FD hierarchy, that were at least once tagged in the collection of CHOs Sect. 6.1. Thus, we only include confirmed food-and-drink-related concepts. For the *negatives*, we collected by random selection abstracts of Wikipedia concepts that are not in the FD tree. We made sure that the selection is not biased towards heavy categories (e.g. *Living people*), which would make the classification unrealistically easy (living people against food and drink concepts would be easy), by limiting the number of samples from the same category to 3. We arrived at a set of about 1200 positive samples and 4700 negatives. We trained a bag-of-words maxent classifier and achieved 89% F1 score, for a train-test split of 80% and 20% of the data, respectively. The dataset being relatively small, we consider that the performance is really good. Also, as the collections of CHOs get populated and more positive examples are collected, the performance will most likely increase.

The most relevant 50 features (stemmed) for classification are:

food, restaur, drink, cook, dish, london, fruit, brand, type, commonli, cuisin, beverag, alcohol, tea, meat, chef, sugar, plant, edibl, term, shape, bread, process, fish, wine, coffe, kitchen, flour, tradition, market, meal, crop asia, largest, varieti, metal, agricultur, consum, typic, heat, anim, tradit, prepar, flavor, grain, vari, popular, kind, britain, bottl.

Clearly, the classifier succeeds to extract the most relevant words used to described FD-related concepts.

With the goal in mind of further improving the tree by removing categories not FD-relevant, we applied the classifier to the rest of the articles from the FD tree, that have not been associated with any CHO from our collection, counting above 90000. We call those *maybes*. The classifier categorizes each *maybe* article as either FD or not FD, which allows for each category in the tree to be evaluated

Table 4. Categories with many articles predicted as non FD (third column), and some articles predicted as FD (second column).

Category	FD	Non FD
Olympic medalists in equestrian	57	344
New York Red Bulls players	64	259
British Darts Organisation players	51	250
Professional Darts Corporation players	43	242
American jockeys	35	236
FC Red Bull salzburg players	34	190
Genes mutated in mice	33	183
Deaths from typhoid fever	25	141
Electro-Motive Diesel locomotives	27	139
Deaths from cholera	34	131

by two counts: the number of articles predicted as FD and the number of articles predicted as not FD.

Since we cannot afford to inspect all categories (above 10000), of interest are two particular types, candidate for removal from the FD hierarchy: fist, those that have no article classified as FD, as many of them could be not FD-relevant; second, large categories with many articles that are classified as not FD (but can have FD articles also), as removing them would decrease the size of the tree by much. For the first type, we manually inspected top 300 categories with 0 FD and more than 8 not-FD articles. Out of them, 34% we judged as not FD-relevant and are candidates for removal. They contain up to 1100 articles. The second type are heavy categories, top 200 sorted by the number of not-FD-classified articles. Out of them, 25% we judged to be candidates for removal, comprising about 9600 articles.

Examples of categories marked for removal (we show these because we consider that it is interesting that they are reachable from the Food and Drink category) are shown in Table 4.

Equestrianism and related topics are reachable from Food and drink via *Agricultural occupations*, *Animal care occupations* and *Horse-related professions and professionals*. It is a large category and mostly irrelevant to the culture of food and drink.

FC Red Bull Salzburg players and *New York Red Bulls players* are linked to Food and drink by their immediate relation to the energy drink, which in turn is related to many sports events.

Various darts topics (*Professional Darts Corporation players*, *British Darts Organisation players*) are related to food and drink because darts are typical restaurant and pub games.

The category *Genes mutated in mice* is subcategory to *Mutated genes*, which leads to *Agriculture* via *Genetically modified organisms* and *Crops protection*.

Clearly the subject turns quickly from agriculture to biology (genetics) and the relation to food and drink culture is lost.

Cholera or typhoid fever are both foodborne illnesses, hence the relation to food and drink. The specific categories *Deaths from cholera* and *Deaths from typhoid fever* are distancing away from the food and drink culture, rather belonging to medicine topics.

The divergence from food and drink to *Electro-Motive Diesel locomotives* occurs around *Agricultural machinery* and *Tractors*.

The lesson we learn is that via the category-category relations topics diverge and change subtly, such that already starting at a distance of 5–6 categories to the root, the relevance to the domain may weaken. In many cases however, the categories remain related to food and drink and get more specific. Discriminating between food-and-drink relevant and irrelevant categories at deep levels down the tree is hard, due to their large number. Hence, the classifier is a valuable tool for ranking and prioritizing the candidates for removal.

Classification of CHOs. The classifier can be used for discovering Europeana CHOs that are FD-related. For most of the CHOs that have a reasonably long description (at least a couple of sentences), we can assume that the classifier can estimate if they are related to FD with high confidence. This constitutes an automated filter for selection of objects and enriching the current collection of CHOs. Further on, via our annotation pipeline, the CHOs will be enriched with FD concepts and the evidence supporting categories in the FD tree will become more substantial. To conclude the cycle, the classifier will be updated based on the new evidence and become better. Hopefully some convergence will be reached after many such iterations, meaning that the classifier and the labels for the categories in our hierarchy will stabilize. We leave this for future work.

8   Food and Drink Modeling for Other Languages - Outlook

Modeling food and drink for many other European languages is future work for Europeana Food and Drink. In this section we present preliminary analyses and approaches.

The most natural approach to modeling FD in other languages is to repeat the procedure for an arbitrary Wikipedia in language X. The *sameAs* relations between the categories in various Wikipedias allows us to use the already existing FD hierarchy in English as a reference, both for curation and for validation of new FD trees. Ideally, there will be a one-to-one match between the trees. In practice, this is far from the truth; the category structure is different for each language. Moreover, other Wikipedias are significantly poorer (see Table 1), which means that the best outcome is a FD hierarchy in the new language which is a subtree of the English FD hierarchy (via *sameAs* relations). Our experiments show that this assumption is also not true. The following subsection shows that there is little overlap between the English reference and the FD in other languages (at least, for the three languages we tested).

8.1   Top-Down Category Harvesting from FD Root

For few European languages we extracted the tree of FD categories reachable from the root equivalent to Food and drink in those languages. In German, the root category is 'Essen und Trinken', in Bulgarian the root is 'Hrana i napitki', in Italian the root is 'Categoria:Alimentazione'. We will call these the raw FD hierarchies, for their respective languages.

In the German Wikipedia, from the FD root we reach 1252 categories, on 8 levels (see Table 5). Similarly, in the Italian Wikipedia, from the root we reach 1352 categories, on 7 levels. By comparison, in the Bulgarian Wikipedia 17849 categories are reachable from the FD root, on 24 levels. By comparison, the Bulgarian FD tree is more than 10 times larger in terms of number of categories. We do not have an a priori estimate of the 'right' size of the FD tree in a specific language, because it is influenced by the overall size of the particular Wikipedia, by the conservativeness of SKOS relations between categories, by the richness of the FD culture of the native speakers of the language, etc. However, the difference between the German and Italian on one side, and the Bulgarian raw FD hierarchies on the other side is interesting and deserves investigation.

We report some statistics about the *sameAs* relations between FD categories in different languages. We consider three types of relations, depicted in Fig. 7: (a) two categories that share a *sameAs* relation, in English and language X, are in the FD hierarchies of their respective languages; in the Figure they are shown in green; (b) categories in one FD hierarchy, the *sameAs* of which is not in the FD hierarchy of the other language; in the figure, they are shown in red, one example for each tree; (c) categories that are in one of the FD trees, but they do not have *sameAs* correspondent in the other language; in the Figure, they are shown in gray.

Figure 8 shows the distribution of categories for each level of the FD tree, for English (the curated tree), German, Bulgarian and Italian (raw hierarchies).

Figure 9 shows the distributions of the *sameAs* properties in the German, Bulgarian and Italian trees, in comparison to English. (Figure 9a) shows by level, the number of Bulgarian FD categories that have *sameAs* match in the English FD tree, in green; the number of Bulgarian FD categories that have a *sameAs* pair outside the English FD hierarchy in red; and in gray, the number of Bulgarian FD categories that do not have *sameAs* pair in English. The overall picture is that the vast majority of the raw FD Bulgarian categories have a *sameAs* pair in English, outside the English FD tree. On manual inspection, we concluded that many of those are related to water, hydrology, oceanography, etc., topics that we removed from the English FD hierarchy early during the project. Conversely, a large percentage of the English FD tree does not have *sameAs* pairs in Bulgarian (94%), see (Fig. 9b), gray area.

The statistics for the German raw FD hierarchy are quite different from the Bulgarian. More than 16% of the German raw FD categories have *sameAs* pairs in the English FD tree (Fig. 9c). Very few German raw FD categories have a *sameAs* pair outside the English tree (less than 4%). However, only 4% of the English FD categories are in the German raw FD (Fig. 9d), which is less than for Bulgarian.

Table 5. *sameAs* statistics for various languages. X is the language, second column shows categories that are

Language	FD in X and EN	FD only in EN	FD only in X	FD cat in X
X = de	285	603	56	1252
X = bg	239	103	11616	17849
X = it	434	331	45	1352

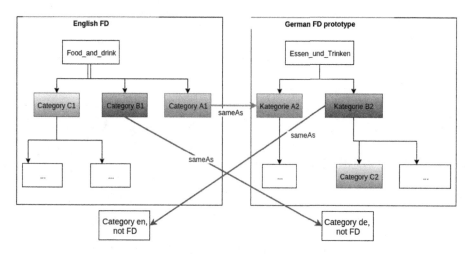

Fig. 7. *sameAs* relations between two FD trees, eg. in English and German. Categories in green are related by *sameAs* and are both in the FD trees. FD categories with *sameAs* correspondents outside the other FD tree are shown in red. Categories without *sameAs* match are depicted in gray. (Color figure online)

Our analysis shows that the Italian FD hierarchy has the highest coherence with the English FD. 32% of the Italian raw FD categories have a *sameAs* pair in the English FD, 3% have a *sameAs* pair outside the English FD and 65% do not have a *sameAs* pair in English (Fig. 9e). 8% of the English FD have a *sameAs* pair in the Italian raw FD, 6% have a *sameAs* pair outside the Italian FD and 86% of the English FD do not have a *sameAs* in Italian.

8.2   Article-Driven Reconstruction Approach

The previous Subsection showed that the *sameAs* correspondence between the FD hierarchies in English and some target language are probably not sufficient for an automatic construction of the FD in the respective language.

An alternative approach is a bottom-up reconstruction of a FD tree in language X, by following the steps:

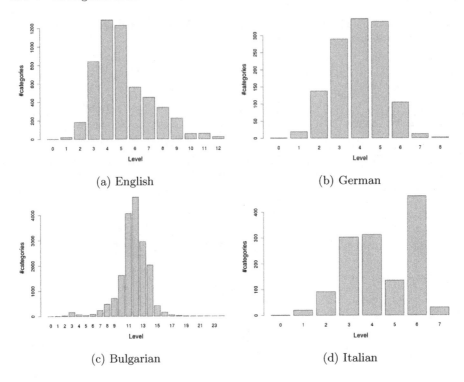

(a) English   (b) German

(c) Bulgarian   (d) Italian

Fig. 8. Overall statistics by level of the FD tree in various languages.

1. start from all FD articles from the English FD, call that set A_{en}
2. getting their *sameAs* pairs in language X, call that set A_X
3. with the Wikipedia in language X represented as a graph, for which nodes are categories, leaves are articles and relations are category-category SKOS relations or article-category relations, infer (using a Steiner tree [13] for example) a minimal connected tree that contains all A_X leaves. Call this FD_X
4. add to FD_X all other articles contained in the categories of FD_X

The implementation of step 3. Is not trivial, the Steiner tree problem being NP-complete in most of the cases. Approximations are available, for large graphs [13].

The procedure described above would ensure maximal coverage for the English FD articles and is fully automated. However, there may be FD articles in language X that are specific to some culture and therefore not have a *sameAs* pair in English. Those would have to be discovered and added separately.

We suggest that a hybrid approach between the top-down category harvesting and bottom-up, article-driven reconstruction is optimal.

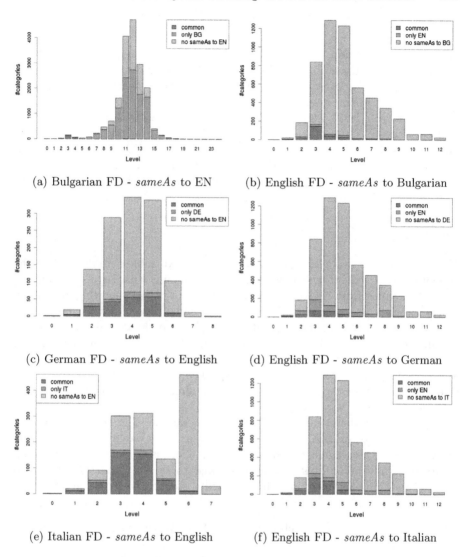

(a) Bulgarian FD - *sameAs* to EN

(b) English FD - *sameAs* to Bulgarian

(c) German FD - *sameAs* to English

(d) English FD - *sameAs* to German

(e) Italian FD - *sameAs* to English

(f) English FD - *sameAs* to Italian

Fig. 9. Overall statistics of category *sameAs* by level of the FD tree in various languages. (Color figure online)

9 Evaluation

Ideally, we would compare the effectiveness of the presented approach to an already existing algorithm but there is no published work dealing with this particular task. To further complicate the situation, the iterative nature of the algorithm and intentionally nebulous definition of the domain preclude the use of many typical evaluation approaches.

9.1 Method

In the end the domain generated by the algorithm was refined sufficiently to function well with the available data but for the purposes of evaluation we settled on the alternative approach of using annotators to more objectively evaluate the quality of the resulting gazetteer.

The finalized Food and Drink domain consists of 14,368 categories and 185,020 articles. A 100 of each were randomly selected and were presented to three independent annotators that judged whether each individual article or category should be part of the Food and Drink domain. The inter-annotator agreement was 97% for categories and 98% for articles. In the cases of annotator disagreement, the choice of the two agreeing annotators was taken as correct.

9.2 Results

The results of the evaluation are summarized in two tables. Table 6 shows the evaluation of the category sample. It has three columns with *Level* denoting the shortest distance from a given category to the root, *Count* showing how many of the sample categories were in that sample and *Correct* showing how many of those were judged by the annotators to belong to the domain. It shows an overall accuracy of 72% but more interestingly it very clearly demonstrates the effect of *semantic drift* mentioned in Sect. 4.1. Categories within five steps of the source are very accurate then meaning is quickly lost in the next few steps until categories 8 or more steps away appear to be almost entirely irrelevant to the domain.

Table 7 shows the evaluation of the articles sample. The columns have the same meaning except *Level* simply chooses an article's parent category closest to the source. Once again the *semantic drift* effect is evident but the overall accuracy is only 56%. This can be attributed to the fact that the article to category relation effectively introduces an extra step in the semantic drift.

Table 6. Category sample results   **Table 7.** Article sample results

Level	Count	Correct
All	100	72
1	0	0
2	3	3
3	13	13
4	24	24
5	21	18
6	17	10
7	10	3
8+	12	1

Level	Count	Correct
All	100	56
1	0	0
2	4	4
3	12	12
4	21	19
5	13	9
6	14	9
7	4	1
8+	32	3

The evaluation made it clear that the main factor in a category's accuracy is the distance from the root. This means that the top-down expert pruning discussed in Sect. 5, which minimizes *semantic drift* and indirectly distance from the root, really is an effective tool for refining the hierarchy. However, the evaluation also demonstrated that while we had pruned the hierarchy sufficiently for working with our data, there is still room for improvement. That can be done by either performing further pruning steps or, as suggested by the data, simply putting a maximum limit on the distance from the root.

10   Comments and Future Work

We presented ongoing work on developing a FD categorization, with the purpose of classifying Cultural Heritage items from Europeana. To this end, we introduced a lightweight, SKOS categorization that borrows Wikipedia categories related to FD. Our preliminary results show that Wikipedia categories are rich enough to provide a good initial coverage of the domain. In fact, we showed that there are a large number of irrelevant categories that need to be removed by supervised curation. We developed an interactive visualization tool that allows experts to remove irrelevant categories and update the knowledge base.

We also presented a bottom-up, data-driven method for scoring categories with respect to concepts identified in Cultural Heritage collections, such as Horniman museum artefacts. We showed that by using this scoring scheme, a sub-hierarchy of FD is supported by evidence and thus confirmed to belong to the domain. This of course does not mean that the remaining categories are not food-and-drink relevant. Clearly, as more resources (e.g. recipes, books, see Sect. 2) are being processed and mapped to our classification scheme, more evidence will be gathered, for more accurate estimation of relevance of categories.

We evaluated the scoring schemes qualitatively, by showing that the categories that are 'activated' with large scores are those that describe the main topics of the Horniman thesaurus terms, namely agriculture, food serving, fishing and hunting, etc. These topics were not explicitly input to our framework, only the concrete terms like spoon, bread, cup, fishing hook, etc. A quantitative evaluation is future work, after the semantic search for FD concepts is open to the public. Then, we plan to submit various scoring schemes with various decay parameters and compare them based on user feedback.

Despite the reasonable coverage of the domain, we identified concepts – or sets of concepts – that belong to FD, but are not found under the FD root. For example, some hunting weapons are not accessible directly from the FD root. Horniman items representing spears could not be tagged, and they should, being tools for obtaining food. We have added a number of Wikipedia parent categorizations to enlarge the FD hierarchy, e.g. placing "Hunting" under FD, "Livestock" under "Agriculture" (which is under FD), etc. We also split some articles and added categorizations and labels (redirects) to match specific objects that we encountered. For example:

- Created pages "Shepherd's crook" and "Tumbler (glass)" by splitting text from existing pages. Added label "Crook"
- added to "Leash" the note "Leashes are often used to tether domesticated animals left to graze alone" as justification for adding category "Livestock"

We may add "private" secondary roots to the categorization: a direct, custom connection of type `broader` to the *Food and Drink* root is a possible way to add secondary roots.

A big challenge for the EFD project is building a multilingual categorization for up to 11 languages. Our prototype is currently limited to English, but we presented some preliminary analysis and two approaches towards automatic or semi-automatic construction of the FD hierarchy in an arbitrary language. We suggested a top-down approach that builds the FD from a root category and a bottom-up approach that reconstructs relations between articles, taking advantage of the 'parallel' Wikipedias for other languages via the *sameAs* relations. We noticed that the inter-language links are not very rich for the three languages we tested: German, Bulgarian and Italian, a large percentage (above 85%) pf the English FD hierarchies having no pair in the other languages.

Acknowledgements. The research presented in this paper was carried out as part of the Europeana Food and Drink project, co-funded by the European Commission within the ICT Policy Support Programme (CIP-ICT-PSP-2013-7) under Grant Agreement no. 621023.

References

1. Agirre, E., Barrena, A., De Lacalle, O.L., Soroa, A., Fern, S., Stevenson, M.: Matching Cultural Heritage items to Wikipedia (2012)
2. Alexiev, V.: Europeana Food and Drink Classification Scheme, Europeana Food and Drink project, Deliverable D2.2 (2015). http://vladimiralexiev.github.io/pubs/Europeana-Food-and-Drink-Classification-Scheme-(D2.2).pdf
3. Cheng, C.P., Lau, G.T., Pan, J., Law, K.H., Jones, A.: Domain-specific ontology mapping by corpus-based semantic similarity. In: 2008 NSF CMMI Engineering Research and Innovation Conference (2008)
4. Fridman Noy, N., Musen, M.A.: An algorithm for merging and aligning ontologies: automation and tool support. In: Workshop on Ontology Management at the 16th National Conference on Artificial Intelligence (AAAI 1999) (1999)
5. Medelyan, O., Manion, S., Broekstra, J., Divoli, A., Huang, A.-L., Witten, I.H.: Constructing a focused taxonomy from a document collection. In: Cimiano, P., Corcho, O., Presutti, V., Hollink, L., Rudolph, S. (eds.) ESWC 2013. LNCS, vol. 7882, pp. 367–381. Springer, Heidelberg (2013). doi:10.1007/978-3-642-38288-8_25
6. Medelyan, O., Milne, D., Legg, C., Witten, I.H.: Mining meaning from wikipedia. Int. J. Hum.-Comput. Stud. **67**(9), 716–754 (2009)
7. Miles, A., Bechhofer, S.: SKOS simple knowledge organization system reference. W3C Recommendation, 18 August 2009
8. Mousavi, H., Kerr, D., Iseli, M., Zaniolo, C.: Harvesting domain specific ontologies from text. ICSC 2014, pp. 211–218 (2014)

9. Mousavi, H., Kerr, D., Iseli, M., Zaniolo, C.: OntoHarvester: an unsupervised ontology generator from free text, CSD Technical report #130003, University of California Los Angeles (2013)
10. Parekh, V., Gwo, J.: Mining domain specific texts and glossaries to evaluate and enrich domain ontologies. In: Proceedings of the International Conference of Information and Knowledge Engineering (2004)
11. Pinto, H.S., Martins, J.P.: A methodology for ontology integration. In: Proceedings of the 1st International Conference on Knowledge Capture, K-CAP 2001 (2001)
12. Ribeiro, R., Batista, F., Pardal, J.P., Mamede, N.J., Pinto, H.S.: Cooking an ontology. In: Euzenat, J., Domingue, J. (eds.) AIMSA 2006. LNCS, vol. 4183, pp. 213–221. Springer, Heidelberg (2006). doi:10.1007/11861461_23
13. Gubichev, A., Neumann, T.: Fast approximation of Steiner trees in large graphs. In: Proceedings of the 21st ACM International Conference on Information and Knowledge Management, pp. 1497–1501 (2012)

What's New? Analysing Language-Specific Wikipedia Entity Contexts to Support Entity-Centric News Retrieval

Yiwei Zhou[1]([⊠]), Elena Demidova[2,3], and Alexandra I. Cristea[1]([⊠])

[1] Department of Computer Science, University of Warwick, Coventry, UK
{Yiwei.Zhou,A.I.Cristea}@warwick.ac.uk
[2] University of Southampton, Southampton, UK
[3] L3S Research Center, Hannover, Germany
demidova@L3S.de

Abstract. Representation of influential entities, such as celebrities and multinational corporations on the web can vary across languages, reflecting language-specific entity aspects, as well as divergent views on these entities in different communities. An important source of multilingual background knowledge about influential entities is Wikipedia—an online community-created encyclopaedia—containing more than 280 language editions. Such language-specific information could be applied in entity-centric information retrieval applications, in which users utilise very simple queries, mostly just the entity names, for the relevant documents. In this article we focus on the problem of creating language-specific entity contexts to support entity-centric, language-specific information retrieval applications. First, we discuss alternative ways such contexts can be built, including *Graph-based* and *Article-based* approaches. Second, we analyse the similarities and the differences in these contexts in a case study including 219 entities and five Wikipedia language editions. Third, we propose a context-based entity-centric information retrieval model that maps documents to aspect space, and apply language-specific entity contexts to perform query expansion. Last, we perform a case study to demonstrate the impact of this model in a news retrieval application. Our study illustrates that the proposed model can effectively improve the recall of entity-centric information retrieval while keeping high precision, and provide language-specific results.

1 Introduction

Entities with world-wide influence, such as celebrities and multinational corporations, can be represented differently on webpages or in other documents originating from various cultures and written in different languages. These various representations can reflect language-specific entity aspects as well as views on the entity in different language-speaking communities. In order to enable a better representation of the language-specific entity aspects for information retrieval applications, methods to systematically identify an entity's context—i.e. the aspects in the entity's descriptions typical in a specific language—need to be developed.

© Springer International Publishing AG 2017
N.T. Nguyen et al. (Eds.): TCCI XXVI, LNCS 10190, pp. 210–231, 2017.
DOI: 10.1007/978-3-319-59268-8_10

For example, in the English news articles, the entity "Angela Merkel", the Chancellor of Germany, is often associated with US and UK politicians such as "Barack Obama" and "David Cameron". Also, recent discussions of European importance, such as the Greek financial situation, are included. On the contrary, although the news articles from German media also include European topics, they frequently focus on the domestic political topics, featuring discussions of political parties in Germany, scandals arising around German politicians, local elections, finances and other country-specific topics. Taking another example, in the case of multinational companies, such as GlaxoSmithKline (a British health-care company), aspects related to the local activities are prevalent in the news articles in specific languages. These aspects range from the effectiveness of the various vaccines developed by the company, to the sports events sponsored by this company in a specific country.

In this article we focus on the problem of creating language-specific entity contexts to support entity-centric, language-specific information retrieval applications. Whilst this work is based on our prior research [29], where we introduced language-specific entity contexts, this article additionally introduces a *context-based entity-centric information retrieval model* that applies these contexts to improve the overall recall and provides language-specific results, which differs our research from all former relevant studies.

In order to obtain a comprehensive overview over the language-specific entity aspects and their representations, multilingual background knowledge about this entity is required. We choose Wikipedia as a knowledge base to obtain such background knowledge. Wikipedia—a multilingual encyclopaedia available in more than 280 language editions—contains language-specific representations of millions of entities and can provide a rich source for cross-cultural analytics. For example, recent studies focused on the manual analysis of the controversial entities in Wikipedia and identified significant cross-lingual differences (e.g. [22]). As entity representations in different Wikipedia language editions can evolve independently, they often include overlapping as well as language-specific entity aspects. We discuss different ways of creating these contexts using Wikipedia, including *Article-based* and *Graph-based* approaches and propose a measure to compute the context similarity. We use this measure to analyse the similarities and the differences of the language-specific entity contexts in a case study using 219 entities of four different entity types and the representations of these entities in five languages. Demonstrating the benefits of finding entity contexts for five languages has been considered enough to illustrate the principles and methods, which can then be transferred to other languages and other entities. Our experiments show that the proposed *Graph-based* entity context can effectively provide a comprehensive overview over the language-specific entity aspects.

Moreover, we propose a *context-based information retrieval model*, which applies language-specific contexts to support entity-centric information retrieval applications. This model enables retrieval of the documents that describe information relevant to the entity, even if the entity is not mentioned by name. This information can include relevant events, which are likely to impact the entity, or are otherwise related to it. At the same time, while using this model, the relevance of the documents mentioning the entity name is only marginally reduced. We implement the proposed model on an information retrieval application, which includes: (i) targeted retrieval of entity-centric information using language-specific contexts; (ii) an overview of the language-specific entity aspects in the each retrieved document. We perform a case study to demonstrate the impact of this model in the context of news articles retrieval through the application. Our results illustrate that language-specific—and in particular *Graph-based*—entity contexts can enhance the recall of the information retrieval application, while keeping high precision, providing positive results are news articles that describe current events relevant to the entity, even if the entity is not explicitly mentioned. We further propose *Result Specificity* to measure the level of language specificity of the proposed information retrieval model when serving users with different language backgrounds. Our results show that our context-based information retrieval model is able to provide highly language-specific results through exploiting language-specific contexts.

2   Creation of the Language-Specific Entity Context

In this section we define the language-specific entity context, present a measure of the context similarity and discuss alternative ways to extract such contexts from the multilingual Wikipedia.

2.1   Language-Specific Entity Context Definition

We define the language-specific entity context as follows:

Definition 1. *The context $C(e, l_i)$ of the entity e in the language l_i is represented through the weights of aspects $\{a_1, \ldots, a_M\}$ relevant to e, $C(e, l_i) = (w(a_1, e, l_i), \ldots, w(a_M, e, l_i))$.*

In this article, we consider entity aspects being *noun phrases* that co-occur with the entity in a given language. In addition, we can also consider the titles of the *in-linked* Wikipedia articles as an additional source of the entity aspects. The weights of the aspects are based on two factors: (1) the language-specific *aspect frequency*, i.e. the frequency of the co-occurrence of the aspect and the entity in a language, and (2) the *language frequency*—the number of languages in which the entity contexts contain the aspect. The first weighting factor prioritises the aspects that frequently co-occur with the entity in a particular language. The second factor assigns higher weights to the language-specific aspects of the entity not mentioned in many other languages.

Inspired by the term frequency–inverse document frequency $(tf - idf)$, given a multilingual data collection containing the languages $\mathbb{L} = \{l_1, \ldots, l_N\}$, the weight $w(a_k, e, l_i)$ of the entity aspect a_k in the language-specific context $C(e, l_i)$ is calculated as follows:

$$w(a_k, e, l_i) = af(a_k, e, l_i) \cdot log \frac{N}{lf(a_k, e, \mathbb{L})}, \tag{1}$$

where $af(a_k, e, l_i)$ is the language-specific *aspect frequency*, which represents the frequency of the co-occurrence of the aspect a_k and the entity e in $C(e, l_i)$; N is the number of languages in the multilingual collection $\mathbb{L}$; $lf(a_k, e, \mathbb{L})$ is the *language frequency*, which represents the number of languages from $\mathbb{L}$ in which the contexts of e contain the aspect a_k.

As for the titles of the manually-defined *in-linked* articles, which are also used to represent aspects, we assign them with an average language-specific *aspect frequency* computed for the noun phrases.

2.2   Context Similarity Measure

In order to compute the similarity between language-specific entity contexts, we use a vector space model. Each axis in the vector space represents an aspect a_k. We represent the context $C(e, l_i)$ of the entity e in the language l_i as a vector in this space. An entry for a_k in the vector represents the weight of the aspect a_k in $C(e, l_i)$. Then the e's context similarity between languages l_i and l_j is computed as the cosine similarity of the context vectors:

$$Sim(C(e, l_i), C(e, l_j)) = \frac{C(e, l_i) \cdot C(e, l_j)}{|C(e, l_i)| \times |C(e, l_j)|}. \tag{2}$$

In order to allow for cross-lingual similarity computations, we represent the aspects in a common language using machine translation. To simplify the description in this article, we always refer to the original language of the entity context, keeping in mind that the similarity is computed in a common language representation.

2.3   Article-Based Context Creation

Wikipedia articles describing an entity in different language editions (i.e. the articles that use the named entity as titles) can be a useful source for the creation of the language-specific context vectors. Thus, we first propose the *Article-based* context creation approach, which simply uses the articles describing the entity in different language editions of Wikipedia. We use all sentences from an article describing the entity in a language edition as the only source of the *Article-based* language-specific entity context.

One drawback of this approach is the possible limitation of the aspects coverage due to the incompleteness of the Wikipedia articles. Such incompleteness can be more prominent in some language editions, making it difficult to create fair cross-lingual comparisons. For example, when reading the English Wikipedia article about the entity "Angela Merkel", a lot of basic aspects about this politician, such as her background and early life, her domestic policy and her foreign affairs, are provided. However, not all aspects about Angela Merkel occur in this Wikipedia article. We can observe, that other articles in the same Wikipedia language edition mention other important aspects. For example, the Wikipedia article about "Economic Council Germany" mentions Angela Merkel's economic

policy: "Although the organisation is both financially and ideologically independent it has traditionally had close ties to the free-market liberal wing of the
conservative Christian Democratic Union (CDU) of Chancellor Angela Merkel".
Even the English Wikipedia article about an oil painting, "The Nightmare",
which does not seem connected to "Angela Merkel" at the first glance, also mentions "Angela Merkel" as: "On 7 November 2011 Steve Bell produced a cartoon
with Angela Merkel as the sleeper and Silvio Berlusconi as the monster." The
aspects contained in the examples above do not occur in the English Wikipedia
article entitled "Angela Merkel". As this example illustrates, just employing the
Wikipedia article describing the entity can not entirely satisfy the need to obtain
a comprehensive overview over the language-specific aspects.

2.4   Graph-Based Context Creation

To alleviate the shortcomings of the *Article-based* approach presented above
and obtain a more comprehensive overview of the entity aspects in the entire
Wikipedia language edition (rather than in a single article), we propose the
Graph-based context creation approach. The idea behind this approach is to
use the link structure of Wikipedia to obtain a comprehensive set of sentences
mentioning the target entity and to use this set to create the context. To this
extent, we use the *in-links* to the Wikipedia article describing the entity and the
language-links of this article to efficiently collect the articles that are probable to
mention the target entity in different language editions. We extract the sentences
mentioning the target entity using state-of-the-art named entity disambiguation
methods and use these sentences to create language-specific contexts.

To illustrate our approach, we use the creation of the context in the English
edition of Wikipedia for the entity "Angela Merkel" as an example. For the
Wikipedia article in English entitled "Angela Merkel", there are several *in-links*
from other articles in English that mention the entity. Besides that, there are also
language-links from the articles describing "Angela Merkel" in other Wikipedia
language editions to this entity's English Wikipedia article.

In Fig. 1, we use the arrows to represent the *in-links*, and dashed lines to
represent the *language-links*. The black nodes represent articles in English, while
the white nodes represent the articles in other languages.

Overall, the creation of the *Graph-based* context for "Angela Merkel" using
these links includes the following steps:

1. *Graph Creation.* We create a subgraph for "Angela Merkel" from Wikipedia's
   link structure in the following way: we first expand the node set from the
   article in English describing the entity (the central node) to all language
   editions of this Wikipedia article; we further expand the node set with all the
   articles having *in-links* to the nodes in the node set; we finally expand the
   node set with all the articles having *language-links* to the existing nodes in
   the node set, if they have not been included into the node set yet. Different
   types of edges are also added between the nodes based on the *in-link* and the
   language-link relationships.

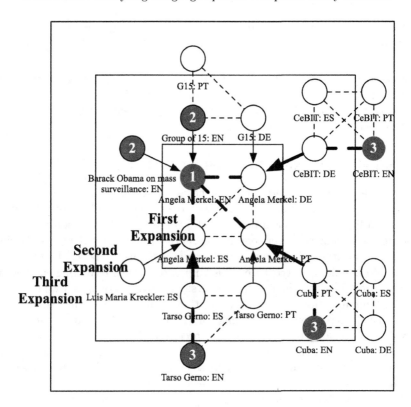

Fig. 1. An Example of the Graph-Based Context Creation from the English Wikipedia for the entity "Angela Merkel".

2. *Article Extraction.* To efficiently extract as many mentions of Angela Merkel from the English Wikipedia as possible, we first extract the article of the central node (with number 1 in Fig. 1), and then start the graph traversal from it.

   Second, all the articles in the graph that have paths of length 1, and the path types are *in-link* to the central node (with number 2 in Fig. 1), are extracted;

   Third, all the articles in the graph that have paths of length 3, the articles are in English, and the path types are *language-link—in-link—language-link* (marked as bold lines in Fig. 1) to the central node (with number 3 in Fig. 1), are also extracted. These articles, although they do not have the direct *in-link* paths to the central node, are in English and their other language editions have *in-links* to articles describing "Angela Merkel" in other languages; Therefore, these articles are likely to mention "Angela Merkel".

3. *Context Construction.* We employ DBpedia Spotlight [13] to annotate the extracted articles to identify the sentences mentioning "Angela Merkel". All the noun phrases extracted from sentences mentioning "Angela Merkel", form the English *Graph-based* context of "Angela Merkel". In addition, we add the names of the linked articles to the entity context.

3   News Retrieval Using Language-Specific Entity Context

In this section we present several retrieval scenarios for answering entity-centric queries over news collections in a common language. Then we describe our approach to address selected scenarios using language-specific entity contexts presented in Sect. 2.

3.1   Entity-Centric News Retrieval

When users are interested in the current news about a named entity, they could simply provide the entity name as the query to a retrieval application. On a daily basis, only a limited number of news articles that explicitly mention this named entity are published. However, one named entity is typically related to various other named entities and events, as we observed during the context creation using the Wikipedia link structure. This kind of relationships among entities and events is represented by the entity contexts, the creation of which we described in Sect. 2. Our intuition is that by using these contexts, we could significantly increase recall of retrieved documents for the entity-centric queries in a news retrieval application, while keeping high precision. Moreover, some documents could only marginally mention an entity, without providing any comprehensive information for the specific entity; In these cases, the entity's contexts can help retrieval application to focus on more relevant documents.

When only using an entity name as the query, traditional information retrieval systems can only return news articles with the named entity's occurrence, which can barely satisfy the users' needs of a comprehensive knowledge about the named entity. For example, when using "Angela Merkel" as the query, it would be beneficial to return news articles like http://www.thelocal.de/20151202/germany-fear-terrorism-if-army-fights-in-syria, which describe the current situation in Germany. Although the content of this article contains neither the term "Angela" nor the term "Merkel", it reports about an event that has potentially large impact on her political decisions. In order to tackle this problem, our context-based information retrieval model incorporates the entity's contexts from Wikipedia into the search and ranking process. As a result, the articles that are similar to the entity context will obtain higher ranks, even if the entity is not mentioned explicitly.

While using entity contexts for retrieval applications, the relevance of a news article to a named entity may be controversial among people with different language backgrounds. For example, a news article containing information about a recent VW scandal affecting the biggest German car production company http://www.thelocal.de/20151202/what-the-vw-scandal-means-for-germanys-economy can be considered as relevant by most German people, as they can think that the German Chancellor should take direct measures to boost the national economy hurt by the scandal. However, the relevance of this article to the query "Angela Merkel" can be considered to be low among the English-speaking communities.

These users could think this to be a company problem, and it could be hard for them to understand if this scandal has a big impact at the national level.

We tackle this problem by using language-specific entity contexts in news retrieval. The users of the retrieval application can select their preferred language-specific entity context when searching for a named entity. The returned news articles and their ranks are then language-specific, based on the background knowledge from the corresponding language edition of Wikipedia.

Besides the retrieval of relevant articles, it is also useful to provide information regarding the aspects of the entity influencing their relevance. That is particularly important in case the entity itself is not mentioned in the article. Our context-based information retrieval model addresses this problem by creating an overview of each news article discussing language-specific entity aspects and uses the most relevant entity aspects to annotate it.

3.2   Approach to Context-Based Information Retrieval

For each document d_i from document set $\mathbb{D}$, we extract all the *noun phrases* in the text as potential related *aspects* to query entities (the named entities whose names are provided as the queries), and then index all the documents by the *aspects*. For a query entity e, and a chosen l_i, we represent each document d_i by the same set of aspects in $C(e, l_i)$, with each aspect a_k weighted by:

$$w(a_k, d_i) = af(a_k, d_i) \cdot log\frac{N}{lf(a_k, e, \mathbb{L})}, \tag{3}$$

where $af(a_k, d_i)$ is the number of matches of aspect a_k with the noun phrases from d_i. In this way, d_i can be represented as $C(d_i, e, l_i) = (w(a_1, d_i), \dots, w(a_M, d_i))$.

We apply the same vector space model and similarity metric as in Sect. 2.2 to compute the similarity between $C(d_i, e, l_i)$ and $C(e, l_i)$. $Sim(C(d_i, e, l_i), C(e, l_i))$ will be used to measure the level of relevances between the query entity and documents. All the documents have similarities with $C(e, l_i)$ higher than a threshold will be returned. Their ranks will be decided based on $Sim(C(d_i, e, l_i), C(e, l_i))$.

The top weighted aspects in d_i will also be returned to provide an overview of what aspects d_i is discussing about e.

4   Entity Context Analysis

The goal of the entity context analysis is to compare the *Graph-based* and the *Article-based* context creation approaches. To this extent we analyse the similarities and the differences of the contexts obtained using these approaches in a case study.

4.1   Dataset Description

To facilitate our analysis, we selected a total number of 219 entities with worldwide influence that evenly come from four categories as our target entities. These categories include: multinational corporations, politicians, celebrities and sports stars. For our study we selected five European languages: English, German, Spanish, Portuguese and Dutch, as our target languages. For each category, we included entities originating from the countries that use one of these target languages as official languages. As our approach requires machine translation of the contexts to enable cross-lingual context similarity computation, we chose Google Translate—a translation service that provides good quality for the involved language pairs.

Based on the approach described in Sect. 2, we created the entity-centric contexts for the entities in our dataset from the five Wikipedia language editions listed above using the *Graph-based* and the *Article-based* approach. The average number of sentences extracted from the Wikipedia article describing the entity using the *Article-based* approach was around 50 in our dataset. With our *Graph-based* context creation approach that utilised Wikipedia link structure to collect sentences mentioning the entity from multiple articles, the number of sentences referring to an entity was increased by the factor 20 to more than 1,000 sentences per entity in a language edition, on average. This factor reflects the effect of the additional data sources within Wikipedia we use in the *Graph-based* approach for each entity processed. The total number of sentences collected by the *Graph-based* approach is 1,196,403 for the whole dataset under consideration.

4.2   Context Similarity Analysis

The cross-lingual context similarity resulting from the *Article-based* and the *Graph-based* context creation approaches are presented in Tables 1 and 2, respectively. To enable cross-lingual context similarity computation, we translated all entity contexts to English. Due to the space limitations, we present example similarity values for four selected entities (one per entity type) for the seven language pairs. In addition, we present the average similarity and the standard deviation values based on all 219 entities in the entire dataset.

From Table 1, we can observe that using the *Article-based* context creation approach, the average similarity values of the language pairs including English are always higher than those of the other language pairs. Using these computation results, we can make several observations: First, as the *Article-based* contexts are more similar to English than to other languages, the English edition builds a reference for the creation of the articles in other language editions. This can be further explained by the fact that the English Wikipedia has the largest number of users, articles, and edits compared to other language editions[1]. Second, as other language pairs are less similar, the overlapping aspects between the English edition and the other language editions appear to be language-dependent. Finally, although the cosine similarity values can be in the interval

---

[1] http://en.wikipedia.org/wiki/List_of_Wikipedias.

Table 1. Cross-lingual context similarity using the *Article-based* context creation approach. The table presents the similarity values for four selected entities of different types, as well as the average similarity and the standard deviation for the whole dataset of 219 entities. The language codes representing the original context languages are as follows: "NL"—Dutch, "DE"—German, "EN"—English, "ES"—Spanish, and "PT"— Portuguese.

Entity	*Article-based* cross-lingual similarity						
	EN-DE	EN-ES	EN-PT	EN-NL	DE-ES	DE-NL	ES-PT
GlaxoSmithKline	0.43	0.34	0.29	0.29	0.31	0.22	0.26
Angela Merkel	0.68	0.66	0.84	0.54	0.60	0.59	0.66
Shakira	0.71	0.58	0.84	0.75	0.48	0.64	0.58
Lionel Messi	0.71	0.86	0.81	0.89	0.71	0.68	0.82
Average of 219	**0.50**	**0.47**	**0.43**	**0.45**	0.38	0.38	0.37
Stdev of 219	0.16	0.17	0.19	0.19	0.15	0.16	0.17

Table 2. Cross-lingual context similarity using the *Graph-based* context creation approach. The table presents the similarity values for four selected entities of different types, as well as the average similarity and the standard deviation for the whole dataset of 219 entities. The language codes representing the original context languages are as follows: "NL"—Dutch, "DE"—German, "EN"—English, "ES"—Spanish, and "PT"— Portuguese.

Entity	*Graph-based* cross-lingual similarity						
	EN-DE	EN-ES	EN-PT	EN-NL	DE-ES	DE-NL	ES-PT
GlaxoSmithKline	0.72	0.73	0.59	0.61	0.63	0.62	0.55
Angela Merkel	0.64	0.62	0.42	0.60	0.75	0.82	0.51
Shakira	0.91	0.94	0.90	0.88	0.94	0.91	0.94
Lionel Messi	0.63	0.76	0.77	0.68	0.70	0.62	0.76
Average of 219	0.52	**0.59**	0.54	0.50	0.56	0.52	**0.64**
Stdev of 219	0.24	0.22	0.21	0.23	0.23	0.23	0.19

$[0, 1]$, the absolute similarity values achieved by the *Article-based* approach reach at most 0.5, even for the language pairs which are supposed to have relatively high similarity, such as English and German. Such relatively low absolute similarity values indicate that although the articles contain some overlapping entity aspects, they also include a significant proportion of divergent aspects.

In contrast to the *Article-based* approach, the *Graph-based* approach collects a more comprehensive overview of the entity aspects spread across different articles in a language edition. From Table 2, we can see that the most similar context pair is Spanish and Portuguese. Intuitively, this could be explained by the closeness of the cultures using these two languages, and a more comprehensive overview of the covered entity aspects in both languages compared to the

Article-based approach. We can also observe that the average similarity values significantly increase compared to the *Article-based* approach and can exceed 0.6 in our dataset.

From a single entity perspective, some entities may achieve higher similarity values than the average similarity for some language pairs, when more common aspects are included in the contexts on both sides. For example, this is the case for EN-NL, DE-ES and DE-NL pairs for the entity "Angela Merkel". Other entities may have lower similarity values for some language pairs, especially when distinct aspects are included into the corresponding contexts, such as the EN-DE, ES-ES, and EN-PT pairs for "Lionel Messi".

To illustrate the differences in the language-specific *Graph-based* entity contexts, we select the highly weighted aspects from the contexts of the entity "Angela Merkel" constructed using the *Graph-based* approach, as shown in Table 3. In this table, the unique aspects that appear with high weights in all contexts of the entity "Angela Merkel" are underlined. We can observe that

Table 3. Top-30 highly weighted aspects of the entity "Angela Merkel" in language-specific *graph-based* contexts.

English	Angela merkel, battle, berlin, cdu, chancellor, chancellor angela merkel, church, edit, election, emperor, empire, england, france, george, german, german chancellor angela merkel, germany, government, jesus, john, kingdom, merkel, minister, party, president, talk, union, university, utc, war
German	Academy, angela merkel, article, berlin, cdu, cet, chancellor, chancellor angela merkel, csu, election, example, german, german chancellor angela merkel, german children, germany, government, kasner, merkel, minister, november, october, office, party, president, propaganda, ribbon, september, speech, time, utc
Spanish	Administration, angela merkel, berlin, cdu, chancellor, chancellor angela merkel, coalition, council, country, december, decommissioning plan, decreed, election, energy, france, german, german chancellor angela merkel, german federal election, germany, government, government coalition, grand coalition, merkel, minister, october, party, president, spd, union, year
Portuguese	Ali, angela merkel, bank, cdu, ceo, chairman, chancellor, chancellor angela merkel, china, co-founder, coalition, csu, dilma rousseff, german chancellor angela merkel, germany, government, government merkel, koch, leader, merkel, minister, november, october, party, petroleum, president, saudi arabia, state, union, york
Dutch	Angela merkel, angela dorothea kasner, bundestag, candidate, cdu, chancellor, chancellor angela merkel, coalition, csu, december, fdp, fist, french president, german, german chancellor angela merkel, german christian democrat politician, german federal election, germany, government, majority, merkel, minister, november, october, party, president, right, spd, state, union

the aspects that appear with high weights only in the non-German context—e.g. "England", "Kingdom" and "Dilma Rousseff"—are more relevant to her international affairs in corresponding language-speaking countries. In contrast, the aspects that appear with high weights only in the German context—such as "German children" and "propaganda"—are more relevant to her domestic activities.

Overall, our observations confirm that the *Graph-based* context provides a better overview of the different entity aspects than the *Article-based* context. The *Graph-based* approach can determine the similarity values and the differences of the language-specific contexts, independent of the coverage and completeness of any dedicated Wikipedia article. The results of the t-test confirm the statistical significance of the differences in context similarity values between the *Article-based* and the *Graph-based* approaches for all language pairs except the EN-DE. This exception can be explained by a relatively high coverage of the German Wikipedia articles with respect to the aspects of the represented entities in our dataset.

The analysis results also confirm our intuition that, although the editors of different Wikipedia language editions describe some common entity aspects, they can have different focus with respect to the aspects of interest. These differences are reflected by the complementary information spread across the Wikipedia language editions and can probably be explained by various factors including the culture and the living environment of the editors, as well as the information available to them. Our *Graph-based* context creation approach is capable of capturing these differences from different language editions by creating a comprehensive language-specific aspects overview.

5 Language-Specific Retrieval of News Articles for Entity-Centric Queries

In this section we discuss the impact of the language-specific entity contexts on a news retrieval application. Since results following the same patterns can be observed across all named entities, we randomly selected two named entities, one originated from an English speaking country, and the other one originated from a non-English speaking country, as examples to demonstrate the effectiveness of the context-based information retrieval model.

5.1 Dataset Description

The two named entities we chose were: "Angela Merkel" originated from Germany and "David Cameron" originated from Great Britain. To enable the comparison among different language-specific contexts of an entity, we built two datasets each containing daily news from different sources: the German media news dataset and the British media news dataset. For the German media news dataset, we randomly sampled 300 news articles from three mainstream online English news websites' RSS feeds published on December 2nd, 2015 in Germany.

These websites were: Deutsche Welle[2], Spiegel Online[3] and The Local[4]. Regarding the British media news dataset, we randomly sampled 300 news articles, from two mainstream British online English news websites' RSS feeds on December 10th, 2015 in Great Britain. These websites were: The Guardian[5] and Daily Express[6]. Then, we analysed the performance of English and German contexts of the entities "Angela Merkel" and "David Cameron" on the retrieved results for these two datasets, respectively.

We expected that there were only few news articles per day mentioning a specific entity, even if this entity was prominent. Nevertheless, daily news can contain many relevant articles that discuss events related to the entity. Therefore, we used the following criteria to annotate the articles as "Relevant":

1. *Is the named entity involved in this event?*
2. *Is the named entity one of the direct causes of this event?*
3. *Will the named entity be directly impacted by this event?*

After the annotation, 51 news articles in the German media news dataset were annotated as "Relevant" for the query "Angela Merkel". In the British media news dataset, 71 news articles were annotated as "Relevant" for the query "David Cameron"[7].

5.2   Precision-Recall Analysis

We used a state-of-the-art information retrieval model, BM25 [21] as a baseline. The baseline model retrieved the documents using the original query containing the entity name without expansion (i.e. "Angela" and "Merkel", "David" and "Cameron").

In Fig. 2, we present the interpolated precision achieved by the baseline and the context-based information retrieval model using different contexts at different recall levels for query entity "Angela Merkel". As we can observe in Fig. 2, although the traditional ranking algorithm based on the BM25 scores of the news articles given a query entity can maintain a relatively high precision, the highest recall it can achieve is about 0.45. That is because a lot of news articles, such as http://www.thelocal.de/20151202/germany-to-send-1200-troops-to-aid-isis-fight, http://www.spiegel.de/international/europe/paris-attacks-pose-challenge-to-european-security-a-1063435.html and http://www.thelocal.de/20151029/germany-maintains-record-low-unemployment, report events either directly driven by "Angela Merkel", or would directly impact her. Although these articles do not mention the query entity by name,

---

[2] http://www.dw.com/en/.
[3] http://www.spiegel.de/international/.
[4] http://www.thelocal.de/.
[5] http://www.theguardian.com/.
[6] http://www.express.co.uk/.
[7] The annotated datasets are accessible at: https://github.com/zhouyiwei/WIKIIRDATA.

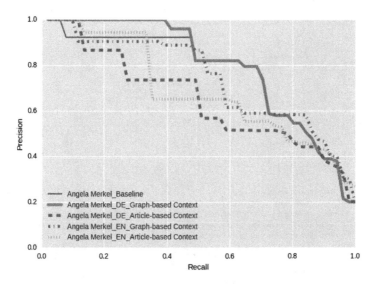

Fig. 2. Precision-recall curve of language-specific context for "Angela Merkel".

they provide indispensable insights on the query entity's current focus or past achievements, such that the users issuing this query would consider them to be relevant, especially when the number of articles mentioning the query entity is small. The context-based information retrieval model using all the contexts, no matter they are *Article-based* or *Graph-based*, no matter they are extracted from English Wikipedia or German Wikipedia, achieved higher recall for this query.

We can also observe that German (DE) *Graph-based* context achieves the overall best performance. For most of the time, it achieves higher precision than other contexts, while achieving the same recall. This is because the German (DE) *Graph-based* context provides a more comprehensive overview of the aspects of "Angela Merkel".

Moreover, the model utilising the German (DE) *Graph-based* context outperforms the baseline with respect to precision at all recall levels for this query entity. This is because "Angela" is quite a common term. By incorporating the background information from Wikipedia, the model can differentiate the Chancellor of Germany from other celebrities, such as Angela Gossow (German singer) and Angela Maurer (German long-distance swimmer), which helps to increase the precision of retrieved results.

The baseline approach ranks the news articles mostly based on the occurrences of the entity name. In contrast, our model considers all the aspects mentioned in the news articles about the named entity. The ranks are generated based on the similarity values between the articles' aspects and the named entity's language-specific Wikipedia context, such that news articles that provide a more comprehensive overview of language-specific aspects are prompted to higher ranks.

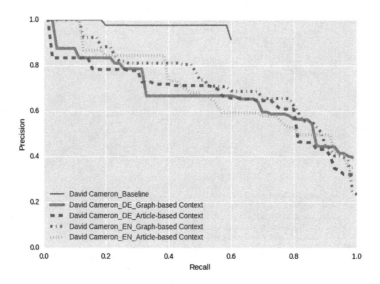

Fig. 3. Precision-recall curve of language-specific context for "David Cameron".

The effectiveness of the context-based information retrieval model can also be observed for the query "David Cameron", presented in the Fig. 3. As shown in Fig. 3, the proposed model can achieve a much higher recall than the baseline for this query as well, while maintaining high precision. As expected, the English (EN) *Graph-based* context, which is local for this query, performs overall better than the other contexts.

We did not observe significant differences among the rest of the contexts for the query "David Cameron". One of the reasons can be the numbers of aspects in the corresponding entity contexts. The English *Graph-based* context of the entity "Angela Merkel" contains 7,317 non-zero weighted aspects, the German one contains 6,614. Both of them are much larger than her English and German *Article-based* contexts, which contain 562 and 1,069 non-zero weighted aspects, respectively. Resulting from that, the German and English *Graph-based* contexts for "Angela Merkel" are much more powerful than its German and English *Article-based* contexts. For "David Cameron", the most populated context is the English *Graph-based* context, which contains 10,365 non-zero weighted aspects, whereas other contexts have much smaller and comparable sizes. The German *Graph-based* context of the entity "David Cameron" only has 1,627 non-zero weighted aspects; the numbers for his English and German *Article-based* contexts are 1,143 and 291. Although all of these contexts can still help to greatly improve the recall while maintaining relatively high precision, their effectiveness is somewhat limited because of their sizes.

Table 4. Top-8 results for the query "Angela Merkel" retrieved using German (DE) and English (EN) *Graph-based* contexts.

Rank	URL and Aspects overview (DE)	URL and Aspects overview (EN)
1	http://www.spiegel.de/international/germany/angela-merkel-changes-her-stance-on-refugee-limits-a-1063773.html (minister, idea, germany, merkel, chancellor)	http://www.spiegel.de/international/germany/angela-merkel-changes-her-stance-on-refugee-limits-a-1063773.html (minister, idea, germany, merkel, chancellor)
2	http://www.thelocal.de/20151130/we-owe-future-generations-a-climate-deal-merkel (prosperity, time, percent, paris, merkel)	http://www.thelocal.de/20151202/german-forces-will-back-france-in-syria-fight (bundeswehr, france, germany, thursday, syria)
3	http://www.thelocal.de/20151202/german-forces-will-back-france-in-syria-fight (bundeswehr, france, germany, thursday, syria)	http://www.thelocal.de/20151130/we-owe-future-generations-a-climate-deal-merkel (prosperity, time, percent, paris, merkel)
4	http://www.thelocal.de/20151202/no-better-life-for-afghans-in-germany-merkel (merkel, migration, dec, security, afghanistan)	http://www.thelocal.de/20151030/the-sailors-who-brought-down-the-german-empire (revolt, attack, government, battle, wilhelmshaven)
5	http://www.thelocal.de/page/view/hamburg-bids-farewell-to-its-most-famous-son (merkel, chancellor, schmidt, flag, terror)	http://www.spiegel.de/international/germany/editorial-on-anti-refugee-sentiment-in-germany-a-1062442.html (hitler, culture, germany, time, country)
6	http://www.spiegel.de/international/germany/editorial-on-anti-refugee-sentiment-in-germany-a-1062442.html (hitler, culture, germany, time, country)	http://www.thelocal.de/20151202/no-better-life-for-afghans-in-germany-merkel (merkel, migration, dec, security, afghanistan)
7	http://www.thelocal.de/20141001/german-cabinet-agrees-cap-on-rent-rises-cities (percent, average, law, oct, property)	http://www.thelocal.de/page/view/hamburg-bids-farewell-to-its-most-famous-son (merkel, chancellor, schmidt, flag, terror)
8	http://www.thelocal.de/page/view/german-astronaut-calls-for-peace-and-tolerance (publicity, vogel, space, space station, photo)	http://www.thelocal.de/20151202/less-than-half-of-german-jets-ready-for-action (report, syria, germany, wednesday, dec)

5.3   Analysis of Language-Specific Results

Table 4 presents the Top-8 results returned by the news retrieval application applying German and English *Graph-based* contexts of the query "Angela Merkel". As we can observe, when using the German

context, German local news such as http://www.thelocal.de/20141001/
german-cabinet-agrees-cap-on-rent-rises-cities and http://www.thelocal.de/
page/view/german-astronaut-calls-for-peace-and-tolerance are included in the
top-ranked results, which is not the case when using the English context. Nevertheless, as the key aspects of the entity are shared across both contexts, the
results at the top of the both rankings are similar.

To better understand the impact of the language-specific contexts on the
retrieved results, we define a measure: *Result Specificity*. *Result Specificity* (*RS*)
is the percentage of unique documents in top-K results retrieved using two contexts:

$$RS(R(e, C(e, l_i)), R(e, C(e, l_j))) = 1 - \frac{|R(e, C(e, l_i)) \cap R(e, C(e, l_j))|}{2 \times K}, \quad (4)$$

where $R(e, C(e, l_i))$ is the set of the results retrieved for the entity e using the
language context $C(e, l_i)$. The higher the *Result Specificity*, the less overlapping
in the retrieved results using language-specific contexts, and the more language-
specific the retrieved documents will be.

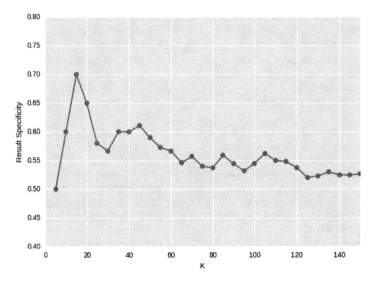

Fig. 4. *Result Specificity* of the top-K retrieved results of German and English *Graph-
based* contexts for the query "Angela Merkel".

Figure 4 illustrates the trends of the *Result Specificity* with an increasing
number of returned results, when using the German and English *Graph-based*
contexts for the entity "Angela Merkel". Whereas the most relevant results are
very similar for both German and English *Graph-based* contexts, the *Result
Specificity* of this pair reaches its maximum of 0.7 when $K = 15$. This means
that these language-specific contexts can retrieve distinct and relevant news

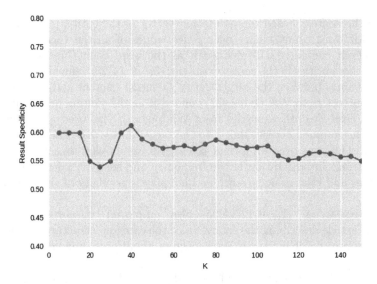

Fig. 5. *Result Specificity* of the top-K retrieved results of German and English *Graph-based* contexts for the query "David Cameron".

articles at the higher ranks. Then, with an increasing K, both relevance and distinctiveness of the retrieved results drop, but the *Result Specificity* still stays above 0.5. On one hand, this is because many aspects in these two contexts overlap (as shown in Table 2, the EN-DE *Graph-based* context similarity value of "Angela Merkel" is 0.64). On the other hand, the most relevant news articles have been included in the retrieved results already by lower K values. With an increasing K, divergent articles with lower relevance are further retrieved.

Similar trends can be observed in Fig. 5 for the query "David Cameron".

6   Related Work

Due to its coverage and diversity, Wikipedia has been acting as an outer knowledge source to build semantic representations of entities/documents in various areas. Examples include information retrieval [4,14,18], named entity disambiguation [1,2,7,8,11,12], text classification [25] and entity ranking [10].

To extract the content of an entity context, many researches directly used the Wikipedia article describing the entity [1,2,8,9,14,25–27]; some works extended the article with all the other Wikipedia articles linked to the Wikipedia article describing the entity [6,7,12]; while some only considered the first paragraph of the Wikipedia article describing the entity [2]. Different from these approaches, our *Graph-based* approach not only employs *in-links* and *language-links* to broaden the article set that is likely to mention the entity, but also performs a finer-grained process: extracting the sentences that mention the entity, such that all the sentences in our context are closely related to the target entity.

As to the context-based representation vector of the entity, [1,11] defined it as the tf-idf/word count/binary occurrence values of all the vocabulary words in the context content; [2,19] defined it as the word count/binary occurrence values of other entities in the context content; [5,6,9,14,25] defined it as the tf-idf similarity values between the target entity's context content and other entities' context contents from Wikipedia; [27] defined it as the visiting probability from the target entity to other entities from Wikipedia; [7,26] used a measurement based on the common entities linked to the target entity and other entities from Wikipedia. Different from all former researches, we employ *aspect weights* that have a different interpretation of the frequency and selectivity than the typical tf-idf values and take co-occurrence and language specificity of the aspects into account.

Some researches [1,2,9,12,14,25] also employed *category-links* to the Wikipedia article describing the entity. Since the category structure of Wikipedia is language-specific, it is hard to gain insights about cross-lingual context similarity for our case.

With the development of multilingual Wikipedia, researchers have been employing it in many multilingual applications [3,16,17,20,23,24]. Similar to the English-only contexts, each dimension in a multilingual context representation vector represented the relatedness of the target entity with a set of entities/words in the corresponding language. However, none of these researches paid attention to the language-specific bias of multilingual Wikipedia, which has been proposed and verified in [28–30]. As different language editions of Wikipedia express different aspects related to the entity, in our research, we take a step further to analyse the differences in the language-specific entity contexts, and realised language-specific information retrieval through language-specific contexts.

As for incorporating the Wikipedia knowledge in information retrieval applications, [4,15,18] applied concept-based approaches that mapped both the documents and queries to the Wikipedia concept space; [14,23] focused only on query extension; [20,24] focused only on mapping documents to Wikipedia concept space. To retrieve documents that did not explicitly mention the query entity by name, but were still relevant to the query entity, we chose to map both the query and the documents to the aspect space. As for the evaluation metrics of these information retrieval models, all these researches used the occurrence of the query entity as a prerequisite of one document to be relevant. Our research, on the other hand, excluded this condition. A document would be annotated as "Relevant" as long as it can satisfy any one of the three criteria in Sect. 5.1. When facing a dataset without enough documents mention the query entity explicitly, our context-based information retrieval model would still be able to return most relevant documents, thus achieved higher recall than former researches under this setting.

7   Conclusions and Outlook

In this article, we proposed context creation approaches for named entities, and used language-specific contexts to support entity-centric information retrieval.

We compared different ways of context creation including the *Article-based* and the *Graph-based* approaches. A Wikipedia article describing the entity in a certain language can be seen as the most straightforward source for the language-specific entity context. Nevertheless, such context can be incomplete, lacking important entity aspects. Therefore, in this article we proposed an alternative approach to collect data for the context creation, i.e. the *Graph-based* approach. Our evaluation results showed significant differences between the contexts obtained using different context creation approaches. We suggested that the *Graph-based* approach was a promising way to obtain a comprehensive, language-specific overview of the entity independent of the Wikipedia article describing the entity. Furthermore, we proposed a context-based information retrieval model that applied such language-specific entity contexts to improve the recall of entity-centric information retrieval applications, while keeping high precision. Our case study illustrated that this model can retrieve documents that contain entity-related information, such as relevant events in the current news articles, even if the entity was not mentioned explicitly. And by selecting contexts of different language editions, our context-based information retrieval model made language-specific results possible.

Even though in this article we used limited number of named entities and languages as examples, our proposed approach and model can be easily extended to all other languages and named entities. In the future work, we plan to improve the context-based information retrieval model, so that it can process multilingual documents; we also plan to apply the model on other domains, to evaluate its effectiveness at a larger scale.

Acknowledgments. This work was partially funded by the COST Action IC1302 (KEYSTONE), the ERC under ALEXANDRIA (ERC 339233) and H2020-MSCA-ITN-2014 WDAqua (64279).

References

1. Bunescu, R.C., Pasca, M.: Using encyclopedic knowledge for named entity disambiguation. In: EACL, vol. 6, pp. 9–16 (2006)
2. Cucerzan, S.: Large-scale named entity disambiguation based on Wikipedia data. In: EMNLP-CoNLL, vol. 7, pp. 708–716 (2007)
3. Daiber, J., Jakob, M., Hokamp, C., Mendes, P.N.: Improving efficiency and accuracy in multilingual entity extraction. In: Proceedings of the 9th International Conference on Semantic Systems, I-SEMANTICS 2013, pp. 121–124. ACM, New York (2013)
4. Egozi, O., Markovitch, S., Gabrilovich, E.: Concept-based information retrieval using explicit semantic analysis. ACM Trans. Inf. Syst. (TOIS) **29**(2), 8 (2011)
5. Gabrilovich, E., Markovitch, S.: Computing semantic relatedness using Wikipedia-based explicit semantic analysis. In: IJCAI, vol. 7, pp. 1606–1611 (2007)
6. Gabrilovich, E., Markovitch, S.: Wikipedia-based semantic interpretation for natural language processing. J. Artif. Intell. Res. (JAIR) **34**, 443–498 (2009). doi:10.1613/jair.2669

7. Han, X., Sun, L., Zhao, L.: Collective entity linking in web text: a graph-based method. In: Proceedings of the 34th International ACM SIGIR Conference on Research and Development in Information Retrieval, pp. 765–774. ACM (2011)

8. Han, X., Zhao, J.: Named entity disambiguation by leveraging Wikipedia semantic knowledge. In: Proceedings of the 18th ACM Conference on Information and knowledge Management, pp. 215–224. ACM (2009)

9. Hu, J., Fang, L., Cao, Y., Zeng, H.-J., Li, H., Yang, Q., Chen, Z.: Enhancing text clustering by leveraging Wikipedia semantics. In: Proceedings of the 31st Annual International ACM SIGIR Conference on Research and Development in Information Retrieval, pp. 179–186. ACM (2008)

10. Kaptein, R., Kamps, J.: Exploiting the category structure of Wikipedia for entity ranking. Artif. Intell. **194**, 111–129 (2013)

11. Kataria, S.S., Kumar, K.S., Rastogi, R.R., Sen, P., Sengamedu, S.H.: Entity disambiguation with hierarchical topic models. In: Proceedings of the 17th ACM SIGKDD International Conference on Knowledge Discovery and Data Mining, pp. 1037–1045. ACM (2011)

12. Kulkarni, S., Singh, A., Ramakrishnan, G., Chakrabarti, S.: Collective annotation of Wikipedia entities in web text. In: Proceedings of the 15th ACM SIGKDD International Conference on Knowledge Discovery and Data Mining, pp. 457–466. ACM (2009)

13. Mendes, P.N., Jakob, M., García-Silva, A., Bizer, C.: DBpedia spotlight: shedding light on the web of documents. In: Proceedings the 7th International Conference on Semantic Systems, I-SEMANTICS 2011, Graz, Austria, 7–9 September 2011, pp. 1–8 (2011)

14. Milne, D.N., Witten, I.H., Nichols, D.M.: A knowledge-based search engine powered by Wikipedia. In: Proceedings of the Sixteenth ACM Conference on Conference on Information and Knowledge Management, pp. 445–454. ACM (2007)

15. Müller, C., Gurevych, I.: Using Wikipedia and Wiktionary in domain-specific information retrieval. In: Peters, C., et al. (eds.) CLEF 2008. LNCS, vol. 5706, pp. 219–226. Springer, Heidelberg (2009). doi:10.1007/978-3-642-04447-2_28

16. Nastase, V., Strube, M.: Transforming Wikipedia into a large scale multilingual concept network. Artif. Intell. **194**, 62–85 (2013)

17. Nothman, J., Ringland, N., Radford, W., Murphy, T., Curran, J.R.: Learning multilingual named entity recognition from Wikipedia. Artif. Intell. **194**, 151–175 (2013)

18. Otegi, A., Arregi, X., Ansa, O., Agirre, E.: Using knowledge-based relatedness for information retrieval. Knowl. Inf. Syst. **44**(3), 689–718 (2015). doi:10.1007/s10115-014-0785-4

19. Ploch, D.: Exploring entity relations for named entity disambiguation. In: Proceedings of the ACL 2011 Student Session, pp. 18–23. Association for Computational Linguistics (2011)

20. Potthast, M., Stein, B., Anderka, M.: A Wikipedia-based multilingual retrieval model. In: Macdonald, C., Ounis, I., Plachouras, V., Ruthven, I., White, R.W. (eds.) ECIR 2008. LNCS, vol. 4956, pp. 522–530. Springer, Heidelberg (2008). doi:10.1007/978-3-540-78646-7_51

21. Robertson, S., Zaragoza, H.: The probabilistic relevance framework: BM25 and beyond. Found. Trends Inf. Retr. **3**(4), 333–389 (2009)

22. Rogers, R.: Wikipedia as cultural reference. In: Rogers, R. (ed.) Digital Methods. The MIT Press, Cambridge (2013)

23. Schönhofen, P., Benczúr, A., Bíró, I., Csalogány, K.: Cross-language retrieval with Wikipedia. In: Peters, C., et al. (eds.) CLEF 2007. LNCS, vol. 5152, pp. 72–79. Springer, Heidelberg (2008). doi:10.1007/978-3-540-85760-0_9
24. Sorg, P., Cimiano, P.: Exploiting Wikipedia for cross-lingual and multilingual information retrieval. Data Knowl. Eng. **74**, 26–45 (2012)
25. Wang, P., Hu, J., Zeng, H.-J., Chen, Z.: Using Wikipedia knowledge to improve text classification. Knowl. Inf. Syst. **19**(3), 265–281 (2009)
26. Witten, I., Milne, D.: An effective, low-cost measure of semantic relatedness obtained from Wikipedia links. In: Proceeding of AAAI Workshop on Wikipedia and Artificial Intelligence: An Evolving Synergy, pp. 25–30. AAAI Press, Chicago (2008)
27. Yazdani, M., Popescu-Belis, A.: Computing text semantic relatedness using the contents and links of a hypertext encyclopedia. In: Proceedings of the Twenty-Third International Joint Conference on Artificial Intelligence, pp. 3185–3189. AAAI Press (2013)
28. Zhou, Y., Cristea, A.I., Roberts, Z.: Is Wikipedia really neutral? A sentiment perspective study of war-related Wikipedia articles since 1945. In: Proceedings of the 29th Pacific Asia Conference on Language, Information and Computation, PACLIC 29, Shanghai, China, 30 October–1 November 2015
29. Zhou, Y., Demidova, E., Cristea, A.I.: Analysing entity context in multilingual Wikipedia to support entity-centric retrieval applications. In: Cardoso, J., Guerra, F., Houben, G.-J., Pinto, A.M., Velegrakis, Y. (eds.) KEYSTONE 2015. LNCS, vol. 9398, pp. 197–208. Springer, Cham (2015). doi:10.1007/978-3-319-27932-9_17
30. Zhou, Y., Demidova, E., Cristea, A.I.: Who likes me more? Analysing entity-centric language-specific bias in multilingual Wikipedia. In: Proceedings of the 30th Annual ACM Symposium on Applied Computing, SAC 2016 (2016)

Author Index

Printed in the United States
By Bookmasters